the voluptuous vegan

the voluptuous vegan

More than 200 Sinfully Delicious Recipes for
Meatless, Eggless, and Dairy-Free Meals

Myra Kornfeld
and George Minot

Illustrations by Sheila Hamanaka

Clarkson Potter/Publishers
New York

Published by Clarkson Potter/Publishers, New York, New York
Member of the Crown Publishing Group

Random House, Inc. New York, Toronto, London, Sydney, Auckland
www. randomhouse.com

CLARKSON N. POTTER is a trademark and POTTER and colophon are reg-
istered trademarks of Random House, Inc.

Printed in the United States of America

Design by Jan Derevjanik

Library of Congress Cataloging-in-Publication Data
Kornfeld, Myra.
The voluptuous vegan : more than 200 sinfully delicious recipes for meatless, eggless, and dairy-free meals / by Myra Kornfeld and George Minot ;
illustrations by Sheila Hamanaka.
Includes bibliographical references.
1. Vegan cookery.   2. Veganism.   I. Minot, George, 1959–   II. Title.
TX837.K67   2000
641.5'636—dc21   00-036405

ISBN 0-609-80489-8

10   9   8   7   6   5   4   3   2

First Edition

To my parents, Charlotte and Irving, who inspired me to follow my passions.

To my husband, Stephen, who supported me through this project in every sense of the word.

To all my dear friends who have ever shared a meal at my table.

acknowledgments

I am so grateful for the generosity, love, and support of many people without whom this book would not be possible.

A heartfelt thanks to everyone at Clarkson N. Potter, especially to editors Christopher Pavone, who meticulously pulled the manuscript into shape, and to Pamela Krauss, who undertook the project and had faith in it from the very beginning; also thanks to her wonderful assistant, Chloe Wigston Smith.

Thanks to all the people who graciously tested the recipes and offered excellent suggestions: Charlotte Kornfeld, Deborah Gavito, Glynnis Osher, Elaine Ryan, Gloria Bugara, Margaret Peot, Diana Miller, Ester Massimilla, Donna Roberts, Sheila Hamanaka, Kathie Peot, and taster Kristin Leigh. A special thanks to an angel in the form of dear friend Alison Rieder, whose generosity and competence in testing the majority of the recipes in this book were invaluable.

Thank you to Linda Erman and Glynnis Osher for supporting me on this project day in and day out, and for love and encouragement every step of the way. Special thanks to Linda for keeping the concept of the book alive and to Glynnis for designing such a voluptuous cover. My gratitude goes to Sheila Hamanaka for her beautiful illustrations, for having such a discerning palette, and for making sure the vast quantities of food coming out of my kitchen never went to waste.

The Natural Gourmet Cookery School in New York City deserves special acknowledgment for being such a vital center devoted to good and healthy cooking; a special thanks to founder Annemarie Colbin for inspiring me to cook healthful and delicious food; to Diane Carlson and Jenny Mattheau, for the opportunity to teach and learn so much from my students; to the students in all the classes I ever taught who encouraged me to write a book in the first place.

I appreciate so much my invaluable experience at the restaurant Angelica Kitchen; thank you to owner Leslie McEachern for giving me free reign to create; to Peter Berley, my colleague and friend, for making my experience there such a blast; to Lynnie Brodeur Martinez, who taught me much about vegan baking.

A special word of gratitude to the following people:

My husband, Stephen, who encouraged my writing, offered consistent and valuable feedback on the manuscript and on the food, and is a source of joy and support in my life.

Melanie Jackson, for being such a wise and terrific agent.

Lorna Sass and Deborah Madison, whose informative books have been an inspiration to me.

Dan Levy and Margaret Peot, for writing "At Myra's Table," a song that always reminds me why I love to cook in the first place.

Finally, my gratitude goes to George Minot for getting this project off the ground, for unflagging enthusiasm and steady calm throughout the effort, for encouraging me to find my voice, and for being an amazing human being.

contents

the voluptuous vegan

introduction

We all need to feed our souls. A person who thinks about satisfying his or her soul is likely to feel more nourished and healthy than someone who treats nourishment as a mere technical problem. Cooking is one of the most basic forms of nurturing—a deeply grounding experience, an active, meditative immersion in nature. It is a means of getting in touch with the rhythms, cycles, and seasons of the world around us. If you live in a city, moreover, cooking is often the only significant way in which you can connect with nature.

The Voluptuous Vegan is about pampering yourself with luscious, healthy food. Although these recipes call for no animal products, nothing here will leave you feeling deprived. This isn't to say that simple cooking is not worthwhile or not an important part of daily sustenance. In fact, a lot of the recipes in this book will show you how to prepare simple fare—but more flavorful versions, and how to make these individual dishes integral parts of voluptuous meals. At the same time, the keystone of this book is the whole meal: carefully designed balanced meals that include a variety of sauces, side dishes, salads, garnishes, swirls, and splashes. In each case, the result is a balanced, delicious, and beautiful ensemble of flavors, textures, and colors. So some of these recipes are elaborate; but this does not mean they're difficult. If you are a beginning cook, they are detailed and clear enough for you to follow. If you're an accomplished cook, they are inventive enough to interest you. Many parts of the meals can be made in advance, so these feasts are ideal for entertaining.

Although the main courses are designed as whole balanced meals, if your time or inclination is limited, single recipes are good in their own right. The chili from the chili casserole, for instance, goes very well with the cornbread from the stuffed squash. I often eat the lentil sauce from the tofu tart on pasta. The Mediterranean salad makes a great light lunch. And the possibilities go on and on. In addition to the section on whole meals, I've included recipes for an array of appealing soups and sumptuous, naturally sweetened desserts. Many of the soups make light meals unto themselves. For example, the minestrone with pesto needs only a wedge of crusty bread, and it's ready to serve; the same is true for the borscht. The desserts range from simple fruit kantens to chocolate layer cakes and filo ensembles.

Although these recipes will certainly serve as a great resource for vegans, you don't have to be a vegan to enjoy this book. There are many reasons you might want to avoid meat or dairy. Maybe you are guided by spiritual or religious conviction—yoga practices, for example, encourage abstinence from animal food to make it easier to meditate. Perhaps you are concerned about the disregard and mistreatment of animals. Some choose vegetarianism because of health concerns—even the USFDA's food pyramid gives primacy to grains, vegetables, and fruit. In addition, more and more information links diets high in animal food with an increased incidence of illnesses. Likewise, some people have an adverse reaction to certain foods and need to find suitable alternatives. But maybe simple vanity motivates you: eating a variety of low-fat, vitamin-rich foods will make you look and feel better. Perhaps you need to cook for someone else who is a vegetarian. Or maybe you simply want to open up your "food vocabulary," to explore the infinite possibilities that the vegetable kingdom has to offer.

Whether you've been living on simple fare but would enjoy genuinely guiltfree culinary pleasure or you want to "lighten up" and avoid meat and dairy, the trove of recipes here will not let you down. This book really shows you how to exclude certain ingredients without compromising your cuisine. While the food is healthful, it's unequivocally rich in taste and attractive in presentation.

The sensuousness of the cooking process starts with a shopping expedition to a grocery store or greenmarket, a place filled with delectable edibles. Start with the best, most luscious natural food you can buy, and let the seasons guide your choices. Whenever possible, use organic food, which feels good in the body, is good for the planet, and is usually the most appetizing. Nonorganic produce is usually heavily sprayed with pesticides that undermine our immune systems and pollute our water supply. But even on taste alone, I have never ceased to marvel at the difference in quality between a can of organic and a can of nonorganic beans.

Try to shop greenmarkets, where farmers who sell directly to the consumer are enthusiastic about what they're growing and ever ready to share information about their often unusual produce. A typical supermarket stocks two or three kinds of tomatoes, whereas your local greenmarket might have as many as fifteen. In addition, an imported tomato from another coast or faraway country cannot compare in vitality and taste to one grown locally and picked just a day before it's sold.

Stay away from unvoluptuous food, such as Aspartame, hydrogenated fats, soft drinks, and artificial "low-fat" products. This includes refined foods, as well as anything that has a long list of unpronounceable additives and preservatives. Keep your larder filled with good quality ingredients that you will use frequently and that will last. This includes beans, grains, shoyu, oil, vinegar, dried chiles, spices, sea vegetables, and miso. A well-stocked pantry makes shopping excursions simpler.

Think voluptuous. It's okay to use coconut milk and salt—to splash love into your food, to call down blessings on your kitchen, your family, and friends, even as you wash and chop and slice. Eat slowly, gorgeously, with gratitude. Nourish one another, as deeply as you can. Dare to be magnanimous and voluptuous of spirit.

ingredients

salt

A voluptuous vegetarian diet—or any diet that is desirable to stay on for a length of time—does not shy away from fat and salt. Salt draws out of food the essential flavors that would otherwise remain neutral or latent. Many people are afraid of seasoning their food properly because of the misconception that salt is bad for you. Salt, however, is your friend, not your enemy: The proper amount added during cooking releases the flavors of the food without making it taste salty (salt added at the table, on the other hand, does not permeate the food properly). Granted, there is too much sodium in many processed and packaged foods. Cut back on these items, and salt your own cooked food properly. Learn to salt to taste, and before long you'll recognize when a dish is at that perfect point.

Different salts taste different. The best salt is **sea salt,** which is highest in trace minerals, and is either evaporated by the sun and wind or dried, additive-free, at low temperatures.

fat

You need fat in a healthy diet. A lot has been made of "good" fats and "bad" fats. The "good," or monounsaturated, oils lower LDL (or "bad") cholesterol without affecting HDL ("good") cholesterol, thus improving your overall cholesterol level.

Olive oil is the best cooking oil, and extra-virgin—taken from the first pressing of the olives—is the best olive oil, in terms of both healthfulness and taste. **Canola oil,** made from rapeseed (similar to mustard seed), is my oil of choice when a no-taste oil is called for. Both of these oils are monounsaturated, as is **peanut oil,** which I like to use for stir-fries. For condiments and dressings, **toasted sesame oil** and **walnut oil** are also good. Use expeller-pressed oils, the kind found in natural food stores, which taste better. Heat-processed oils and those extracted with solvents use hexane to remove the oil, which is then bleached and deodorized in a high-temperature process. The resulting product is highly refined, with a very different molecular structure from anything found in nature.

Though shunned by some because it's a saturated fat, **coconut oil** is an excellent cooking oil that tastes good (pie crusts made with coconut oil are tender and flaky), is highly resistant to chemical changes when heated (so it cooks well and retains its natural integrity), and is known to have many healthful qualities. Coconut oil has no cholesterol and populations that rely on coconut oil as their main fat source have among the lowest incidence of cardiovascular disease. Make sure to use a high-quality coconut oil, unprocessed, and packaged in a dark, opaque, airtight container (see Sources). But never use for consumption coconut oil labeled for body or hair care!

grains

Grains have sustained cultures as long as humans have cultivated land. Complex carbohydrates consisting of bran, germ, and endosperm, grains are a good source of fiber, minerals, and the B-complex vitamin. To be assimilated into the body, grains need to be chewed (and the longer you chew, the sweeter they become). They also should be cooked with a small amount of salt. Make sure to store grains in a cool, dry place, preferably in sealed glass jars or tightly closed airtight sacks. Try to use grains within six months of purchase.

Most grains should be washed before cooking: cover with water in a large bowl, stir and swish around the submerged grains with your hand, then let the water settle for a moment. Any dust, bugs, or loose particles should come to the surface when the grains settle. Pour off the top half of the water along with any floating debris. Then pour the rest through a strainer. Repeat until the runoff water is clear.

Many grains benefit from toasting after washing and before cooking, which can enhance their taste by imparting a light nuttiness, and helps them soften while cooking. To toast, simply warm the grains over a medium-low heat in the dry pot you're going to cook them in. Stir as they toast until any residual washing water is evaporated. Or, sauté the grains in a little oil first. The oil coats the grain and helps to keep the cooked grains separate.

The following grains, used in this book, are widely obtainable in natural food markets, and most can be found at gourmet and specialty stores.

Rice comes in white or brown, in long grain, medium grain, and short grain. While white rice is stripped of its hull, bran, and germ, thus containing fewer nutrients, sometimes its light texture is appropriate in the context of the meal. For this reason, at times I favor types of white rice over brown. White and brown **basmati**, with their nutty aroma and fluffy texture, double in length when cooked. **Arborio**, the white rice used for making risotto, swells when cooked. To retain the starch that gives it its characteristic creaminess, it is not washed before cooking. **Thai jasmine** is another white rice with a distinct fragrant bouquet. **Red Bhutan** is like a short-grain brown rice, only with a deep reddish-brown color and a sweet, nutty taste. **Wild rice** is not technically a rice, but a seed of aquatic grass mostly found around lakes, although now it is cultivated. Its seeds split open and become fluffy after 30 to 40 minutes of cooking. It is high in protein and its wild flavor makes it a favorite gourmet food.

From Colombian and Venezuelan friends, I was taught a wonderful method of cooking brown rice: The rice is washed and dry-toasted as normal. It is then cooked uncovered, in a high ratio (3:1) of water to grain. When the water is almost entirely absorbed, the rice is covered for the last

5 minutes. This makes perfect brown rice every time, and the cooking process is in plain sight, taking any guesswork out of it.

Quinoa, not actually a true cereal grain but used like one, is light and easily digested, and has the highest protein of any grain. It is small, about the size of a sesame seed, but round. It must be washed well, not only to clean but to remove the bitter saponin coating that grows on its outer surface. A fine-meshed strainer is helpful for rinsing quinoa, as the grains are very light and float in the water. I like to cook quinoa in combination with other grains, for example with millet as in the African Groundnut Stew (page 74).

Millet is a small, nutty-flavored yellow grain that is easy to digest (it is good for the stomach and spleen) and gluten free. It is an important staple in Asia and North Africa. It should be toasted before cooking to keep the grains separate; untoasted, the grains are sticky and wonderful for croquettes, as in the Fresh Corn, Millet, and Rice Croquettes (page 64).

Barley comes in two forms, hulled (only the outer hull is removed) and pearled (where the bran is polished off). Pearled barley loses all its fiber and half its protein, fat, and minerals. Pearled barley found in natural food stores has undergone fewer pearlings than the supermarket counterpart, and therefore is much larger and a better choice. Barley is fairly starchy, making it a natural thickener in soups. It is soothing to the digestive tract and liver.

Amaranth, rich in lysine, is a very tiny grain, like a poppy seed. It is difficult to wash because the grains are so tiny and light that they pour off with the water, or get stuck in the holes of even the finest-meshed strainer. The packaged variety is quite clean, so I tend not to wash it. Amaranth has a bit of a gooey quality, so it is best mixed with other grains. I like to toast it and bake it into quick breads (it gives them a nutty crunch), as in the cornbread for the stuffed squash.

Couscous, often mistakenly considered a grain, is in fact a pasta, and should not be washed before cooking. A traditional food of Morocco, couscous is made from semolina that is cooked, dried, and chopped into little grain-like pieces.

Hominy is dried field corn or dent corn, which has larger and starchier kernels than corn-on-the-cob sweet corn. Also called *posole,* hominy has a delicious corn flavor and is great left whole in stews or blended for tamales or *arepas.* **Grits** are broken-up pieces of dried corn. **Masa harina** is finely ground corn flour.

greens

Greens, full of vitamins and minerals, are foods the body craves. Dark, leafy greens such as collards and kale are loaded with calcium and are extremely important in a dairy-free diet. The long list of greens used in the book includes salad greens that are best eaten raw as well as greens that must be cooked; a number of them can be eaten either way.

Always wash greens. It is usually easiest to wash them after they have been cut and trimmed. Place the greens in a large bowl of water and swish them around for a minute or so. Lift them from the water and the dirt will settle to the bottom of the bowl. Some greens that are typically very dirty, such as escarole, spinach, and arugula, should be submerged several times, each in fresh water. Pour the dirty water and sediment from the bowl, rinse the bowl, and refill it with fresh water. Wash the greens again, and possibly again, until no more grit is left at the bottom of the bowl. Herbs such as parsley, cilantro, and basil are usually quite muddy and should be washed in the same way.

It is important to dry your greens, especially if you plan to store them for several hours; they won't spoil if they're well-dried. Salad greens especially need to be dried, since a vinaigrette will get watered down over wet lettuce. Store salad greens wrapped loosely in a towel and put in a plastic bag and refrigerate. Use cooking greens as soon as possible after purchasing or refrigerate in plastic bags.

Greens wilt dramatically when cooked, so count on at least a full pound of greens for two servings. Tender greens such as spinach, chard, and beet greens wilt down even more than heartier ones such as collards and kale.

Here is a quick overview of the greens used in the book:

Romaine is one of my favorite salad greens because the crisp leaves have a flavor that holds up to strong dressings, and the dark leaves are among the most nutritious of lettuces. **Green-leaf** and **red-leaf** are common varieties of loose lettuces with tender leaves. **Lollo rosso** is a dramatic, specialty version of red-leaf lettuce with small, bright, crinkly red leaves. These greens need a more subtle dressing than does romaine. Among the soft, buttery textured leaves for salads are the tender **Bibb** and **butter** lettuces.

Mesclun mixes can include as many as fifteen to twenty different varieties of small, wild, slightly bitter greens. The lettuces are most often previously rinsed and are sold by the pound in farmer's markets, supermarkets, and specialty stores. They make an interesting salad with very little fuss.

Escarole and **curly endive (frisée)**, **dandelion**, and **radicchio** are all members of the chicory family, which is closely related to lettuce. They all have a refreshing bitterness, ranging from light to more pronounced, and they stand up well to assertive dressings made with sharp vinegars and nut oils.

Watercress, arugula, and **sorrel** are leafy herbs with unabashed flavor that mix well with other greens, make great salads unto themselves, and are delicious quickly sautéed. Since they shrink quite a bit when cooked, you need to allow an entire bunch per person. Make sure to chop off the tough stems before cooking. Sorrel has a wonderfully lemony flavor but turns a distinctive olive drab when cooked, so it is usually best cooked with some brighter green such as spinach.

Of the cooking greens, **spinach, beet greens,** and **chard** are tender and quick-cooking, suitable for a quick sauté. They are sweet and versatile and more or less interchangeable. Their stems should be removed but reserved—they make wonderful additions to stocks. Of course, spinach is also good raw.

Cabbages have wonderful texture. Both **red** and **green dutchhead cabbage** (the ones we're all used to) can be eaten raw or cooked, and are available year-round. Braised cabbage wilts into a harmonious blend of spicy sweet flavor. **Napa** (Asian cabbage), with its football shape and crinkly leaves, makes wonderfully tender cole slaw. **Mizuna** and **bok choy** are both members of the cabbage family as well, although mizuna looks more like a salad green and is treated as such—its spiky leaves make an especially dramatic plate garnish. **Bok choy** has green leaves and fleshy, white, edible stems. It is quick-cooking and mild-tasting and makes a wonderful addition to any stir-fry.

Of the frequently used hearty greens, **collards** are the most versatile and the mildest in taste. Collards have large, broad leaves and a stem that needs to be removed. **Kale** has ruffled, grayish leaves and is stronger-tasting than collards, and also has an inedible stem that needs to be removed. Since they usually need to be cooked for 10 to 20 minutes (depending on how tough the leaves are), boiling or braising are better techniques than something like a quick steam. Collards and kale don't lose that many nutrients from the longer cooking time, and their flavors benefit dramatically. Besides, the cooking liquid becomes a nutritious broth. The greens are also delicious sautéed, but you should boil them first to partially cook.

Pungent, peppery **mustard greens** have light green crinkled leaves that are more tender than kale but have a hot, mustardy bite. The larger the green, the stronger the flavor. The small, young leaves are good eaten raw in salad and are often part of a mesclun mix. The larger leaves should be stemmed before cooking for a good 10 to 20 minutes. The longer mustard greens cook, the softer their flavor.

Broccoli rabe, commonly eaten in Italy, is a green with a pronounced bitter flavor (a blanch before further cooking gets rid of some of the bitterness). Its leaves are similar to those of a turnip, with little broccoli-like florettes interspersed among the greens. All parts are edible.

beans

Beans, or legumes, are an important part of a vegetarian diet—high in protein and fiber, versatile, inexpensive, and delicious. Almost every traditional culture has several types of beans that have sustained it for centuries. Beans are readily available at natural food stores, gourmet markets, and ethnic groceries. As heirloom or boutique types become more and more popular, a greater variety of unusual or worthwhile beans appears in markets.

Beans need to be sorted to remove any stones (when you're dealing with whole foods, these little traces of nature are to be expected) and washed before cooking: cover them with water in a bowl, swish them around with your fingers, and drain. As opposed to washing greens, where the sediment will sink to the bottom of the bowl, with beans (as with grains), most sediment will rise to the surface of the water. Pour off the water, refill, and rinse again.

Beans fall into two categories: those that need to be soaked, and those that do not. Those that don't need soaking are all types of lentils (including brown, green, red, and French), and any split bean, such as split peas or moong dhal; these are all relatively quick-cooking. Adzuki beans and black-eyed peas can go either way.

The rest of the beans should be soaked 6 to 8 hours before cooking. Easiest is to soak them overnight, in three times as much water as beans. If there is no time for a 6-hour soak, you can quick-soak: Cover with water, bring to a boil, then turn off the heat and let the beans sit in the water for an hour or two. To make beans most digestible, always drain the soaking liquid, and cook in fresh water. With the exception of limas, beans should always be salted *after* they are cooked. Salting during cooking inhibits the cooking and prevents the beans from softening. For lima beans, however, salting both the soaking and cooking water helps keep the beans' skins intact.

All of the bean recipes in this book give both the stovetop method and a pressure-cooking method, which cooks them especially quickly. In fact, this alone is a good enough reason to own a pressure cooker—it's amazing how much time is saved, and it gives beans a marvelous soft texture and a good thick broth.

To pressure cook, in the pot of a pressure cooker cover the beans with three times as much water as beans. Bring the water, partially covered, to a boil, then lock the lid into place. Pressure will rise inside the pressure cooker. When you wait until the liquid is at a boil before you lock the lid, the pressure gauge will start rising immediately, which takes the guesswork out of when to start timing. When the second ring on the pressure-release valve is revealed, adjust the heat to maintain that level of pressure. Start timing your beans from the instant the pressure cooker is at high pressure. When the cooking time is up, turn off the heat and let the pressure come down at its own rate. This is the natural cooling method and usually takes about 10 minutes for the pressure to decrease. To cool quickly, put the pressure cooker under running water until the pressure is down. (You will be cutting down on the cooking time this way.) But *never* attempt to remove the lid while the pressure valve is up.

Lentils shouldn't be pressure cooked; they turn to mush unless cooked on the stovetop. I personally do not like to cook lima beans in a pressure cooker, since they are so delicate.

Here is a quick rundown of the beans used in the book:

Lentils are shaped like disks or lenses. In India there are more than fifty varieties, but the most familiar ones here are brown and green. Lentils have an earthy flavor and cook quickly. They tend to get mushy, although the tiny, elegant **lentilles du Puy** (French lentils) hold their shape really well. **Red lentils** cook quickly (in about 20 minutes) and turn to mush, so they are good in soups and sauces.

Moong dhal is the hulled and split mung bean. The whole mung bean is dark green, but when split it is a golden yellow inside. Available in Indian markets, the split mung bean is the form most widely used. It is easily digestible, and it is often combined with appropriate spices such as asafetida to make it even more digestible.

Split peas are split dried field peas, available in green or yellow. Their consistency becomes completely creamy when cooked, so they are perfect for soups and sauces.

Adzuki beans are small reddish brown beans with a white stripe along one edge; they have a sweet, almost nutty flavor when cooked. Adzukis are popular in Japanese and Chinese cooking, and according to traditional Chinese medicine, they strengthen the kidneys. It is ancient Chinese folk wisdom that kidneys govern the emotion of fear, so adzuki beans are considered a source of strength that helps people confront their challenges bravely. Thus, they are served on New Year's Eve to bring courage and good fortune in the coming year.

Lima beans, also known as butter beans, come in large and small, and are starchy and creamy. They melt down into a very smooth texture for soups and sauces once the skin starts to loosen. To keep the skins intact, soak and cook them with a little salt in the water.

Chickpeas are creamy, beige, and round beans that are loosely shaped like walnuts; they are versatile, mild, and sweet-flavored. Chickpeas are popular in many cuisines, especially Middle Eastern and Mediterranean. They are ground into **chickpea flour**, an important component in the chickpea crepes (see page 81) and custardy Indian chickpea tart (see page 118).

Black beans hold up against the assertive, hot seasonings found in Mexican and other Latin American foods. They are members of the kidney bean family and can be interchanged with pinto beans in any recipe. Black beans are sweet and hardy, and their deep color contrasts beautifully with many foods; they are one of my favorites.

Black-eyed peas, also known as cowpeas, are quick-cooking, earthy, flavorful, beige peas with a black spot. They were brought to the South, where they thrived and became a part of Southern cuisine. They are most associated with the down-home classic Hoppin' John, a dish of black-eyed peas and rice that, eaten on New Year's Day, is said to bring good luck for the year.

Anasazi beans are mottled maroon and white beans. The name comes from a Navajo word meaning "ancient ones." They were popularized in the Southwest, and they lend themselves well to Southwestern and Latin American flavors. The full flavored beans hold their shape when cooked.

Pinto beans have a beige to pink color with mottled splotches, thus the name *pinto*, meaning "painted" in Spanish. They turn solid pink, however, when cooked. Pintos are synonymous with Southwestern cooking, and they are the most cultivated bean in the United States.

The deep-red **kidney bean** is named for its shape. Its family includes pinto beans and anasazi beans. It is the most common bean used in chili.

equipment and cutting terms

equipment

Decent equipment is far more important than the size of your kitchen. You can have a large kitchen with a lot of counter space, but if your pots are flimsy, or your knife is thin and dull, even the simplest of tasks, such as cooking a pot of rice or chopping vegetables, could be a frustrating experience.

This doesn't mean that you need to go out and spend a fortune right away. Building your kitchen is like furnishing any other part of your home: Start with the essential items, then pick up extra tools and baking supplies as you go along.

I can't emphasize enough how important good equipment is to the cook. "Good" doesn't always mean the most expensive, although sometimes a quality tool is the pricier one. A lot of equipment is not necessary, as long as your few essentials are really serviceable.

POTS, PANS, AND OTHER COOKING VESSELS

Pots, whether good or bad, last a very long time, so you'll never regret an investment in good pots. Heavy-duty pots are so much more forgiving: They disperse heat evenly, and they are much easier to clean if you do happen to burn something. My favorite pots have three layers: a stainless interior that touches the food, a middle layer of aluminum to conduct heat evenly, and an outer layer (of stainless or polished steel, aluminum, or whatever look you like).

You don't need that many different pots when a few good ones will do the job.

- One or two 4-quart pots, or saucepans, referred to in this book as a medium pot. This most useful size is perfect for cooking four to six servings of soup or stew, and will accommodate nearly all the soups in the book, and almost all of the stews.
- At least one 1½- to 2-quart pot for smaller amounts, such as one cup of grain.
- One larger pot (8-quart) is necessary for stocks, larger soups, and cooking large quantities of greens.
- One 10- to 11-inch frying pan and one 2- to 3-quart sauté pan. Both are good pans for sautéing. One has sloped sides, and one has vertical sides with a lid, perfect for braising vegetables.

These are the essential five pots. A cast-iron skillet is great for toasting chiles and dry-toasting nuts and spices. A flat-top **griddle** is fun to have for pancakes and *arepas* (although you could also use a cast-iron skillet). If you don't have an outdoor grill or an indoor gas grill, a **grill pan** (the kind that fits over two burners) is adequate. They often come with a griddle on one side and a grill on the other. Additionally, I like a very tiny pot for making spice oils or reheating small amounts. A very large sauté pan is good if you plan to be cooking for more than eight people. And a **crepe pan** made of cold-rolled steel (black steel) is the best for easy crepe-making. Finally, baking sheets and a steamer insert will come in handy.

A **pressure cooker** is indispensable for vegetarian food, especially beans. Pressure cookers lock in flavor, drastically reduce the cooking time, and give beans a marvelous soft texture and a good, thick broth. Easy and safe to use, pressure cookers are no longer the capricious, volatile devices of the past.

A selection of **Pyrex** baking dishes is useful, especially an **8 by 8-inch**, a **deep 7 by 9-inch** (all casseroles are baked in this pan), and a large **9 by 11-inch** pan. A **9-inch pie plate** is also useful for all the pies.

Cheesecloth, available in most supermarkets, is wonderful for tying herbs in a bouquet garni and for making almond milk or ginger juice, or whenever extra-fine straining is called for.

Parchment paper is a lesser but still-helpful item. It keeps food from directly coming in contact with the baking pan, so food doesn't stick. It helps vegetables roast evenly. Use it to line cake pans or to keep poaching fruit submerged in liquid. You can roll crusts out easily sandwiched between two sheets of parchment paper.

KNIVES AND TOOLS

Knives are another essential supply, but you can get by with a few. No need to purchase an entire set. I use basically three knives—an 8-inch chef's knife, a serrated knife, and a paring knife.

You should have an 8-inch or 10-inch chef's knife, whichever feels more comfortable. The knife should have a good, weighty feel. A serrated knife is also handy for cutting bread, citrus, and tomatoes. Sometimes I like to use a thin-bladed Japanese vegetable knife as well. I don't make a big deal about paring knives, because, like socks in the washing machine, they seem to disappear quite easily. Instead of worrying about it, I keep a few around. And a **mandoline** is a small metal or plastic device useful for cutting vegetables paper thin.

I like to have two kinds of **peelers**. A wide plastic peeler takes a thick layer of skin off at a time, so it is ideal for winter squash or thick-skinned vegetables such as celery root. A classic metal potato peeler is good when you want to take a thin layer off a fruit or vegetable. I especially like them when I want a large piece of lemon zest without getting any of the white pith underneath.

The best citrus **zester** was developed by Suzy O'Rourke, a cooking teacher and recipe developer. It looks like a carpenter's rasp, and it has shallow teeth that make grating zest quick and easy and don't touch the bitter white pith. It is available from Cooking By the Book in New York City and from other cookware suppliers (see Resources and Mail-Order Sources, page 293).

Although a **mortar and pestle** may not be a truly necessary tool (in almost all instances you could substitute a spice grinder), this is a tool I would not be without. There is something very satisfying and soulful about toasting spices and hand-grinding them in a mortar and pestle. The aroma of freshly toasted spices is strong and fragrant when you crush the seeds this way. I favor the marble mortar and pestle, or stone grinding bowls, which can be found in most kitchen supply stores.

An **oven thermometer**, an essential tool, lets you know if your oven is preheated to the desired temperature. It also lets you know if your oven runs hot or cold so you can adjust it accordingly.

A simple **timer** is necessary if you're easily distracted (if you answer the phone when you're cooking, for example), or for when you have several dishes cooking at the same time.

Squeeze bottles are plastic bottles of various sizes available at art, beauty, and cooking supply stores. They are a fun—and to me crucial—tool for embellishing your food. Use for chile-paste dots in your soup, for stripes of cream on your main courses, for patterns on dessert sauces. They are great for salad dressings also. They give your meal a professional look without a lot of bother. Have a few handy for the sheer fun of decorating.

Other small but essential pieces of equipment include wooden spoons, rubber and metal spatulas (and an offset spatula), a wooden or plastic reamer (for juicing citrus) or small citrus juicer, whisks, mixing bowls, metal strainers, and a fluted-edged pastry wheel. Also indispensable are measuring spoons and cups (both dry and wet), scoops, a pastry brush, and a potato masher. Additional useful pastry items are mentioned in the introductions to desserts.

SMALL APPLIANCES

A **blender**, with its narrow base and small, sharp blade, is the best piece of equipment for making your food wonderfully creamy, especially food that has a high proportion of liquid. It is the device of choice to make the smoothest, silkiest-textured soups. Since the base is small, it's great for chile pastes or small amounts of pasty things. It is also useful for emulsifying the wet ingredients in a cake or for mixing a crepe batter.

An **immersion blender** is an inexpensive tool that can speed up a lot of cooking. It can be placed directly into a pot, so it saves you the trouble of transferring liquid from the pot to the blender. It is great for puréeing some soups or sauces—though not if they contain fibrous bits that really need a blender. Use it to purée part of a soup to thicken it, while retaining part whole for texture. You can easily emulsify a salad dressing. An immersion blender is handy for whisking cornmeal into polenta, and chickpea flour for the chickpea "polenta."

A **food processor** is wonderful for puréeing food that is more solid than liquid. For whipping up a tofu crème, for example, or for making the texture of the hominy *arepas* perfect, a food processor is the way to go. It grinds nuts into flour for mixing with crusts, it purées squash filling for pumpkin pies, it finely chops garlic and ginger. It is preferable to have both a food processor and a blender, because they both are perfect for different things.

A **food mill** is used when you want to remove seeds and skin from a sauce or purée. Only the juice and pulp of the fruit and vegetables pass through the mill.

Freshly milled pepper is simple with a **pepper mill**. Pepper mills come in a variety of sizes and shapes. You want one that is adjustable for a finer or coarser grind. Once you get used to freshly ground black pepper, any other kind will taste flat.

A **spice grinder** is a coffee mill used exclusively to grind spices. (Use another one for coffee and the like.) Buy your spices whole—they last longer and you have the option of toasting them whole—and grind them in a spice grinder.

An inexpensive, hand-cranked **pasta machine** is essential for rolling out pasta dough and making ravioli. A **ravioli mold** also makes the process most efficient.

cutting techniques

A **round** is a circular slice. To make rounds, cut across a cylindrical vegetable—be it a carrot, daikon, cucumber, or jalapeño—at even intervals. The basic round cut can be varied by cutting the vegetable on the bias to create elongated or oval disks. This is a **diagonal cut**. This cut exposes a larger surface area of the vegetable, so the vegetables will have a shorter cooking time.

Half-moons are used for elongated vegetables like carrots and parsnips. Cut the vegetable in half lengthwise, then cut each piece across into half-circle pieces. These are half-moons.

Quarter-moons are the same idea as half-moons, except you cut the vegetable in half lengthwise and then cut the halves once more into quarters, before cutting into pieces.

To make **matchsticks**, first cut vegetables or fruit into thin diagonal slices of the same length. Then stack the slices and cut into long thin pieces.

To **dice** is to cut a vegetable into uniform pieces. First cut off a slab to make a flat base to sit solidly on the cutting-board surface. Cut the vegetable into slabs—¼-inch, ⅓-inch, ½-inch, or 1-inch, depending on the size dice you want. Then stack a few slabs on top of each other and cut into matchsticks the same width you cut the slabs. Now cut the matchsticks into cubes—or dice. Be sure to cut the same width at each stage. For example: ¼-inch slabs are cut into ¼-inch matchsticks, which in turn become ¼-inch dice. A ¼-inch dice is considered a small dice. A ⅓-inch is a medium dice, and a ¾-inch is a large dice. An ⅛-inch dice is also called *brunoise.*

A **rough cut** is made by cutting the vegetable without regard to shape. This cut is used for stocks, and for soups and sauces that are going to be puréed. Though the shape doesn't matter, the size of these cuts should be more or less uniform. For a vegetable stock a rough cut is fine, but do not cut vegetables more than an inch thick, so that the vegetable pieces can fully impart their flavor during the cooking time.

To **mince** is to chop into very fine pieces. Garlic, shallots, and fresh herbs are often minced. First slice or chop the vegetables or herbs into small pieces. Hold your knife by the handle with one hand the way you always do, and position the blade above the pile of chopped pieces. Then with your palm or fingers pressing the back edge of the blade, rest the sharp edge of the knife near the tip against the cutting board and chop pieces rapidly, using the curve of the blade to help create a round, rocking motion. Continue chopping, inching left and right, until pieces are uniformly very small.

To **shred** means to slice leaves very thin. This cut is often used on cabbages and leafy greens. To shred cabbage, first quarter the cabbage and cut out the rough centers. Then lay each quarter on one cut side and thinly slice across, repeatedly working the knife from one end of the quarter to the other, until it's all shredded. For Napa, or Chinese cabbage, pull off outer leaves and discard, then thinly slice across.

A **chiffonade** is made by shredding leaves, most often leaves that have been stacked and rolled. First stack same-size leaves together, tightly roll them up, then slice across the rolled leaves, again and again, until the roll has been transformed into wispy little shreds. This technique is used on basil and on large leafy greens such as spinach and chard.

A **roll cut** is a handsome, basic cut for long, thin root vegetables, such as carrots, parsnips, and daikon. First place the peeled root on a cutting board at an angle and make a diagonal cut to remove the stem end. Roll the root halfway over (180 degrees) and slice through on the same diagonal, keeping the knife where it was for the first cut, creating a wedge shape. This is a roll cut. Repeat until the entire root has been cut. If the vegetable is thicker at one end, roll it only a quarter of the way around and then make the diagonal cut. The result will be an irregular piece with angled edges facing different ways. Continue to roll partway and slice on the diagonal. The cut and size varies depending on the angle at which the vegetable rests in relation to the knife.

Onions are a special case. First, to **peel** an onion, cut off the stem end and trim the root end—but leave it intact. Peel off any skin and also the underlying layer if it has brown spots.

To **thinly slice** an onion lengthwise (half moon), cut the peeled onion in half from the root end to the tip. Thinly slice in the direction of the growth lines.

To **dice**, first halve the onion lengthwise through the root. Lay it cut-side down and make even, crosswise cuts (distance apart depends on how small you want the dice to be) all the way through from stem to root end without cutting through the root end. Then turn onion and cut into cubes—dice.

Onion rings are slices cut crosswise against the growth lines.

All recipes in this book call for medium onions, which are about the size of tennis balls.

A medium onion weighs about 6 ounces, and yields about one cup chopped.

soups

Beautiful soup, so rich and green,
Waiting in a hot tureen.
Who for such dainties would not stoop?
Soup of the evening, Beautiful soup.

—Lewis Carroll

Of all the components of a meal, soup is the most versatile. It can be a luscious first course designed to whet your appetite for the delicacies that follow, or it can be a cozy meal unto itself. The soups in this book range from rustic, chunky soups to elegant, smooth-as-silk varieties. Although these soups are strictly vegetarian, there is no lack of flavor here. All sorts of techniques are presented to get the creamy textures and rich, deep flavors comparable to, if not better than, those associated with animal products.

Even when you are working from a recipe, you still have a good deal of room for your own adjustments. You want the soup thicker? Evaporate some of the liquid by cooking longer. You want the soup thinner? Add a little water or broth. Almost every soup in this book can be prepared as a starter to a main course or as a quick and economical way to make a whole meal. Black bean soup is delicious with cornbread (page 102). Add some greens, and the meal is complete. Minestrone is a whole light meal, needing perhaps only a salad. The possibilities for mixing and matching go on and on.

Most soups last from a few days to a week, and many freeze quite well. If you're a Sunday cook who likes to get a head start on the week's cooking, then soup-making is one place where you'll get a substantial return on your time in the kitchen. Moreover, perhaps more than any other food, soups make great leftovers. Most taste even better a day or two after they are made.

All of the soups in this book were made in a heavy-bottomed medium (4-quart) or large (6- to 8-quart) pot. Rather than fill your pot to the brim and risk spilling soup as it cooks or is stirred, choose a pot that is big enough. The heavy bottom on a good pot prevents vegetables from scorching. Therefore, you can sauté vegetables right in the pot. Use cold filtered or bottled water when you make a stock or soup. Don't use hot water here, or, for that matter, anywhere in your cooking, because it picks up whatever residue is in your pipes.

After sautéeing the vegetables for a soup, I usually cover the pot to bring the liquid to a quick boil. I lower the heat and cook my soups partially covered. This allows for minimal evaporation, while it gives the steam an escape valve, thus eliminating messy spillovers caused by a buildup of steam.

Cook your soup at a steady simmer. That is, small bubbles should break the surface regularly. Don't cook at a rolling boil, at which point large bubbles break the surface and ingredients collide with one another. And don't cook at too low a heat, so that no bubbles rise—that's not cooking. Keep an eye on the soup so you can adjust the heat if necessary.

When you reheat a soup, do not recook it. Slowly bring it to a simmer and make sure to taste it. Some soups thicken as they cool and may need some more liquid and reseasoning. Potato soups generally need a quick pick-me-up of lemon and salt.

Don't serve your soup without the garnish. The garnishes are not intended as afterthoughts. They are an integral part of the design and flavor of the soup.

Soup-making is a pleasurable pursuit. Hot or cold, thick or brothy, chunky or smooth, exotic or familiar, soup comes in so many forms. Whether you need a starter for an elegant dinner party or something to soothe your weary spirits after a hard day, a good soup will always suit the occasion.

stocks

An important consideration in a soup is whether or not to use a stock. A stock, of course, injects fuller flavor into a recipe. Some soups, however, have so much flavor on their own that it is not necessary to use one. If you're making a thick bean soup, chances are a stock is not necessary. If it is a light brothy soup with delicate vegetables floating in the middle, chances are you will need one. Fortunately, the stock-making is neither difficult nor time-consuming. You usually need only ten minutes or so to rough-chop the vegetables. A stock is best made in a pot with high sides so that less water is evaporated. Keep your pot uncovered to prevent the stock from clouding. Once the stock is simmering, the remaining cooking time is labor-free. Make a stock while you're prepping the soup ingredients. Or make one while you're at the stove doing something else; you can always freeze it.

You'll find several stock recipes in this book, including a basic vegetable, a Southeast Asian, a Chinese mushroom, and a rich stock. The basic stock is quite versatile and it can be tailored to enhance a specific soup by adding extra ingredients. For example, some good additions for a sweet vegetable soup include parsnips, fennel, and sweet potatoes. When I'm making stock for a particular soup from scratch I'll often use the trimmings from the main flavor components to enhance these key flavors. But this is not necessary; stock can be kept frozen, then defrosted and simmered with vegetable trimmings and herbs from the recipe you are making. Shallots and green beans are suitable for any pottage. Additions for specific soups include ginger, lemongrass, corn cobs, mushroom stems, asparagus, and tomatoes. Avoid spinach, as it makes stock taste grassy, and avoid onion peels, which give stock a bitter taste and turn it dark. Avoid the brassica family, which includes cauliflower, cabbage, Brussels sprouts, and broccoli. Beets, while they are appropriate in some instances, will turn your stock red. And while a stock is a good place to use up bits and pieces of leftover vegetables, do not even think of using anything that is tired or spoiled-looking.

For a richer-tasting stock, sauté the vegetables in a little oil before adding the liquid. The rich stock for the onion soup—which, incidentally, is a good basic rich stock—includes lentils, potatoes, and celery root. Although this stock has a little shoyu (soy sauce) in it, I almost never add salt to my stocks. That way, I have more flexibility later on if I want to reduce the stock to concentrate the flavor.

In a pinch, vegetable bouillon cubes make a satisfactory substitution for basic vegetable stock. The best-quality bouillon cubes I have found are those made from organic vegetables. They are salted; unfortunately, the unsalted varities contain hydrogenated fat and are lacking in flavor. When using the bouillon cubes, omit the salt in the cooking process and adjust salt to taste after your soup is completed. Use 2 bouillon cubes in recipes that call for 4 to 6 cups of stock.

basic vegetable stock

This all-purpose basic stock can be tailored to individual soup recipes with additional vegetables and flavorings.

MAKES 6 CUPS

1   onion, peeled and roughly chopped
1   leek, greens included, cleaned and roughly chopped
2   celery stalks, roughly chopped
2   carrots, roughly chopped
1   bay leaf
2   garlic cloves, halved
1   zucchini, roughly chopped
2   cups chopped Swiss chard
    Handful of flat-leaf parsley
    Handful of thyme sprigs
8   cups water

• Place all the ingredients in a large pot or stockpot and bring to a boil uncovered. Lower the heat and simmer for 45 minutes, until the flavor develops. Strain, pushing the vegetables against the strainer to extract as much liquid as possible. Cool the stock. Refrigerate for up to three days, or freeze for up to four months.

southeast asian stock

Lemongrass, ginger, and lime zest provide the definitively Asian accents.

MAKES 6 CUPS

1 onion, peeled and roughly chopped
2 leeks, sliced, cleaned, and roughly chopped, greens included
1 celery stalk, roughly cut
3 carrots, roughly cut
1 small sweet potato, peeled and roughly cut
1 2-inch piece of ginger, sliced into 3 pieces
3 garlic cloves, unpeeled and halved
1 lemongrass stalk, cut in a couple of pieces and bruised
1 shallot, peeled and diced
1 tablespoon shoyu (see Glossary)
1 1-inch strip of lime zest
8 cups water

• Combine all the ingredients in a large pot. Bring to a boil, lower the heat, and simmer, uncovered, for 45 minutes, until the stock has developed its flavor. Strain the stock, pushing the solids against the strainer to extract as much liquid as possible. Cool the stock. Refrigerate for up to three days, or freeze for up to four months.

chinese mushroom stock

This is a flavorful base for the hot and sour soup on page 38. Chinese black mushrooms are easily obtained at any Asian grocery, and dried shiitake mushrooms are readily available at natural food stores.

MAKES 6 CUPS

1   tablespoon canola oil
3   cups cleaned and roughly chopped leek greens
2   celery stalks, roughly chopped
2   medium carrots, roughly chopped
1   large shallot, chopped
3   garlic cloves, halved
2   2-inch slices of ginger
1   6-inch piece of kombu (see Glossary)
5   dried Chinese black mushrooms or shiitakes
8   cups water
½   cup dry sherry or white wine
1   tablespoon shoyu

• Warm the oil in a large pot or stockpot. Add the leeks, celery, carrots, and shallots and sauté for 10 minutes over low heat until softened. Add the garlic, ginger slices, kombu, mushrooms, water, sherry, and shoyu. Bring the liquid to a boil uncovered, then lower the heat and simmer for 5 minutes. Remove the kombu and continue to simmer 40 minutes longer. Strain, pushing the solids against the strainer to extract as much liquid as possible. Cool the stock. Refrigerate for up to three days, or freeze for up to four months.

rich stock

Celery root, potato, and lentils give this stock a lot of body, especially important for the onion soup (page 33). Although you could use celery instead of the celery root, the root gives a much deeper flavor.

MAKES 5 CUPS

1   tablespoon extra-virgin olive oil
4   cups cleaned and roughly chopped leek greens
3   medium carrots, roughly chopped
    ½-pound piece of celery root (celeriac), peeled and chopped into 1-inch cubes, or two celery stalks, chopped
1   medium potato, cut into chunks (½ pound)
4   garlic cloves, halved
½   cup brown lentils
1   bay leaf
½   teaspoon whole black peppercorns
1   tablespoon shoyu
    Sprigs of fresh thyme
8   stems of fresh flat-leaf parsley

• Warm the oil in a large pot. Add the leeks, carrots, celery root, potato, and garlic and sauté 7 minutes. Add the remaining ingredients along with 10 cups of water. Bring to a boil, then reduce the heat and simmer uncovered for 45 minutes or until the lentils are tender. Strain, pressing against the strainer to extract as much liquid as possible. Cool the stock. Refrigerate for up to three days, or freeze for up to four months.

crimson cabbage borscht with dill tofu "sour cream"

This soup is at once striking and familiar; you'll recognize it as borscht no matter what your background. The deep red color is so voluptuous that it is sure to awaken your senses.

By adding a wedge of crusty bread, I can make a meal out of this hearty winter soup. If you can purchase beets with tops, use both parts of the vegetable; otherwise red chard makes a good substitution for the beet greens.

SERVES 5

2 tablespoons extra-virgin olive oil
2 medium onions, cut into small dice (2 cups)
1 14.5-ounce can chopped tomatoes
2 cups shredded cabbage (¼ medium-size head)
1 bay leaf
3 medium beets, peeled and cut into small dice (½ pound)
1 medium carrot, cut into thin half-moons (½ cup)
1 medium potato (½ pound), peeled and cut into ½-inch cubes (1 cup)
1½ cups cooked great northern beans or white kidney beans, or 1 15-ounce can
6 cups Basic Vegetable Stock (page 20)
  Salt
2 tablespoons mirin or sherry
2 cups chopped beet greens (from 3 medium beets) or Swiss chard
  Freshly ground black pepper
1 tablespoon fresh lemon juice
1 recipe Dill Tofu "Sour Cream" (recipe follows)

• Warm the olive oil in a medium pot. Add the onions and sauté over medium-low heat for 10 minutes, or until the onions are softened and just starting to brown. Add the tomatoes and cabbage and cook about 5 minutes, until the cabbage is wilted and the tomatoes have reduced.

• Add the bay leaf, beets, carrots, potatoes, beans, and stock. Cover and bring the liquid to a boil. Lower the heat to a simmer, add a teaspoon of salt, and simmer, partially covered, for 15 minutes, or until the potatoes are tender. Add the mirin and beet greens and cook an additional 5 minutes.

• Finish the soup by adjusting the salt to taste and add black pepper and lemon juice. Serve with a big dollop of the "sour cream."

dill tofu "sour cream"

A snowy dollop of dairy-free sour cream rounds out many soups. Soft tofu makes a medium thick cream, but you could substitute silken tofu, which results in a slighty lighter cream.

½ pound soft tofu
2 tablespoons fresh lemon juice
3 tablespoons canola oil
2 teaspoons brown rice vinegar
¾ teaspoon sea salt
¼ teaspoon freshly ground white pepper
¼ cup chopped fresh dill

• Place all the ingredients except the dill in a food processor fitted with a metal blade. Process until creamy and smooth. Add the dill and pulse to combine. Transfer to a container and refrigerate until you are ready to use.

cream of the harvest soup

This velvety soup flirts with spicy and warming tastes. Sautéing the ginger, garlic, cumin, and coriander in a separate pan and adding them near the end of cooking creates an exciting burst of flavor for the finished product. Red chile paste boldly complements the orange soup; I keep it in a squeeze bottle so I can squirt in a few drops and make decorative swirls with the back of a knife or toothpick. Sometimes I add sautéed or roasted shiitake mushrooms as a garnish.

SERVES 4 TO 6

4 tablespoons extra-virgin olive oil
2 onions, halved and sliced into thin half-moons (2 cups)
   Salt
1 2¼- to 2½-pound butternut squash, peeled, seeded, and cut into chunks (about 6 cups)
2 medium-size sweet potatoes, peeled and cubed (3 cups)
1 medium parsnip, peeled and cubed (1 cup)
7 cups Basic Vegetable Stock (page 20)
1 bay leaf
2 dried ancho chiles
2 dried pasilla chiles
5 garlic cloves, peeled
1 1-inch cube of peeled ginger
2 teaspoons ground coriander
2 teaspoons ground cumin
1 tablespoon fresh lemon juice

• Warm 1 tablespoon of the olive oil in a large pot. Add the onions and a light sprinkle of salt and sauté over medium-low heat for about 10 minutes, until the onions are just starting to brown. Add the squash, sweet potatoes, parsnip, stock, and bay leaf, cover, and bring to a boil over high heat. Reduce the heat and simmer, partially covered, about 20 minutes, until the vegetables are tender.

• Meanwhile, remove the stems and seeds from the chiles. Place in a pot and cover with water. Bring the water to a boil, turn off the heat, and allow the chiles to sit for about 15 minutes to soften. Drain, reserving 1 cup of the soaking liquid. Purée the chiles with the reserved liquid in a blender or food processor. Pour into a squeeze bottle or glass jar and refrigerate until ready to use.

• While the soup is simmering, purée the garlic and ginger in a food processor, or mince by hand. (A food processor is definitely easier.) Warm the remaining 3 tablespoons of oil in a medium skillet. Add the puréed garlic and ginger and the coriander and cumin and sauté them about a minute, until fragrant. Add the spice mixture to the soup when the vegetables are cooked.

• Remove the bay leaf. Use an immersion blender or a conventional blender to purée the soup. Add the lemon juice and 1½ teaspoons salt. Let sit a few minutes, then taste and correct seasoning if necessary.

• Ladle the soup into warm bowls. Squeeze a squiggle of chile paste onto each portion or spoon on a dollop.

squash, fennel, and apple soup

Smooth and sweet, this deep orange soup tastes far richer than its simple ingredients would lead you to believe. Even if you're not wild about fennel, you'll love the way it blends and adds its own particular flavor here. Every component is important, so don't leave anything out—neither the fresh sage nor the tart apple matchsticks.

I like to make the stock for this soup just as I'm starting to cut the vegetables so I can include squash and fennel trimmings as well as sage.

Adding white rice to a soup to thicken and improve the texture is a classic French technique. A tiny bit cooked into the soup makes the final blended version absolutely creamy.

SERVES 5 TO 6

1 teaspoon fennel seeds
1 tablespoon extra-virgin olive oil
1 medium onion, chopped (1 cup)
½ medium fennel bulb, finely chopped (1 cup)
2 Granny Smith apples, 1 peeled and cubed, 1 for the garnish
2 garlic cloves, minced
1 pound winter squash, preferably kabocha, peeled, seeded, and cubed (3 cups)
4 cups Basic Vegetable Stock (page 20)
2 tablespoons raw white rice
  Salt and freshly ground black pepper
  Pinch of cayenne pepper
  Finely chopped sage for garnish
  Apple matchsticks (see Note)

KABOCHA SQUASH IS MY FAVORITE HERE, FOR ITS INTENSE FLAVOR AND BRIGHT ORANGE COLOR.

• Place the fennel seeds in a small, dry skillet and toast until fragrant. Crush the seeds in a mortar and pestle or in an electric spice grinder. Set aside.

• Warm the oil in a medium saucepan. Add the onions and fennel and sauté 5 to 7 minutes over medium-low heat until they begin to soften. Add the cubed apple, garlic, and ground fennel seed and sauté another 5 minutes.

• Add the squash cubes, stock, and rice; turn up the heat, and cover. When the liquid reaches a boil, add 1 teaspoon of salt, lower the heat to a simmer, and partially cover. Cook 10 to 15 minutes, until the squash is tender.

• Purée the soup in batches in a blender, making sure not to fill the blender more than halfway. Use a conventional blender here for best results to make a silky-smooth texture. Return the soup to the pot and add more salt to taste, black pepper, and cayenne.

• Serve garnished with chopped sage and apple matchsticks. For an artful presentation pile matchsticks in the center of each bowl.

To make apple matchsticks, cut an unpeeled apple into thin slabs on both sides of the core. Pile the slabs and cut crosswise into thin matchsticks. The little pieces of skin left at the tip resemble the tips of matchsticks.

french lentil soup

This is not just a regular lentil soup. The lentils may be small, but the flavor is big. It's easy to make, and the fresh herbs and reduced red wine scent your kitchen most deliciously as it cooks. It's an absolute favorite in my household.

You can substitute brown lentils, but the French lentilles du Puy make this hearty soup surprisingly light.

SERVES 4 TO 6

1 cup French lentils, sorted and washed
Bouquet garni of 5 fresh thyme sprigs, 3 rosemary sprigs, 1 bay leaf, and 5 flat-leaf parsley stems
6 cups water
2 tablespoons olive oil
2 medium onions, cut into small dice (2 cups)
3 garlic cloves, minced
¼ teaspoon hot red pepper flakes
½ cup dry red wine
1 tablespoon tomato paste
1 14.5-ounce can whole tomatoes, drained, or 2 medium-size fresh tomatoes, peeled and seeded
Salt and freshly ground black pepper
3 cups thinly sliced chard leaves (half the leaves of a 1-pound bunch)
1 teaspoon finely chopped fresh rosemary
1 teaspoon finely chopped fresh thyme

FOR MINIMUM WASTE, BUY TOMATO PASTE IN A TUBE. THAT WAY YOU CAN USE WHAT YOU NEED AND STORE THE REST CONVENIENTLY IN THE REFRIGERATOR.

- Place the lentils in a medium pot. Add the bouquet garni and water. Cover, bring to a boil, then lower the heat to a simmer. Partially cover and simmer for 25 to 35 minutes, or until the lentils are soft. Discard the bouquet garni.

- Meanwhile, warm the olive oil in a medium skillet. Add the onions, garlic, and red pepper flakes and sauté over medium-low heat for 8 to 10 minutes, or until the onions are softened and begin to brown.

- Add the red wine, turn up the heat, and cook for a few minutes, uncovered, until the wine is reduced by about half. Add the tomato paste and tomatoes. Cook a few minutes more, breaking up the tomatoes with the back of a spoon.

- Add the tomato mixture to the pot with the lentils along with 1½ teaspoons salt and black pepper to taste. Simmer a few minutes to marry the flavors. Adjust the salt to taste.

- Add the chard leaves, rosemary, and thyme and turn off heat. Let the chard leaves sit in the soup for five minutes before serving. The hot soup will wilt the leaves sufficiently.

smoky chestnut and sweet potato soup

This soup has all the soothing comfort of mashed sweet potatoes, while a splash of rum at the end lends grown-up relief. Best of all, the dried chestnuts and their cooking liquid give the soup a smoky anchor.

Dried chestnuts are available in gourmet stores, Italian groceries, and natural food stores, especially through autumn. They are either sold loose from a bin or in packages. Unlike fresh chestnuts, they come already peeled, so they are convenient to use. Soak the dry chestnuts as if they were beans (either overnight or with the quick-soak method). This will reduce the cooking time considerably and make it easier to remove any skin left on the chestnuts. You should remove any bits that float to the top of the soaking water. Any skin left in the grooves of the chestnuts that you cannot pick off will disappear when the soup is blended.

This soup can also be prepared quickly in a pressure cooker; see Note for details.

SERVES 4 TO 6

¼ cup hazelnuts

1 tablespoon extra-virgin olive oil

1 medium onion, cut into small dice (1 cup)

1 celery stalk, thinly sliced on the diagonal (½ cup)

¼ teaspoon nutmeg (if using fresh, swipe back and forth 30 times on a nutmeg grater), plus more for garnish

2 medium-size sweet potatoes (1 pound), peeled and cut into 1-inch chunks (3 cups)

1 cup dried chestnuts, soaked overnight or by the quick-soak method (see page 8)

1 bay leaf
  Salt and freshly ground black pepper
  Pinch of cayenne pepper

1 tablespoon rum

IN A PRESSURE COOKER, SAUTÉ THE ONIONS AND CELERY, THEN ADD THE NUTMEG AND SWEET POTATOES AS ABOVE. ADD CHESTNUTS AND BAY LEAF AND ENOUGH WATER TO THE CHESTNUT SOAKING LIQUID TO MAKE 5 CUPS. LOCK THE LID, WAIT FOR HIGH PRESSURE, THEN LOWER THE HEAT JUST ENOUGH TO MAINTAIN HIGH PRESSURE. COOK 15 MINUTES. ALLOW THE PRESSURE TO COME DOWN NATURALLY OR USE A QUICK-RELEASE METHOD. FINISH AS ABOVE.

- Preheat the oven to 350°F. Spread the hazelnuts on a baking sheet and place in the oven for 7 to 10 minutes, until the skins darken, get papery, and begin to crack. Transfer the nuts to a dishtowel or paper towel and rub between your hands to loosen the skins. (Don't worry if every last bit of skin does not come off.) Chop the nuts and set aside for the garnish.

- Warm the oil in a medium saucepan. Sauté the onions and celery about 10 minutes, until softened. Add the nutmeg and sweet potatoes and cook a couple of minutes more.

- Skim off any pieces of chestnut skin that have floated to the top of the soaking liquid. Drain the chestnuts, reserving the liquid. Add the chestnuts to the pot with the bay leaf. Add enough water to the chestnut soaking liquid to make 8 cups, add to the pot, and bring to a boil. Lower to a simmer and cook, partially covered, until the chestnuts and sweet potatoes are soft, about 45 minutes. (The sweet potatoes will soften earlier than the chestnuts.)

- Remove the bay leaf. Purée the soup in a blender or with an immersion blender. Return the soup to the pot and, if necessary, add water to thin the soup to the desired consistency. Season with salt, pepper, and a pinch of cayenne. Add the rum and cook an additional 5 minutes.

- Serve hot, sprinkled with additional grated nutmeg and the toasted hazelnuts.

wild mushroom and rice soup

This is a perfect beginning to a holiday meal. The mix of wild mushrooms infuses it with a deep, earthy taste, and carrots mixed in at the last minute give it a little crunch. Make sure to cut the vegetables small; they look elegant and taste best this way. The mâche, a tender, tiny, round-leafed lettuce, makes a delicate garnish in the middle of the plate.

Since the rice continues to absorb liquid as it sits, store the broth and solids separately if the soup is prepared in advance.

SERVES 6

1 pound mixed wild mushrooms (shiitakes, portobellos, oysters, chanterelles)
2 tablespoons shoyu
4 tablespoons extra-virgin olive oil
½ ounce dried porcini mushrooms
1 medium onion, cut into small dice (1 cup)
1 cup cleaned and finely chopped leeks, white part only
2 garlic cloves, minced
2 celery stalks, cut into ¼-inch dice (1 cup)
½ pound winter squash (butternut squash, kabocha, hokaiddo), peeled and cut into ¼-inch dice (1 cup)
2 teaspoons finely chopped sage leaves
1 teaspoon salt
  Freshly ground black pepper to taste
¼ cup Madeira
½ cup wild rice, rinsed
6 cups water or Basic Vegetable Stock (page 20)
2 medium carrots, peeled and cut into ¼-inch dice (1 cup)
1 scallion, thinly sliced
  Mâche for garnish (optional)

IT IS ESPECIALLY IMPORTANT TO CUT THE SQUASH PIECES VERY SMALL SO THAT THEY WILL MELT INTO AND THICKEN THE SOUP.

• Preheat the oven to 375° F. Wipe the mushroom caps with a damp paper towel. If using portobello or shiitake mushrooms, remove the stems and save for stock or discard. Finely chop the mushrooms by hand. Do not use a food processor—it will chop them too fine. The pieces should be roughly ¼ inch. Place in a bowl and toss with the shoyu and 2 tablespoons of the oil. Spread in a baking dish and roast for about 30 minutes. (No need to toss the mushrooms as they cook.) Remove the mushrooms from the baking dish and set aside.

• Place the dried porcini mushrooms in a bowl. Pour 2½ cups of boiling water over them and let them sit for 20 minutes. Line a strainer with 2 layers of paper towels and pour the porcinis and liquid through, reserving the liquid. Rinse the porcinis to remove any remaining dirt. Chop them into small pieces.

• In a large pot, warm the remaining 2 tablespoons of oil. Add the onions, leeks, garlic, and celery and cook over medium-low heat for 10 minutes or until the vegetables have softened. Add the squash, sage, salt, and pepper and cook a couple of minutes more.

• Stir in the roasted mushrooms, chopped porcinis, and Madeira and continue to cook. When the Madeira has almost evaporated, add the wild rice, water or stock, and 2 cups of the porcini soaking liquid. (If you don't have 2 cups, make up for it with water.)

• Cover the pot and bring to a boil, then reduce the heat and simmer, partially covered, for 50 minutes, or until the rice is cooked. Add another cup of water if necessary to reach the desired consistency. Add the carrots and simmer another 2 minutes, just enough to soften them slightly.

• Add salt if needed and ladle the soup into bowls. Serve with scallions and a cluster of mâche in the middle.

butternut–lemongrass soup

The creamy comfort of autumn squash fuses with bright Southeast Asian flavors for a soup with a glowing orange color, a delicate coconut flavor, and a surprising limey tanginess. Purée it in an ordinary blender for the most velvety texture. Roast the squash and make the stock while you prep the remaining ingredients; the soup cooks up quickly after that.

SERVES 4 TO 6

1   2½- to 3-pound butternut squash (3 cups cooked)
3   tablespoons extra-virgin olive oil
1   large shallot, cut into small dice (¼ cup)
1   cup cleaned and chopped leeks, white part only
2   garlic cloves, minced
2   tablespoons chopped lemongrass
1   small sweet potato, peeled and cut into chunks
1   14-ounce can coconut milk
4   cups Southeast Asian Stock (page 21)
1½ teaspoons salt
1   red bell pepper
     Freshly ground black pepper
2   tablespoons fresh lime juice
¼   cup basil chiffonade

THE BOTTOM THIRD (THE THICKER PART) OF THE LEMONGRASS IS THE PART THAT YOU USE. MAKE A LONG SLIT IN THE STALK AND PEEL OFF THE TOUGH OUTER LAYER. FINELY CHOP THE INNER LAYERS. THE REST OF THE LEMONGRASS IS GOOD FOR STOCK.

FRESH LEMONGRASS DRIES OUT AFTER 2 WEEKS IN THE REFRIGERATOR. IT FREEZES FOR UP TO 6 MONTHS.

• Preheat the oven to 400° F. Cut the squash in half, rub it with 2 tablespoons of the oil, and bake it, cut side down, about 45 minutes, until the squash is tender. When cool enough to handle, remove the seeds from the squash and discard them. Scrape the flesh from the skin and set it aside.

• Heat the remaining tablespoon of oil in a medium saucepan and sauté the shallots and leeks over medium-low heat for about 5 minutes, or until the leeks are softened but not browned. Add the garlic and lemongrass and sauté an additional few minutes.

• Add the squash, sweet potato, coconut milk, and stock and cover. Bring to a boil, lower the heat, add the salt, and simmer about 15 minutes, partially covered, until the sweet potato is soft.

• Meanwhile, roast the bell pepper over an open flame or in the oven (see page 188). Place in a paper or plastic bag to sweat for about 20 minutes. Discard the skin, stem, and seeds from the pepper and chop into ¼-inch squares.

• Purée the soup in a blender or with an immersion blender. Add black pepper to taste and the lime juice. Adjust salt to taste.

• Ladle the soup into bowls and garnish with the red pepper squares and basil chiffonade.

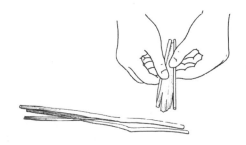

winter white soup

This golden soup boasts green flecks of dill and swirls of red pepper purée. You don't need to use a stock, although it would be even more delicious with one. Since the pepper purée and the soup are both thick, it is easy to make fun designs by pulling a toothpick through dollops of the purée.

SERVES 4 TO 6

1 medium head of garlic
4 tablespoons extra-virgin olive oil, plus 1 teaspoon for the garlic
  Salt
1 pound cauliflower, cut into small florets (4 cups)
1 cup cleaned and chopped leeks, white part only
2 tablespoons chopped shallots
1 medium potato, peeled and chopped into 1-inch cubes (1½ cups)
½ pound celery root (1 medium), peeled and cubed (page 93) (2 cups)
6 cups water or Basic Vegetable Stock (page 20)
  Bouquet garni of 1 bay leaf, ¼ teaspoon black peppercorns, a few thyme leaves, and flat-leaf parsley stems
1 medium red bell pepper
2 hot red peppers, such as red jalapeños or serranos, or New Mexican red or green jalapeños
  Freshly ground black pepper
2 teaspoons fresh lemon juice
2 tablespoons snipped fresh dill, plus extra for garnish

• Preheat the oven to 375° F. Remove the outer papery skin from the head of garlic and cut off the top fifth. Place on aluminum foil and drizzle the exposed flesh with 1 teaspoon of the olive oil and a pinch of salt. Wrap up the foil, place on an oven rack, and roast for about 30 minutes or until soft.

• In a medium bowl, toss the cauliflower with 2 tablespoons of the olive oil and ½ teaspoon of salt. Arrange on a cookie sheet lined with parchment paper and roast for 30 minutes, stirring every 10 minutes, until golden brown.

• Warm the remaining 2 tablespoons of oil in a large pot. Add the leeks and shallots, sprinkle with salt, and cook for 7 minutes over low heat until the leeks are soft but not brown. Add the potatoes, celery root, water or stock, roasted cauliflower, and bouquet garni. Squeeze the baked garlic cloves from their skins and add them to the pot.

• Cover and bring to a boil over high heat. Reduce to a simmer and add 1½ teaspoons salt. Simmer 45 minutes, partially covered, until the celery root and potatoes are tender.

• Meanwhile, roast the bell pepper and hot peppers over an open flame or in the oven (see page 188). Place in a paper or plastic bag and sweat for about 20 minutes. Discard the skins, stems, and seeds. Transfer the peppers to a blender and purée; you should have ¾ cup. Set aside.

• When the vegetables have softened, discard the bouquet garni. Purée the soup in batches. Fill the blender less than half full and hold a towel against the top to prevent spillage. (An immersion blender would also work quite well but the texture from the blender is extra velvety.)

• Return the soup to the pot, adjust the seasonings if necessary, and add freshly ground black pepper to taste, the lemon juice, and the 2 tablespoons of chopped dill. Simmer a few minutes to combine. Serve garnished with red pepper purée and additional snipped dill.

onion sonata

This soup has six types of onions slowly cooking, melding, and browning into a tasty harmony. You won't miss the usual brown stock; the rich vegetable stock made with lentils carries lots of flavor. I've made this soup numerous times for people used to the classic version, and it's always a hit.

SERVES 4 TO 6

1 tablespoon extra-virgin olive oil
3 cups thinly sliced onions (3 medium)
3 cups cleaned and chopped leeks, white part only (5 medium)
¾ cup minced shallots
6 garlic cloves, minced, plus 1 garlic clove, peeled and left whole
1 cup scallions cut into 1-inch lengths (4 medium)
6 cups Rich Stock (page 23)
1 tablespoon shoyu
1 tablespoon molasses
1½ teaspoons salt
12 to 18 thinly sliced pieces of baguette (3 slices per serving)
Freshly ground black pepper
Snipped fresh chives, for garnish

- Warm the oil in a heavy-bottomed medium pot. Add the onions and leeks and sauté over low heat for 10 minutes, or until softened. Add the shallots, minced garlic, and scallions and cook slowly for about 30 minutes, stirring from time to time, until the onions have wilted and cooked down. Turn up the heat during the last 10 minutes if necessary to allow the onions to brown. It's okay if some brown bits are stuck to the bottom.

- Add the stock, shoyu, and molasses. Scrape the bottom of the pan with a wooden spatula to loosen any bits that have stuck. Cover the pot. When the liquid reaches a boil, lower the heat, add the salt, and simmer, partially covered, for 30 minutes.

- While the soup simmers, preheat the oven to 350° F. Arrange the bread slices on a baking sheet and toast 10 minutes, or until the bread is crisp. Remove from the oven and rub each slice of bread with the peeled garlic clove.

- Taste the soup, and add more salt if necessary. Add a generous sprinkling of pepper. If the soup is too thick, add more stock to thin it to a desirable consistency.

- To serve, place 3 slices of garlic toast in each bowl. Ladle soup over the toast and sprinkle with snipped chives.

Rubbing toasted bread with a peeled clove of garlic is a traditional French technique for infusing the bread with a fresh, strong garlic flavor. For a great appetizer, you can flavor toasts this way before adding your favorite topping.

creamy chickpea soup with moroccan spice oil

I make this soup constantly; it's one of those recipes that suits so many kinds of meals and is a snap to prepare in the pressure cooker (see Note). The Moroccan spice oil dots and floats on the surface, making the mild chickpeas come alive with flavor.

SERVES 4 TO 6

2　tablespoons extra-virgin olive oil
1　medium onion, diced (1 cup)
4　garlic cloves, minced
1　cup dried chickpeas, soaked overnight in water to cover by 3 inches
1　bay leaf
½　cup roughly chopped flat-leaf parsley, plus more for garnish
8　cups water or stock for the stovetop method; 6 cups for the pressure cooker
1½　teaspoons salt
¼　cup fresh lemon juice
　　Moroccan Spice Oil (recipe follows)

• Warm the oil in a medium pot (depending on whether you are using pressure cooker or stovetop) and sauté the onions and garlic over medium-low heat for about 10 minutes, until the onions are soft and beginning to brown.

• Drain the chickpeas and discard the soaking water. Add the chickpeas, onion mixture, bay leaf, the ½ cup parsley, and water to the pot, cover, and bring to a boil. Lower the heat to a simmer, leave the lid slightly askew to allow for steam to escape, and cook until the chickpeas are soft, about 1½ to 2 hours. Stir in the salt.

• Remove the bay leaf and, working in batches, blend the soup until very creamy. Do not fill the blender more than half full, and hold down the blender lid with a towel. Return the soup to the pot and add the lemon juice. Adjust salt to taste.

• Ladle the soup into bowls and drizzle ½ teaspoon of the Moroccan spice oil into each serving. Sprinkle with chopped parsley and serve.

☞ TO PREPARE THE SOUP IN A PRESSURE COOKER, SAUTÉ THE ONION AND GARLIC AS ABOVE, ADD THE SOAKED AND DRAINED CHICKPEAS, BAY LEAF, PARSLEY, AND WATER OR STOCK TO THE PRESSURE COOKER, COVER, AND BRING THE LIQUID TO A BOIL. LOCK THE LID INTO PLACE. PRESSURE WILL COME UP TO HIGH VERY RAPIDLY. COOK FOR 12 MINUTES AT HIGH PRESSURE, AND LET PRESSURE COME DOWN NATURALLY. ADD THE SALT TO THE SOUP, THEN FINISH AS ABOVE.

moroccan spice oil

Spice oil keeps well for a month. Just a drizzle on simple beans, grains, or vegetables will turn them into exciting fare.

2 teaspoons whole cumin seeds
2 teaspoons whole coriander seeds
1 teaspoon whole fennel seeds
1 teaspoon ground cinnamon
1 teaspoon ground ginger
½ teaspoon hot red pepper flakes
¼ cup extra-virgin olive oil

- In a heavy, dry skillet, toast the cumin, coriander, and fennel seeds over medium-high heat until they release a strong, fragrant aroma, about 3 minutes. Be careful not to burn the spices. Immediately transfer the seeds to a spice grinder or use a mortar and pestle and grind along with the cinnamon, ginger, and red pepper flakes.

- Return the spices to the skillet along with the oil and heat for a few minutes, just until the oil is warmed through. Strain the oil right away through a fine strainer lined with cheesecloth and store in a tightly closed jar.

a word about puréeing soups

Soup can be puréed a number of ways. A blender gives the creamiest results, but the soup should be cooled a few minutes before puréeing. Fill the container only half-full and hold a towel over the top to prevent hot liquid from spurting out. Pulse the blender a few times before running.

The simplest way to purée is to use an immersion blender. Just place the immersion blender in the pot and purée until you have the desired consistency. No transferring between pots, no mess.

Passing the soup through a food mill is a good method if your recipe has a lot of potatoes, as it will keep it from becoming gummy. You can also pass a soup that has already been blended through a food mill for a very smooth end product. This gets rid of any seeds or bits of skin.

If you use a food processor, process only the solids with just enough broth to loosen them. To let steam escape, be careful not to overfill the processor or to block the feed tube.

colombian black bean soup

I confess I have a weakness for this soup. Maybe it's the way the smoky chile cooked whole contributes a lovely, delicate heat. Maybe it's the lime and orange tang, or the subtle flavor the cumin adds when it's toasted whole and then ground. Maybe it's the lush, thick consistency. At any rate, it always gets great reviews!

In Colombia and Venezuela, sour orange is used to lend freshness and exotic flavor. While sour oranges are not widely available in the United States, combining lime juice with orange juice creates a similar flavor. If you have access to sour oranges (try Caribbean markets), by all means use them.

This soup, like all bean soups, will thicken in the refrigerator, so when you reheat it, you will need to add a little water and probably some salt.

SERVES 4

1½ cups dried black turtle beans, soaked overnight or by the quick-soak method

1 habanero chile, fresh or dried

6 cups water (see Note)

2 teaspoons cumin seeds

1 tablespoon extra-virgin olive oil

1 medium onion, cut into small dice (1 cup)

4 garlic cloves, minced

½ medium green bell pepper, cut into small dice (½ cup)

1 celery stalk, cut into small dice (½ cup)

Salt and freshly ground black pepper

3 tablespoons fresh orange juice

3 tablespoons fresh lime juice

Coarsely chopped fresh cilantro leaves

Scallions, thinly sliced on the diagonal

Chopped orange and lime pieces

THE HABANERO CHILE IS ONE OF THE WORLD'S HOTTEST. IT COMES FRESH OR DRIED, AND IF DRIED, IS OFTEN SMOKED. WHEN ADDED WHOLE TO A POT OF BEANS, IT FLAVORS THEM WITH A LOVELY, DELICATE HEAT AS THEY COOK. A SMOKED HABANERO IS MY FAVORITE FOR THIS SOUP, BUT ANOTHER SMOKY, HOT DRIED CHILE SUCH AS A CHIPOTLE OR A OAXACAN PASILLA WOULD WORK WELL, TOO.

• Drain the soaked beans and place in a medium saucepan with the chile and the water. Bring to a boil over high heat, lower heat, and simmer for about an hour, partially covered, until tender. Discard chile. Remove 1½ cups of the beans with a slotted spoon to a blender. Add 1 cup of the cooking liquid and blend until smooth. Return the purée to the bean pot.

• Toast the cumin seeds in a small, dry skillet over medium heat, stirring constantly, until fragrant; be careful not to let them burn. In a mortar and pestle or electric spice grinder, grind the seeds to a powder.

• Warm the oil in a medium sauté pan. Add the onions and garlic and sauté over medium-low heat for 7 minutes, or until the onions are softened. Add the cumin, green pepper, and celery and cook an additional 5 minutes, until the vegetables are soft.

• Add a couple of ladles of beans with cooking liquid to the sauté pan and simmer a few minutes, stirring with a wooden spoon to loosen any bits sticking to the pan. Stir the contents of the sauté pan back into the bean pot.

• Add 1½ teaspoons salt and a sprinkle of black pepper and simmer, uncovered, 15 minutes. Stir in the orange and lime juices and add salt to taste. Ladle into bowls, sprinkle with chopped cilantro and sliced scallion, and top with a few pieces of chopped orange and lime.

☞ IN A PRESSURE COOKER: COMBINE THE BEANS AND CHILE AS ABOVE AND ADD 4 CUPS OF WATER. BRING TO A BOIL, LOCK THE LID, AND BRING UP TO HIGH PRESSURE. LOWER THE HEAT ENOUGH TO MAINTAIN PRESSURE AND COOK 11 MINUTES. ALLOW THE BEANS TO COME DOWN FROM PRESSURE NATURALLY OR USE THE QUICK-RELEASE METHOD. REMOVE THE CHILE AND DISCARD. CONTINUE AS ABOVE FROM STEP 2.

masala root soup

When you prepare this Indian-inspired soup, an aromatic blend of spices awaits you. Since the vegetables are quick-cooking and there aren't many to chop, you can make it in short order. Don't toast the coconut garnish; a little white mound along with green cilantro leaves contrasts beautifully with the bright orange backdrop.

SERVES 6

2   tablespoons canola oil
1   medium onion, cut into small dice (1 cup)
⅛   teaspoon asafetida (optional)
½   teaspoon yellow mustard seeds
1   teaspoon whole cumin seeds
1   teaspoon curry powder
1   teaspoon ground coriander
½   teaspoon turmeric
¼   teaspoon ground cinnamon
3   medium carrots, peeled and coarsely chopped
2   medium sweet potatoes (1½ pounds), peeled and coarsely chopped
6   cups water (see Note)
    Salt
1   tablespoon fresh lemon juice
    Cayenne pepper
    Unsweetened shredded coconut
    Coarsely chopped fresh cilantro leaves

• Warm the oil in a medium saucepan. Add the onions and sauté for 7 minutes, or until they are translucent. Add the spices and cook for a couple minutes more, then stir in the carrots, sweet potatoes, and water.

• Cover and bring to a boil over high heat. Add 1½ teaspoons of salt, then lower the heat to a simmer and cook, partially covered for 12 to 18 minutes, or until the vegetables are tender.

• Purée the soup using an immersion blender or blender. (This is an ideal time to use the immersion blender since the sweet potatoes are very creamy.)

• Adjust salt to taste. Add the lemon juice and cayenne to taste. Serve with a generous sprinkle of coconut flakes and cilantro leaves.

⚬ TO PREPARE THE SOUP IN A PRESSURE COOKER, SAUTÉ THE ONIONS AND SPICES AS ABOVE, THEN ADD 4 CUPS OF WATER, THE CARROTS, AND THE SWEET POTATOES. BRING THE WATER TO A BOIL AND ADD 1½ TEASPOONS OF SALT. LOCK THE LID INTO PLACE AND COOK 10 MINUTES OVER HIGH PRESSURE. LET THE PRESSURE COME DOWN NATURALLY. PROCEED WITH THE RECIPE AS ABOVE.

ASAFETIDA (HEENG), FOUND IN INDIAN STORES, IS AVAILABLE IN POWDERED OR LUMP FORM. I RECOMMEND COOKING WITH THE READY-TO-USE POWDER. IN INDIA, IT IS USED BY GROUPS OF PEOPLE WHO ABSTAIN FROM ONIONS AND IS ALSO HIGHLY VALUED AS A DIGESTIVE AID.

yams and sweet potatoes

A yam is a large tuber that has starchy, pale yellow flesh. Different varieties grow in tropical and subtropical climates—in fact, it is difficult to get a yam outside a Latin market.

In our markets, however, sweet potatoes are often confused with yams. The tubers with a dry, mealy flesh are often called sweet potatoes, while the ones with the moister, denser flesh are usually call yams. Garnet and Jewel are two varieties with deep orange-red flesh and skin.

In all my recipes, the sweet potatoes intended are the orange-fleshed ones (they probably will be called yams in the market). Garnet and Jewel can be used interchangeably for the sweet potatoes in the recipes.

hot and sour soup

I love hot and sour soup, but I often find the versions I'm served in restaurants too viscous. If you like it super thick, increase the kudzu to 2 tablespoons. In all other ways, this vegetarian version retains the most important characteristics of the classic.

Hot sesame oil, readily available in natural food stores, lends a delicious flavor. Traditional hot and sour soups often have bamboo shoots added; the broccoli stems included here have a similar texture.

For a festive touch, I've added dumplings made of wonton skins filled with minced vegetables. If you want, make the wontons and the stock in advance and freeze them. The soup itself requires little labor. Otherwise, put the stock on to cook first, then assemble the wontons. Make the soup last.

SERVES 4

8 dried black Chinese mushrooms
1 ounce enoki mushrooms (optional)
4 cups Chinese Mushroom Stock (page 22)
2 tablespoons red wine vinegar
1 tablespoon shoyu
1 medium carrot, peeled and thinly sliced
1 medium broccoli stem, peeled and thinly sliced
¼ pound firm tofu, pressed for 30 minutes
¼ cup scallions cut into 1-inch slices
   Freshly ground black pepper
   Salt
2 teaspoons hot sesame oil or 2 teaspoons sesame oil with a large pinch of cayenne
1 rounded tablespoon kudzu
¼ cup water
   Dumplings (recipe follows)

BLACK MUSHROOMS ARE A CRITICAL INGREDIENT IN THIS DISH. THEY ARE UBIQUITOUS IN CHINESE MARKETS AND CAN ALSO BE MAIL-ORDERED. ENOKI MUSHROOMS ARE LITTLE PEARL-TIPPED CAPS PERCHED ON TOP OF STEMS. THEY OFTEN COME PACKED IN THE DIRT THEY WERE GROWN IN, SO THE LAST INCH OR SO OF THE STEMS MUST BE REMOVED.

• In a medium bowl, pour 1½ cups boiling water over the black mushrooms and soak for 30 minutes. Pour the mushrooms and liquid through 2 layers of paper towels placed in a strainer. Reserve liquid. Rinse the mushrooms to get rid of any last bits of dirt. Discard the stems and slice the caps thin. Cut into ⅜-inch cubes. Remove the bottom inch or so from the enoki stems and slice in half lengthwise.

• In a medium saucepan, combine the stock with 1 cup of the reserved mushroom liquid, the red wine vinegar, and the shoyu. Add the carrots, broccoli, tofu, black mushrooms, and enoki mushrooms. Cover and bring to a boil over medium-high heat, then lower the heat and simmer, partially covered, for 5 minutes, or until the vegetables are tender. Add the scallions, a generous sprinkling of black pepper, and salt to taste.

• In a small bowl, mix the sesame oil with the kudzu and water. Add to the soup, stirring constantly, and cook over medium-high heat a couple of minutes, or until bubbles appear on the surface and the liquid has turned from cloudy to clear. Turn off the heat.

• Bring a few inches of water to boil in a large skillet or saucepan. Add the dumplings and cook 3 to 4 minutes, or until cooked through. Serve the soup with 3 dumplings floating in each bowl.

dumplings

These dumplings make great appetizers, and they are equally delectable in soups. They contain arame, a nutritious sea vegetable well worth introducing into your diet (see Glossary). Use the square wonton wrappers to make the dumplings tortellini-shaped.

Fuchsia-colored umeboshi vinegar, the brine of pickled umeboshi plums, is a versatile condiment. A small amount of its sour-salty flavor provides a pick-me-up to a variety of dishes from the dumpling filling here to soups, sauces, and dressings. It is readily available in natural food stores.

MAKES 15 DUMPLINGS

1   large or 2 small heads of bok choy
½   cup dried arame, soaked for 15 minutes
1   tablespoon toasted sesame oil
2   garlic cloves, minced
1   tablespoon shoyu
1   tablespoon mirin (sweet Japanese sake)
½   cup water
½   teaspoon umeboshi vinegar
15 square wonton wrappers

• Separate the leafy greens from the white stem ends of the bok choy. Very finely chop enough of the stems to make 1 cup, then cut the greens into fine ribbons. Reserve separately.

• Drain the arame, discarding the soaking liquid, and chop fine. Warm the oil in a medium saucepan. Add the bok choy stems, garlic, and arame and sauté over medium-low heat for 10 minutes. Add the shoyu, mirin, and water and cook a few minutes, until the liquid evaporates. Add the bok choy leaves and stir until they wilt and are cooked through. Add the vinegar and remove from the heat.

• Arrange several wonton wrappers on a work surface. Place 1 heaping teaspoon of filling in the center of each wrapper. Moisten the edges with a little water and press together firmly to form a triangle. Make sure each wonton is completely closed. Fold the long points together, moistening with a little more water; the dumpling will look like a tortellini. Repeat with the remaining filling and wrappers. The wontons are now ready to cook or freeze for future use (see Note).

☞ LOOK FOR WONTON WRAPPERS WHOSE SOLE INGREDIENTS ARE FLOUR AND WATER. SOME HAVE EXTRANEOUS INGREDIENTS ADDED. THE WRAPPERS CAN BE STORED FOR A FEW DAYS IN THE REFRIGERATOR, OR FOR A COUPLE OF MONTHS IN THE FREEZER.

TO FREEZE FILLED WONTONS, LAY THE WONTONS ON A TRAY AND PLACE THEM IN THE FREEZER FOR A COUPLE OF HOURS. WHEN THEY ARE FROZEN SOLID YOU CAN THEN STACK THEM OR PLACE THEM IN FREEZER BAGS. WHEN READY TO COOK, REMOVE AS MANY AS NEEDED AND DROP INTO BOILING WATER WITHOUT DEFROSTING. THIS METHOD WORKS FOR JUST ABOUT ANYTHING. FREEZING INDIVIDUALLY BEFORE STACKING KEEPS EVERYTHING FROM HARDENING INTO ONE BIG LUMP.

mushroom-barley soup with fennel and coriander

Here is the absolute simplest of recipes that really demonstrates the magic of cooking. Starting with so little yields so much hearty flavor.

Barley expands to three or four times its volume when cooked, and its natural starch thickens the soup beautifully. You could use hulled, which has only its outer layer or husk removed, or pearled, with both the outer layer and the bran layer removed. I prefer the hulled for the chewier texture; if you do use pearled, buy it from a natural food store, since the quality is superior to that of the barley found in supermarkets.

It is best to start with whole spices and grind them in a spice grinder or coffee mill, especially since fennel seed is difficult to find already ground. You can also grind the seeds in a mortar and pestle, but first toast the spices in a dry skillet to make them easier to crush.

SERVES 4

8 dried shiitake mushrooms (about 1 ounce)

½ cup barley, hulled or pearled

7 cups water

1 6-inch piece of kombu (page 200)

1 teaspoon ground coriander

1 teaspoon ground fennel seeds

3 tablespoons shoyu

1 medium carrot, peeled and cut into small dice (½ cup)

1 medium parsnip, peeled and cut into small dice (¾ cup)

1 tablespoon barley or mellow barley miso mixed with 3 tablespoons water

½ teaspoon brown rice vinegar Salt

1 scallion, cut thin on the diagonal

- Break off the stems from the shiitake mushrooms and discard or save for a future stock. Snap each mushroom cap into small pieces by hand (the mushrooms expand a lot when they're cooked).

- In a medium pot or saucepan, combine the mushroom pieces, barley, water, kombu, coriander, fennel, and shoyu. Cover, bring to a boil over high heat, then reduce the heat and simmer, partially covered, for 10 minutes.

- Remove the kombu and cook 20 minutes longer.

- Add the carrots and parsnips. Continue cooking until the barley is completely tender, about 20 more minutes.

- Add the dissolved miso, stirring constantly to avoid lumps, then add the vinegar and salt to taste. Sprinkle in scallions and serve.

MISO ADDS COMPLEXITY OF FLAVOR TO THE SOUP. IT CLUMPS WHEN ADDED TO HOT LIQUID, SO IT MUST BE DISSOLVED BEFORE YOU STIR IT INTO THE SOUP. MISO COMES IN MANY VARIETIES, FROM LIGHT TO DARK. MELLOW BARLEY IS A GOOD ALL-AROUND TYPE OF MISO.

gingery split pea soup

You won't miss the traditional flavorings in this lush version of split pea soup; dried chile provides the essential smoky flavor. Cooked to a golden creaminess, the split peas are enhanced with sautéed vegetables and finished with a little miso, which contributes its distinctive, salty richness.

See Resources and Mail-Order Sources (page 293) for a mail-order source if you can't find dried chipotle chiles.

SERVES 4 TO 6

1 cup yellow split peas

1 medium russet potato, peeled and cut into small dice (1 cup)

1 chipotle chile or other dried smoked chile, such as a pasilla de Oaxaca

1 2-inch chunk of ginger, unpeeled, cut into 3 slices

6 cups water
Salt

2 tablespoons extra-virgin olive oil

1 medium onion, cut into small dice (1 cup)

2 garlic cloves, minced

1 medium carrot, peeled and cut into small dice (½ cup)

1 celery stalk, cut into small dice (½ cup)

½ teaspoon balsamic vinegar

1 teaspoon barley or mellow barley miso, dissolved in 1 tablespoon water

½ cup chopped fresh flat-leaf parsley

• In a medium pot, combine the split peas, potatoes, chile, ginger, and 5 cups of the water. Cover and bring to a boil over high heat. Lower the heat and simmer covered 45 minutes to 1 hour, stirring occasionally, until the split peas are completely soft and broken down. Add 1 teaspoon salt. Remove the chile and ginger slices and discard.

• Warm the oil in a medium skillet. Add the onions, garlic, carrot, and celery and sauté about 10 to 12 minutes over medium-low heat until the vegetables are soft and beginning to brown. Then add the vegetables to the split peas along with the remaining 1 cup of water.

• Stir in the balsamic vinegar and miso. Taste and adjust salt if necessary. Reheat if necessary, then stir in the chopped parsley and serve hot.

AS AN ALTERNATE METHOD, ADD THE SPLIT PEAS TO A PRESSURE COOKER WITH THE POTATOES, CHILE, GINGER, AND 4 CUPS OF WATER. BRING THE LIQUID TO A BOIL, COVER THE POT, AND COOK AT HIGH PRESSURE FOR 11 MINUTES. LET THE PRESSURE COME DOWN NATURALLY. REMOVE THE LID AND ADD 1 TEASPOON OF SALT. REMOVE THE CHILE AND GINGER SLICES AND DISCARD. PROCEED AS ABOVE.

My favorite smoked chile is the pasilla de Oaxaca, a chile grown only in the Oaxaca region of Mexico and available primarily from mail-order sources (see page 293). It is very wrinkled, has a mahogany-red color, and measures 3 to 4 inches long and 1 to 1½ inches across. It has a very strong fruity, smoky flavor—it smells like tobacco—and a sharp, lingering heat. One chile gives this soup a deep, subtle, smoky quality.

asparagus potage
with garlic "cream"

I'm always excited when spring rolls around and I can start eating and cooking with asparagus again; I make this lush soup the minute the first stalks make their way to market. This thick green potage is best made with slender asparagus, since the delicate tips make a lovely garnish. A tarragon garlic "cream" gives the soup extra-rich flavor.

SERVES 6

1 pound asparagus, hard ends removed
  Salt
2 tablespoons extra-virgin olive oil
¾ pound leeks, cleaned and finely chopped, white part only (2 cups)
½ pound potatoes, preferably low-starch, thin-skinned potatoes, peeled and cut into 1-inch dice
4 cups Basic Vegetable Stock (page 20)

tarragon garlic "cream"

1 medium head of garlic, separated into cloves and peeled
3 tablespoons extra-virgin olive oil
1 cup water
5 sprigs of fresh tarragon

  Freshly ground black pepper
1 teaspoon fresh lemon juice
  Chopped fresh flat-leaf parsley for garnish

- Cut 1½ inches of the tip of each asparagus spear. Bring a saucepan of salted water to a boil; add the asparagus tips and blanch uncovered until tender (rinse in cold water to stop cooking). Set aside.

- Warm the oil in a medium pot. Add the leeks and a pinch of salt, and sauté over medium-low heat for 7 minutes, or until the leeks are softened but not browned. Add the potatoes, asparagus stems, and stock, and bring to a boil. Lower the heat, stir in 1 teaspoon of salt, and simmer, partially covered, for 30 minutes, or until the potatoes are tender.

- Make the garlic cream: In a small saucepan, combine the garlic, oil, water, and tarragon. Simmer, uncovered, for 20 to 30 minutes, or until tender. Transfer to a blender and purée, adding a little liquid from the vegetable pot if needed. Stir the cream into the soup and mix well. Purée the soup in a blender or with a hand-held immersion blender.

- Return to the pot. Adjust salt to taste, and season with pepper and lemon juice. Add the reserved asparagus tips and reheat if necessary. Serve sprinkled with chopped parsley.

≈ GARLIC MUST BE PEELED BEFORE ALMOST ALL USES. TO LOOSEN THE SKIN, WHACK THE GARLIC CLOVE (SAME GOES FOR A SHALLOT BULB) WITH THE FLAT SIDE OF A KNIFE BLADE AGAINST A CUTTING BOARD, PRESSING ONCE HARD WITH THE HEEL OF YOUR HAND. THEN PEEL THE SKIN AND CUT OFF THE ROOT END AND ANY BROWN SPOTS. THE CLOVE CAN NOW BE MINCED, SLICED, OR CHOPPED. BEFORE CHOPPING, REMOVE ANY GREEN SHOOT THAT MAY BE GROWING THROUGH THE GARLIC.

A MEDIUM CLOVE OF GARLIC YIELDS ABOUT ONE TEASPOON MINCED, AND AN AVERAGE HEAD USUALLY HAS ABOUT TWELVE SUCH CLOVES IN ADDITION TO A FEW TINY ONES NEAR THE CENTER. I HAVE NOTICED A TENDENCY FOR GARLIC TO BECOME BLOATED NOWADAYS, WITH HEADS SOMETIMES CONTAINING EXTRA-LARGE CLOVES. YOU SHOULD SUBSTITUTE ONE LARGER CLOVE FOR TWO OR THREE OF THE MEDIUM SIZE.

minestrone with
basil-oregano pesto

I think of this soup as an Italian potpourri, a bowl brightly filled with a variety of ingredients and colors. Good as a starter or as a light meal, the soup has pesto swirled in, an accent that takes it just over the top. Make sure to cut the vegetables quite small so that the flavors blend in every bite.

This is one instance where I use organic canned chickpeas for the convenience. Any of the soup pastas or small pastas on the market would work fine here; I use colorful vegetable alphabets for a subtle, silly touch.

· SERVES 6

2 tablespoons extra-virgin olive oil
1 onion, cut into small dice (1 cup)
3 garlic cloves, minced
1 teaspoon dried thyme
1 teaspoon dried rosemary
¼ teaspoon hot red pepper flakes
7 canned plum tomatoes with 1 cup juice from the can reserved, or 1 14.5-ounce can whole tomatoes with liquid
5 cups water
1 medium-size low-starch potato, peeled and finely diced (1 cup)
1 medium carrot, finely diced (½ cup)
1 small zucchini, finely diced (1 cup)
1 teaspoon salt

pesto
1 cup pine nuts
1 cup fresh oregano
2 cups packed fresh basil leaves
2 garlic cloves, peeled
1 tablespoon mellow barley miso
½ cup extra-virgin olive oil
Salt

2 cups shredded Swiss chard leaves
¼ cup small pasta
1½ cups cooked chickpeas or 1 15-ounce can, drained and rinsed
Freshly ground black pepper
1 teaspoon fresh lemon juice

• Warm the oil in a medium pot. Add the onions and sauté over medium-low heat for 7 minutes, or until softened and translucent. Add the garlic, thyme, rosemary, and red pepper flakes and sauté a few minutes more.

• Add the tomatoes and juice, breaking up the tomatoes with the back of a spoon. Cook for 10 minutes, stirring often until the tomatoes are softened and the liquid is reduced by half.

• Add the water, potatoes, carrots, and zucchini, bring to a boil, and add the salt. Reduce the heat and simmer, partially covered, for 15 minutes, or until the vegetables are tender.

• Meanwhile, make the pesto. Preheat to oven to 350° F. Spread the pine nuts on a baking sheet and toast for 5 to 7 minutes, until lightly golden. To the bowl of a food processor fitted with a metal blade add the pine nuts, oregano, basil, garlic, miso, and oil. Process until smooth, then add salt to taste. Remove the pesto to a container and set aside.

• Add the Swiss chard, pasta, and chickpeas to the soup. Adjust the salt to taste and add a generous sprinkle of pepper. Cook a few minutes more, until the pasta is al dente, then add the lemon juice.

• Ladle into bowls and swirl in a heaping tablespoon of pesto.

☞ MISO IS THE SURPRISE INGREDIENT THAT MAKES THE PESTO RICH AND FULL-BODIED. THE PESTO IS ALSO DELICIOUS ON PASTA OR OVER SIMPLE STEAMED GRAINS OR VEGETABLES. THE RECIPE MAKES ENOUGH TO ALLOW FOR A HEAPING PORTION PER PERSON. EXTRA PESTO CAN BE REFRIGERATED FOR A FEW DAYS OR FROZEN. I LIKE TO FREEZE IT IN ICE-CUBE TRAYS BEFORE REMOVING IT TO A RESEALABLE PLASTIC BAG.

miso soup with greens

I find myself hankering for miso soup whenever I've indulged in too much rich food; this traditional Japanese staple makes the body feel balanced and nourished. It's no wonder it has such a long and venerable tradition in Japan, where so many types of miso make it possible to produce the soup differently every time. This tangy, rich version, while familiar, will go well beyond your expectations of what a miso soup can be. Here I've suggested hatcho miso, a dark rich miso, and mellow barley, which has a much lighter taste. It is a good idea to experiment with different types of miso to determine your favorites. Garnishes that are good in miso soup include small pieces of cubed tofu, slivered snow peas, napa cabbage, and slivers of daikon. With a delicate soup like this one, it's best to slice the garnishes thinly.

The live culture in miso is killed when it boils, so be sure to add the miso at the last minute over a gentle heat. Also, if you are serving only a portion of the soup, put the miso only in the portion that you will use.

SERVES 4 TO 6

8   dried shiitake mushrooms
1   6-inch piece of kombu
3   scallions, thinly sliced on the
    diagonal
1   medium onion, cut in half and
    thinly sliced
2   tablespoons shoyu
2   tablespoons mirin (Japanese
    sweet sake)
8   cups water
1   6-inch piece of wakame
½   pound bok choy (½ head)
1   carrot, peeled, halved, and cut
    into thin half-moons
1   cup watercress leaves
    3 to 4 tablespoons hatcho miso,
    or 4 to 5 tablespoons mellow
    barley miso

WAKAME EXPANDS MORE WHEN SOAKED THAN
DO OTHER SEA VEGETABLES. AFTER JUST 10
MINUTES IT BECOMES A LARGE, FLOPPY LEAF
WITH A RIGID SPINE, WHICH YOU SHOULD
REMOVE.

• Combine the shiitakes, kombu, two thirds of the scallions, the onions, shoyu, mirin, and water in a medium pot. Bring to a boil over high heat, then reduce the heat and simmer, uncovered, for 20 minutes. Strain the broth and discard the vegetables, reserving the shiitake mushrooms. You should have about 6 cups of broth. Return to the pot and set aside.

• Soak the wakame in cold water for 10 minutes. Drain, then cut out the hard spine and chop the wakame into small pieces. You should have about ¼ cup. Cut the bok choy leaves away from the stems. Cut the stems into ¼-inch dice and the leaves into small pieces. You should have 1 cup chopped stems and 2 cups chopped leaves.

• Remove and discard the stems from the shiitakes and thinly slice the caps.

• Heat the broth in a medium pot. Add the shiitakes, bok choy stems, carrots, and wakame. Simmer, partially covered, for 5 minutes. Uncover and add the watercress leaves, bok choy leaves, and the remaining scallions to the hot broth.

• Mix 3 tablespoons of the miso with a small amount of the hot soup in a small bowl. Dissolve the miso thoroughly, then add it to the soup pot. Taste and add more miso if desired, dissolving it in a bit of hot liquid each time.

vietnamese noodle soup

The rich broth and a cornucopia of fresh condiments here will transport you to Southeast Asia. Add a side of Thai tofu triangles for a great lunch or light supper. Don't be intimidated by the long list of ingredients; the soup actually goes together very quickly.

A flavorful sweet stock is the first and most important step. If you already have a basic vegetable stock, you could simmer that with some lemongrass and ginger.

SERVES 5 TO 6

4   cups Southeast Asian Stock
    (page 21)
1   jalapeño, stem removed, sliced
    into thin rounds (seeds included)
1   lemongrass stalk, cut into 2 or
    3 pieces and bruised
3   tablespoons shoyu
1   tablespoon maple syrup
1   14-ounce can unsweetened
    coconut milk
2   ounces rice noodles
3   tablespoons creamy peanut butter
2   tablespoons fresh lime juice
    (about 1 lime), plus 1 lime cut into
    wedges for garnish
    Pinch of cayenne pepper
    (optional)
    Salt
2   cups shredded napa cabbage
    (¼ medium head)
½   cup thinly sliced snow peas
1   cup mung bean sprouts
1   scallion, thinly sliced diagonally
2   tablespoons chopped fresh mint
    leaves
¼   cup fresh cilantro leaves, roughly
    chopped
¼   cup chopped roasted, unsalted
    peanuts

USE A CHEF'S KNIFE TO "BRUISE" THE LEMON-
GRASS. LAY THE FLAT OF THE BLADE OVER THE
LEMONGRASS, AND, WITH THE HEEL OF YOUR
HAND GIVE IT A FIRM SMACK TO CRUSH THE
FIBERS OF THE STALK. DO THIS IN SEVERAL
PLACES ALONG THE STALK.

• Add the stock to a medium pot. Add the jalapeño, lemongrass, shoyu, maple syrup, and coconut milk. Bring to a boil over high heat, lower the heat, and simmer, partially covered, for 15 minutes.

• Meanwhile, place the noodles in a heatproof bowl. Pour boiling water over them to cover, and let soak for 10 minutes. Put up additional water to boil so that it is ready when your soup is.

• Remove the lemongrass from the soup and discard. Place the peanut butter in a small bowl. Add ½ cup of hot soup to the peanut butter and whisk them together until the peanut butter is well dissolved. Add the peanut butter mixture to the soup along with the lime juice. Add a pinch of cayenne and sprinkle of salt to taste.

• Drain the noodles. Put the napa cabbage, snow peas, bean sprouts, and noodles in a strainer. Pour boiling water over just to heat them. If you are eating only a portion of the soup, pour boiling water only over the portion of vegetables you are going to eat. (This keeps the vegetables from cooling down the broth.)

• Divide the vegetables and noodles among soup bowls. Pour the hot soup over each portion. Garnish with scallions, mint, cilantro, and chopped peanuts. Serve with wedge of lime.

potato, sorrel, and watercress soup

In the rustic simplicity here, every ingredient is essential, and so is the seasoning. The dill is an absolute must. This is a soup to make in spring and summer, when sorrel—which has a lemony flavor and looks like a cross between arugula and spinach—makes its way to market. It's important to use two kinds of potatoes—one that holds its shape, and one that melts down. They should be cut small for the best result.

    The sorrel and watercress are both fresh green when they are added at the last moments of cooking. They instantaneously wilt, and the sorrel darkens while the watercress brightens. This striking visual effect is paralleled in the taste. Sorrel's singular tart flavor contrasts nicely with the peppery watercress.

SERVES 4 TO 6

2   tablespoons extra-virgin olive oil

1   medium onion, cut into small dice (1 cup)

2   leeks, cleaned and cut into small dice (2 cups)

3   garlic cloves, minced

1   pound potatoes, low- to medium-starch, such as red bliss, white creamer, Yukon gold, or Yellow Finn, peeled and cut into small dice (3 cups)

½   pound russet or Idaho potatoes, peeled and cut into small dice (1½ cups)

4   cups water

2   teaspoons salt

2   cups chopped watercress, thick stems removed

2   cups thinly sliced sorrel (2 ounces)
    Freshly ground black pepper

¼   cup chopped fresh dill

REMEMBER TO PUT POTATOES IN WATER AFTER DICING TO KEEP THEM FROM TURNING BROWN.

• Warm the olive oil in a medium pot. Add the onions and leeks and sauté over medium heat for 8 minutes, or just until the leeks are softened but not browned. Add the garlic and cook 2 more minutes.

• Add the potatoes and water, cover, and bring to a boil over high heat. Reduce the heat, add the salt, and simmer, partially covered, for 20 minutes, or until the potatoes are tender.

• Remove the pot from the heat. Stir in the watercress, sorrel, and a generous sprinkle of pepper. Mash about half of the potatoes with the back of a wooden spoon to break the potatoes down and thicken the soup. Taste and add a little more salt if necessary. Serve with a generous sprinkle of fresh dill.

roasted corn soup

When I make this recipe, I feel like I'm participating in a late-summer harvest festival. The act of shucking and roasting and cutting kernels off the cobs is such an invigorating experience. This soup is a salute to corn, and it's a great recipe to make at the height of summer, when corn is succulent and sweet, as roasting it intensifies the flavor. Adding the sofrito, rich and red, is like stirring a sunset into your golden soup.

The soup really benefits from a stock. Strip two ears of corn first (step 2) so that you can add the corn cobs to your stock while you're making it. Otherwise, simmer the cobs for 15 minutes in an already prepared stock while you roast the rest of the corn. The soup comes together very quickly after these preliminary steps.

SERVES 4 TO 6

6   ears corn
1   red bell pepper, halved, stems, seeds, and white membrane removed
1   poblano chile, halved, stems, seeds, and white membrane removed, or 2 jalapeños
4   tablespoons extra-virgin olive oil
2   scallions, thinly sliced, plus 2 scallions, cut into 1-inch pieces
3   garlic cloves, minced
2   medium tomatoes, peeled, seeded, and cut into ½-inch dice (2 cups)
1½ teaspoons salt
    Freshly ground black pepper
2   medium shallots, minced (¼ cup)
3½ cups Basic Vegetable Stock (page 20)
½   pound russet potatoes, peeled and cut into ¼-inch dice (1 cup)

TO GIVE THE SOUP A PARTICULARLY BRILLIANT GLOW, YOU CAN WARM 1 TABLESPOON OF ANNATO SEEDS IN THE OLIVE OIL. WHEN THE OIL TAKES ON A BRIGHT ORANGE COLOR AFTER A COUPLE OF MINUTES, STRAIN IT AND USE FOR SAUTÉING.

• Preheat oven to 375°F.

• Shuck 2 ears of corn, and cut the kernels off the cobs. Transfer the kernels to a blender and purée with ½ cup of water. Set aside.

• Place the remaining 4 ears of corn on a tray and roast for about an hour to an hour and 15 minutes, until the husks on the corn are parched and brown. Remove corn from the oven and let cool for a few minutes. Strip and discard the husks and silk, then cut the kernels off the cobs and set them aside.

• Meanwhile, make the sofrito: Cut the red bell pepper into ¼-inch slices. Cut each slice lengthwise into 1-inch-long pieces. Cut the poblano into slivers. Cut each sliver lengthwise into 1-inch pieces. Warm 2 tablespoons of the olive oil in a medium skillet. Add the red bell pepper, the poblano, and the thin slices of scallion and sauté until the peppers are softened, 8 to 10 minutes. Add the garlic and tomatoes and cook for 5 to 10 minutes, until the tomatoes have broken down and thickened. Season to taste with a sprinkling of salt and pepper. Set aside until the the rest of the soup is completed.

• Warm the remaining 2 tablespoons of oil in a medium pot or saucepan. Add the shallots and the 1-inch pieces of scallion and sauté for 3 to 4 minutes over medium heat, until the shallots just start to brown.

• Add the corn kernels, corn purée, stock, and the diced potato. Cover, bring to a boil over high heat, reduce the heat, add salt, and simmer, partially covered, about 10 minutes, or until the potatoes are cooked. Stir in the sautéed tomato mixture and add a sprinkling of pepper. Taste and adjust salt if necessary.

pinto bean and grilled vegetable soup

If you like chiles as much as I do, you'll love this soup's lively bite. A combination of fresh and dried chiles gives this pinto bean, vegetable, and chile combo south-of-the-border flair. The recipe calls for a poblano, also known as a fresh pasilla; if you can't get this, substitute a jalapeño cut into thin strips.

If you have neither a grill nor a grill pan—or if you simply don't have the inclination to grill—you can roast: preheat the oven to 400°F., cut the vegetables small, toss them with the oil, salt, and pepper, then roast, turning every 10 minutes, until softened. If you're doing it this way, cut the kernels off the cob and include them with the other vegetables.

SERVES 6

4 tablespoons extra-virgin olive oil
¼ cup minced shallots
1 teaspoon chile powder, preferably New Mexican
1 teaspoon dried thyme
1½ cups dried pinto beans, soaked
6 cups water (see Note)
1 guajillo chile (or pasilla or ancho), stem and seeds removed
1½ teaspoons salt
1 ear of fresh corn
1 medium red onion, peeled and cut into ½-inch rings
1 small to medium zucchini, cut lengthwise into ½-inch slices
½ poblano chile, cut in half, membrane removed, and cut into 1-inch strips
   Freshly ground black pepper
2 teaspoons fresh lime juice

• Warm 2 tablespoons of the oil in a medium saucepan. Add the shallots and sauté over medium heat for about 4 minutes, or until lightly golden. Add the chile powder and thyme and cook a couple more minutes, until fragrant.

• Add the beans, water, and guajillo to the pot. Bring to a boil over high heat. Lower the heat and simmer, partially covered, until the beans are soft, about 1 hour. Add the salt.

• Meanwhile, peel back the husks on the corn but do not tear them off. Tear out and discard the corn silk and pull the husks back over the cobs. Twist the husks at the tip to keep them in place. Soak in water for 15 minutes.

• Combine the red onions, zucchini, and poblano strips in a medium bowl. Toss with the remaining 2 tablespoons of oil. Sprinkle with salt and pepper.

• Heat the grill or grill pan (the kind that fits over two burners). Place the soaked corn on the grill and grill for 15 to 20 minutes, depending on the heat, turning occasionally so that the corn inside the husks steams and cooks. Pull back the husks for the last few minutes and grill directly on the heat to caramelize the sugars in the corn. Add the red onions, zucchini, and poblano strips in a single layer (make sure each vegetable touches the grill) and leave them until they have grill marks seared into them. Turn and grill on the other side. Remove the vegetables from the grill and cut them into bite-size pieces. Shuck the corn. Cut the kernels off the cob. Set aside.

- When the beans are cooked, remove the guajillo chile and place it in a blender. Remove 1 1/2 cups of the beans with a slotted spoon and add that to the blender as well. Add 1 cup of bean cooking liquid, and blend until smooth. Return the blended beans to the pot on the stove.

- Add the grilled or roasted vegetables to the soup and let the soup simmer a few minutes to allow the flavors to marry. Taste and add more salt if necessary. Remove from the heat, add the lime juice, and serve.

   ☞ PRESSURE COOKER METHOD: SAUTÉ THE SHALLOTS, CHILE POWDER, AND THYME IN A PRESSURE COOKER AS ABOVE. ADD THE BEANS, 4 CUPS OF FRESH WATER AND THE DRIED GUAJILLO TO THE COOKER. COVER AND BRING THE WATER TO A BOIL, THEN LOCK THE LID IN PLACE AND COOK OVER HIGH PRESSURE FOR 4 MINUTES. LET PRESSURE COME DOWN NATU-RALLY. ADD 1 1/2 TEASPOONS SALT. PROCEED AS ABOVE.

gazpacho

A few years ago, I traveled around southern Spain in the dog days of summer. I discovered that nothing was so refreshing as a chilled bowl of gazpacho. After pouring the gazpacho, the waiters, drawing from a tray of neatly separated garnishes, would meticulously place a spoonful of each in the center. Although gazpacho comes in different versions, chunky or creamy, I love the creamy variety served all over Andalusia. Though quintessentially Spanish, gazpacho is refreshing anywhere on a hot day. Make it from July through September, during the heart of tomato season, when tomatoes are ripe and succulent.

My gazpacho is a twist on the classic. The roasted red pepper lends both a smoky flavor and an especially bright color. No cooking is required; you simply toss a bunch of ingredients in a blender and blend until smooth. It could hardly be simpler.

The soup holds up for days in the refrigerator.

SERVES 4 TO 6

4   thick slices of white sourdough bread, preferably stale

2   pounds red tomatoes (6 medium)

2   cups cold water

1   large roasted red pepper (see page 188)

1   scallion, finely chopped

2   tablespoons paprika

2   garlic cloves

4   tablespoons red wine vinegar

¼   cup plus 1 tablespoon extra-virgin olive oil

¼   cup chopped fresh basil leaves

2   teaspoons salt

Finely chopped red onion, for garnish

Finely chopped green bell pepper, for garnish

Finely chopped tomatoes, for garnish

THE BREAD THICKENS THE SOUP AND CREATES A CREAMY, SMOOTH TEXTURE.

• Remove the crusts from the bread. Place 2 slices of the bread in a small bowl, cover with water, and soak for 5 minutes. Remove the bread and squeeze it like a sponge to get rid of excess water. Discard the water.

• Remove the stems from the tomatoes. Transfer the tomatoes, soaked bread, and water to a blender and blend to break up the tomatoes. You probably will need to do this in 2 batches.

• Remove the charred skin from the red pepper. Discard the stem and seeds and chop the roasted pepper into 1-inch pieces.

• To the blender add the red pepper, scallions, paprika, garlic, vinegar, ¼ cup of the oil, the chopped fresh basil, and salt and blend until smooth.

• Transfer to a container and chill thoroughly. Taste and add more salt if necessary.

• To make the croutons: Preheat oven to 350° F. Cut the remaining bread slices into ½-inch cubes. Put the remaining tablespoon of olive oil in a small bowl. Place the bread cubes in the bowl and lightly toss around so that all the bread touches the oil. Spread the cubes on a baking sheet and bake about 15 minutes or until crispy and golden.

• Serve the soup garnished with a spoonful of red onion, green pepper, tomato, and croutons.

main-course menus

The meals in this section are not just main courses; these ensembles are veritable feasts. Each menu reflects an artful balance of tastes, texture, and colors. These dishes fuse flavors and ingredients from around the world. For instance, a French chickpea crepe with a robust, earthy Eastern European filling is paired with bright red beets and a pungent, creamy horseradish topping. Spicy Mexican tamales are paired with side dishes such as a cucumber and jicama salad and sweet glazed squash. These complete main courses need only a starter or a soup, and a dessert, to make them ideal for dinner parties. These recipes will entice just about anyone who loves to eat and delight even the most committed vegetarian. The lush nature of the food belies the fact that these are healthful recipes, each of which provides an optimal combination of nutrients. They also present interesting and unusual ways of cooking foods that you might have been wanting to include in your diet, but so far have been reluctant to cook (such as soy, for instance).

Do not be daunted by the fact that each meal is composed of multiple components—that's what makes it gorgeous and exciting! You will find that each individual part is quite practicable and once you have become familiar with a recipe, it comes together much more quickly. And don't forget that while these parts are readily coordinated into ensembles (which add up to more than their parts), you may choose to prepare only some of the parts. You will also find that many of these components make ideal complements to recipes already in your repertoire, so feel free to mix and match at will!

When you are preparing a full ensemble, make sure to read the Cook's Notes first. They will guide you through the menu in logical steps so that everything is ready to serve at the same time. Read through the entire set of recipes in a main course before you get ready to cook. This will help you not only to envision the meal, but to anticipate what the next step will be. Note also that many of the steps can be done in advance.

This is the quintessential dinner-party food, but of course it should not be limited to parties. The recipes are fun to make on any day or for any occasion. The meals in this book are great for the Sunday cook who can prepare some of the recipes in advance, then do the finishing touches and serve the ensemble on the same day. Whenever I have a dinner party, I almost always prepare a good portion of the meal in advance, thereby eliminating much last-minute stress.

Don't think it is always necessary to go all out. Each dish stands solidly on its own. I often make dishes such as the potato salad from the crepe menu, the ginger-baked tofu from the African Groundnut Stew, or the chile from the chile casserole menu on their own.

No matter how interesting a recipe may be, you are the artist and the magician. The personal energy of the cook is always an integral part of what ends up on the plate. When you cook, envision any and all who will eat your food. Picture them in a state of delirious rapture as they savor each and every bite. The more joyful the energy and concentration that goes into your cooking, the more you put into the process of creating, the more truly voluptuous your meals will become.

Succotash

Spicy Polenta with Chile Paste

Guacamole

SERVES 4 OR 5

This version of succotash is best made at the height of summer, when farmers' stalls are bursting with ripe tomatoes, sweet corn, and golden summer squash. It's a thoroughly modern version of the traditional thick corn and bean stew favored by the Narragansett tribe of Rhode Island. The name derives from the Narragansett word *M'sickquatash,* which means both "fragments" and "whole boiled corn," suggesting that the mélange of ingredients has always included fresh corn.

This is not just any old stew; it is fit for a special occasion, especially when served with the supporting cast of spicy sweet polenta and traditional guacamole. In my experience, people who are normally averse to lima beans won't mind them here, although you can always substitute white beans.

cook's notes

- Soak the lima beans overnight or use the quick-soak method (page 8).
- Put the beans on to cook and make the chile paste.
- Make the polenta and let it set up.
- Make the guacamole and prep the stew ingredients.
- As you start to cook the stew, put the polenta in the oven to heat through.
- This is especially beautiful served in a wide soup bowl or pasta plate. Ladle stew onto the plate. Place a polenta round (or square) in the middle of the plate and spoon a mound of guacamole on top. Tuck a sprig of arugula or mizuna under the polenta and sprinkle with chopped parsley.

succotash

The mild but flavorful stew contrasts with the spicy polenta; it also goes well with simple cornbread or corn grits. Lima beans are best cooked by the stovetop method for this recipe. They cook in less than an hour, and their liquid makes a flavorful stock. Keep a good eye on the stew during the last few minutes to be sure you cook the vegetables until just tender, no longer, so that when you serve it, the stew is at its vibrant best. Add ¼ teaspoon of salt to the soaking liquid to help keep the lima beans' skins intact. It also helps to cook them with a little salt in the winter—something not usually recommended for beans.

SERVES 4 OR 5

1 cup baby lima beans, soaked
6 garlic cloves, peeled
1 bay leaf
Salt
2 tablespoons extra-virgin olive oil
1 medium onion, finely diced (1 cup)
2 medium carrots, peeled and cut in a roll cut (see page 15)
2 celery stalks, cut into ½-inch diagonal pieces
1 red bell pepper, stems, seeds, and membrane removed, cut into 1-inch chunks
1 yellow bell pepper, stems, seeds, and membrane removed, cut into 1-inch chunks
¾ pound plum tomatoes or 2 medium tomatoes, peeled, seeded, and chopped
1 medium zucchini, cut into ½-inch rounds
1 medium yellow squash, cut into ½-inch rounds
1 cup fresh corn kernels
1 ear of corn, cut into 1-inch wheels
Freshly ground black pepper
1 tablespoon fresh lemon juice
Pinch of cayenne pepper
Spicy Polenta with Chile Paste (page 55)
Chopped fresh flat-leaf parsley
Arugula or mizuna or young dandelion leaves, for garnish

• Skim off any bits of skin that have floated free from the beans and drain. Place the beans and 5 cups of fresh water in a medium saucepan. Add the garlic and bay leaf, cover, and bring to a boil over medium heat. Reduce the heat, add ¼ teaspoon salt, and simmer, partially covered, for about 30 to 45 minutes, or until the beans are just cooked. Add 1 teaspoon of salt, and let the beans sit, covered, for a few minutes to allow the beans to absorb the salt. Drain, reserving the cooking water. Discard the bay leaf.

• Warm the oil in a large pot or saucepan. Add the onions, carrots, celery, and peppers and sauté over medium-high heat for about 10 minutes, or until the onions are translucent. Add the tomatoes and cook an additional 5 minutes. Add the drained beans, along with the cooked garlic and 2 cups of cooking liquid, and bring to a boil. (If your liquid is still hot from cooking the beans, this only takes a moment.) Add the zucchini, yellow squash, corn kernels, and corn wheels. Lower the heat to a simmer and cook for 5 minutes, or until the vegetables are tender. Adjust salt to taste, add black pepper to taste, and add the lemon juice and cayenne.

• Serve the polenta in the center of the stew. Sprinkle parsley over the dish. Arrange a couple of pieces of arugula or other greens poking out from under the polenta.

AN INTERESTING WAY TO SLICE CELERY ON THE DIAGONAL IS TO PLACE THE CELERY ON ITS SIDE RATHER THAN FACE DOWN. THIS MAKES FOR HANDSOME, ARROW-SHAPED CUTS.

IF YOU USE A SUMMER SQUASH (OR CROOKNECK) THAT IS MUCH WIDER AT ONE END, CUT THE THICK END IN HALF LENGTHWISE. CUT HALVES INTO ½-INCH SLICES.

spicy polenta with chile paste

Carrot juice gives this polenta a touch of sweetness and a beautiful orange color. It also tastes great with the Smoky Black Beans (see page 196) or makes a great appetizer when cut into bite-size pieces, baked, and topped with a Fresh Tomato Sauce (see page 224).

Polenta is one of those versatile foods that can be made days in advance and kept in the refrigerator. Simply cut and heat what you need. You'll get the most out of the batch if you divide the polenta into squares. However, for an elegant dinner-party look, I prefer cutting it into rounds with a 3½-inch cookie cutter.

SERVES 4 OR 5

¾　cup cornmeal
¾　cup quick-cooking corn grits
2　cups fresh carrot juice (available at natural food stores; do not use canned)
2½ cups water
1　teaspoon salt
2　tablespoons extra-virgin olive oil
¼　cup Chile Paste (page 56)

THE CORN GRITS MAKE THE POLENTA COOK UP QUICKLY, AND THE CORNMEAL SMOOTHS OUT THE TEXTURE. THESE TWO COMBINED MAKE FOR A QUICK-COOKING POLENTA THAT HAS A PERFECT CONSISTENCY.

• Oil a 9 × 11-inch baking pan and set it aside.

• Mix together the cornmeal and corn grits in a bowl. Combine the carrot juice and water in a medium saucepan and bring to a boil over high heat. Add the salt and olive oil. Slowly whisk the cornmeal and corn grits into the carrot juice and water, stirring continuously until everything is incorporated and smooth. You can use an immersion blender in the beginning to break up little lumps or chunks that may form. Lower the heat and cook for 15 minutes, stirring constantly with a wooden spoon and making sure the polenta doesn't stick to the bottom of the pot; the polenta will start to pull away from the sides of the pot.

• Pour the polenta into the prepared baking pan and use a small metal spatula to smooth the top. Work quickly, because the polenta sets up fast. Immediately spread the chile paste evenly over the top in a thin layer. Let the polenta sit at room temperature until cool and set, or refrigerate for 30 minutes.

• Preheat the oven to 350° F. Cut the polenta into desired shapes and arrange on an oiled baking sheet. Bake the polenta until it is heated through.

chile paste

This is an all-around great chile paste to have on hand; the recipe makes more than you'll need for the polenta, but you can keep the rest refrigerated for weeks. Use it for the Baked Tempeh and Creole Sauce (pages 68–69), and for other sauces, instant chili, enchiladas, or anything that needs a touch of picante.

This recipe relies on my absolute favorite combination of chiles; I like the combo of the smoky hot chipotles with the milder anchos and pasillas. Don't worry if you don't have all of these chiles on hand; experiment with whatever chiles you do have or enjoy.

You want this to be of spreading consistency, so use only the liquid as necessary.

1   dried ancho chile (you may substitute mulato)
1   dried pasilla chile (you may substitute guajillo or New Mexican)
3   dried chipotle chiles
¼   cup extra-virgin olive oil
1½ teaspoons balsamic vinegar
    Pinch of salt

- Remove the stems and seeds from all the chiles. Place in a small saucepan, cover with water, and bring to a boil. Turn off the heat and let the chiles sit in the hot liquid for about 15 minutes, or until softened. Drain, reserving the soaking liquid.

- Transfer the chiles to a blender. Add ¼ cup of the soaking liquid and the olive oil, vinegar, and salt. Purée until smooth.

guacamole

This guacamole is an all-purpose variety; its mild flavor goes well with the spicy polenta. I use this basic condiment for just about everything: for dipping, filling, pita topping, and burritos. Have your lime juice ready before cutting the avocados—it keeps the green flesh from turning brown.

SERVES 4 OR 5

2   ripe avocados, preferably Hass
2   to 3 tablespoons fresh lime juice
½   teaspoon salt, plus more to taste
½   cup scallions, thinly sliced on the diagonal
¼   cup finely chopped fresh cilantro
1   garlic clove, minced
1   medium tomato, seeded and chopped

- Cut the avocados in half, scoop out the flesh into a mixing bowl, and break it up with a fork. Gently stir in the remaining ingredients. Do not mash the avocado too much—you want to keep the guacamole chunky. Taste and adjust the salt if necessary and add the extra lime juice if desired.

  ☞ GUACAMOLE IS BEST MADE AND EATEN THE SAME DAY. HOWEVER, REFRIG-
  ERATING IT WITH A PIECE OF PLASTIC WRAP PRESSED DIRECTLY ONTO THE
  SURFACE WILL HELP KEEP THE COLOR BRIGHT.

Hominy, Tomatillo, and Squash Stew

Ginger-Lime Tofu "Cream"

Tortilla Crisps

Lime-Marinated Cucumber Spears

SERVES 6

This menu is a real crowd pleaser and it is easy to scale up the recipe. I like to present the whole meal in one large soup bowl with the cucumber and tortilla crisps sticking out of the stew like sails on a boat. The recipe is a twist on a chile, with hominy and frozen tofu soaking up the flavors, adding good texture, and replacing the more traditional ingredients. I've used it as a good ice breaker for a bunch of guests who don't know each other—fishing out little corn wheels puts everyone in a good mood. This is an ideal dish to serve in autumn, as the corn wheels bring in a taste of late summer.

cook's notes

- Freeze the tofu.

- Soak the hominy overnight or use the quick-soak method (see page 8).

- Put the hominy on to cook first. While it is cooking, prep everything else.

- Make the stew.

- Assemble the ginger-lime "cream," tortilla crisps, and cucumber spears just before serving.

- Serve the stew in a bowl garnished with watercress and cucumber spears. Place a dollop of cream in the middle and arrange crisps vertically in the center.

hominy, tomatillo, and squash stew

This stew is light, bright, with lots of body. You have to plan ahead, as you'll need to have some frozen tofu and soaked hominy on hand. In fact, it's always a good idea to keep some tofu in the freezer so you can use it on a whim. If you've never frozen tofu, you will be amazed at how the texture magically transforms into something completely different (see Note).

Choose a squash with edible skin, since leaving the skin on helps the squash maintain its shape.

SERVES 6

½ pound frozen tofu (see Box)
1 cup whole hominy, soaked overnight
1 dried chipotle chile or another dried smoked hot chile
1 mild dried chile such as pasilla or ancho
1 tablespoon extra-virgin olive oil
2 medium onions, diced (2 cups)
 Salt
2 garlic cloves, minced
1 teaspoon dried oregano
1 teaspoon ground coriander
½ pound tomatillos, husked and halved (quartered if large)
1 pound winter squash (red kuri, buttercup, kabocha, delicata), cut into large cubes (about 4 cups)
½ cup fresh corn kernels (1 ear), plus 1 ear of corn cut crosswise into 1-inch wheels
1 medium red bell pepper, stem, seeds, and membrane removed, cut into ¾-inch squares
2 scallions, cut into 1-inch pieces
1 teaspoon umeboshi vinegar
 Watercress, for garnish
 Chopped fresh cilantro for garnish

IF YOU SCALE UP THE RECIPE, DON'T SCALE UP THE TOTAL LIQUID. EVAPORATION DECREASES WITH THE AMOUNT YOU SCALE UP. ADD A LITTLE EXTRA TO START, THEN ADD MORE IF NEEDED.

• Squeeze the tofu to remove any excess water. Crumble the tofu into large pebbly pieces by hand or in a food processor fitted with a metal blade. (A food processor is definitely easier.) Set aside.

• Drain the soaked hominy and place in a medium pot with 8 cups water. Bring to a boil and simmer, partially covered, for about 1½ hours, or until the hominy is tender. Reserve the cooked hominy and cooking liquid separately.

• Meanwhile, cut the stems off the chipotles and ancho, discard the seeds, and place the chiles in a pot. Cover with water, bring to a boil, then turn off the heat and let the chiles soak for 15 minutes in the hot liquid until they are softened. Transfer the chiles to a food processor or blender with ¼ cup of the soaking liquid and purée; set aside.

• Warm the oil in a medium pot. Add the onions and a little salt and sauté over low heat for about 5 minutes, or until the onions are translucent. Add the garlic, oregano, and coriander and sauté for another 5 minutes, or until the onions are soft and starting to brown. Add the crumbled tofu, chile purée, and tomatillos, combine well, and cook another 5 minutes.

• Add the squash, hominy, and reserved cooking liquid plus enough water to make 3 cups. Cover the pot, bring to a boil, then reduce the heat and simmer, partially covered, for 15 minutes, or until the squash is tender.

• Add the corn kernels, corn wheels, and bell peppers and cook 5 minutes. Add the scallions, salt to taste, and umeboshi vinegar. Cook 5 minutes, or until the peppers are softened.

• Serve with a garnish of watercress and chopped cilantro.

ginger-lime tofu "cream"

This ginger-lime "cream," stirred into the stew, imparts richness and a spicy citrus burst. Although I tend to use silken tofu in many of my dishes, I prefer a firmer texture for this recipe, as it gives it more body. However, you can use whichever type you have on hand. Make this lime and ginger–spiked cream at least 20 minutes before serving to let the flavors develop.

½   pound soft tofu
2   tablespoons fresh lime juice
3   tablespoons canola oil
2   teaspoons brown rice vinegar
¾   teaspoon salt
¼   teaspoon white pepper
2   teaspoons minced peeled ginger

• In a food processor fitted with a metal blade, combine all the ingredients. Whirl together until creamy, scraping down the bowl once or twice. Place in a bowl, cover, and refrigerate until ready to serve.

freezing tofu

Freezing tofu completely changes its texture. It becomes chewy, can be crumbled easily, and absorbs flavors even more readily. Firm tofu freezes best. To freeze tofu, remove it from the water it is packaged in, wrap it in plastic, and place it in the freezer. It will turn somewhat yellow in the process of freezing, which is fine. When you are ready to use it, defrost the tofu overnight in the refrigerator or by steaming it for 15 to 20 minutes. When the tofu is cool enough to handle, squeeze out as much water as you can with your hands. It is now ready to be crumbled by hand or in the food processor.

tortilla crisps

Although it is not as quick as frying, this method does produce crispy chips, with much less fat.

SERVES 6

6 6-inch corn tortillas
1 tablespoon canola oil

• Preheat the oven to 350° F. Cut the tortillas into long triangles an inch wide at the base. Place in a medium bowl and drizzle with canola oil, tossing to coat evenly. Place on a parchment-covered baking sheet and bake for about 20 minutes, or until crispy.

lime-marinated cucumber spears

Cucumbers dashed with lime provide a crisp green crunch. They taste best within a few hours of preparation.

SERVES 6

1 large cucumber
1 tablespoon fresh lime juice
1 tablespoon chopped fresh cilantro
Salt

• Peel the cucumber and cut it in half lengthwise. Use a teaspoon to scrape out the seeds, then cut each half into 1/2-inch spears. In a medium bowl, toss the cucumbers with the lime juice, cilantro, and a pinch of salt.

Warm Chickpea Salad with Artichokes and Sun-Dried Tomatoes

Fresh Corn, Millet, and Rice Croquettes

Jalapeño-Potato-Tofu "Cream"

Olive Tapenade

SERVES 4

I'm convinced that the Impressionist artists were drawn to the south of France not only for the famous light, but also for the quality of the food. Once they got a taste of Provence, they weren't going to budge. This menu evokes some of the goodness of the sun-drenched region with chickpeas, artichokes, sun-dried tomatoes, olives, and rosemary. The centerpiece, the warm chickpea salad, makes a good lunch or light supper.

cook's notes

- Advance preparation: If you are using dried chickpeas, soak them overnight or use the quick-soak method (see page 8) an hour in advance.
- Put the chickpeas on to cook. While they cook, prep the salad ingredients. Make the salad.
- Put the millet and rice on to cook. Boil the potato while you blend the tapenade.
- Get everything ready for the potato "cream," so you will be prepared when the potato is cooked.
- Form and bake the croquettes.
- To serve, place mesclun in the center of each plate, top with chickpea salad, and arrange three croquettes around it. Spoon potato "cream" and tapenade onto each croquette.

warm chickpea salad with artichokes and sun-dried tomatoes

If you have a pressure cooker and you've soaked your beans, making the salad from dried chickpeas is a breeze. Otherwise, this recipe is a good opportunity to use canned chickpeas. Though it can be eaten at room temperature, I prefer this salad warm, so just before serving I toss it in a pan over medium heat just until it is heated through. Serve on a bed of baby mixed greens, or mesclun.

SERVES 6

¼ cup sun-dried tomatoes (about 8 or 9)
3 cups cooked chickpeas, or 2 15-ounce cans, drained and rinsed
4 tablespoons fresh lemon juice
12 baby artichokes or 4 to 5 regular artichokes
3 tablespoons extra-virgin olive oil
1 onion, minced (1 cup)
4 garlic cloves, minced
1 celery stalk, cut in thin diagonal slices (½ cup)

salad dressing

3 tablespoons fresh lemon juice
¼ cup extra-virgin olive oil
1 tablespoon minced fresh rosemary
   Salt and freshly ground black pepper

Mesclun for garnish

COOKING THE CHICKPEAS IN ADVANCE MAKES THIS SALAD A SNAP. FOR 3 CUPS OF COOKED CHICKPEAS, START WITH 1½ CUPS DRIED. AFTER SOAKING, COOK THEM IN A PRESSURE COOKER FOR 10 MINUTES OVER HIGH PRESSURE AND LET THE PRESSURE COME DOWN NATURALLY. WHEN THE BEANS ARE TENDER, SALT THEM WHILE THEY ARE STILL IN THE COOKING WATER SO THAT THEY CAN ABSORB THE SALT.

• Place the sun-dried tomatoes in a small pot. Cover with water and bring to a boil over medium heat. Turn off the heat and let sit for about 10 minutes, or until the tomatoes are softened. If your sun-dried tomatoes are already soft and moist—and these are the best kind—there is no need to soak them. Slice the tomatoes thin and combine with the chickpeas in a medium bowl.

• Fill a bowl with 4 cups of water and add 2 tablespoons of the lemon juice. Trim the artichokes (see page 63), cut in half (cut larger artichokes into eighths), and place in the acidulated water. Bring a pot of water to a boil and add the remaining 2 tablespoons of lemon juice. Add the artichokes and boil until they are just tender, about 3 minutes for the baby and 4 minutes for the larger. Drain the artichokes and set aside.

• Warm 1 tablespoon of the olive oil in a medium skillet. Add the onions, garlic, and celery and sauté over medium-low heat for about 10 minutes, until the onions are soft and beginning to brown and the celery is tender. Add to the bowl with the chickpeas.

• Wipe out or wash the skillet and heat the remaining 2 tablespoons of olive oil in it. Add the artichokes and cook over medium heat without stirring until they are browned. Turn and brown them on the other side. Add them to the chickpeas.

• In a small bowl combine the dressing ingredients. Pour over the chickpea salad and stir well to combine the flavors. Let the salad sit for a few minutes to allow the flavors to marry.

• To serve, return the salad to the skillet and heat if desired, stirring just until it is heated through. Arrange on a bed of mesclun.

trimming artichokes

Before trimming the artichoke, have a bowl with acidulated water (3 tablespoons lemon juice to 1 quart water) ready to drop the artichoke in as it's trimmed. Snap off the tough outer leaves by pulling them downward until they break off at the base. Keep pulling off leaves until you get to the tender yellow ones where only the top third part of the leaf is green. (It is better to take off too many leaves than too few). Slice off the green top of the artichoke, then cut off all but an inch or so of the stem. Trim with a paring knife where the leaves were pulled off, and also the green outer skin of the stem. Smooth any rough areas around the base with your knife. Cut the artichokes in half, and place the half you're not working with in the acidulated water. Cut out the choke—the hairy fringe including the spiky inner purple leaves—with a paring knife. You are now ready to cut the artichoke into smaller pieces.

If you are using baby artichokes, trim them in a similar manner, breaking and peeling off the outer layers of leaves until the tender, pale green inner leaves show. Trim the stem and cut in half. No need to remove the choke, which is not fully formed in baby artichokes.

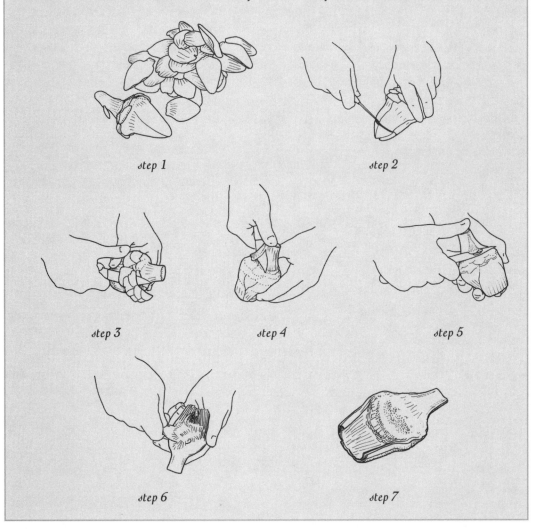

step 1

step 2

step 3

step 4

step 5

step 6

step 7

fresh corn, millet, and rice croquettes

These mini croquettes are designed to be served three per plate, with the chickpea salad in the middle, but you can make them larger if you want. The fresh corn keeps them moist and they hold together well because—and this is important—the grains are not toasted. Croquettes are easily reheated in an oven or skillet, and are even good eaten right out of the refrigerator. They also taste great accompanied by Black Beans with Epazote (page 89) or with simple beans and salsa.

SERVES 6

2/3 cup millet
1/3 cup basmati rice
1 teaspoon salt
3 cups water
2 tablespoons extra-virgin olive oil, plus oil to brush croquettes
1 onion, cut into small dice (1 cup)
3 garlic cloves, minced
1 cup fresh corn kernels (2 ears corn)
1 scallion, sliced thin on the diagonal
Freshly ground black pepper

• Cover the millet and rice with water in a bowl. Stir and swish them around, then let the water settle for a moment. Pour off the water, catching the grains at the last moment with a strainer. Place in a medium pot with the salt and water and bring to a boil, uncovered, over moderate heat. Lower the heat and simmer for about 15 minutes, uncovered, until most of the liquid is evaporated. Cover, turn the heat down to very low, and cook 5 more minutes with the lid on.

• Preheat the oven to 350° F.

• Meanwhile, warm the oil in a medium skillet. Add the onions, garlic, and corn and cook over medium heat, stirring, for about 8 minutes, or until the onions are starting to brown. Stir in the scallions and cook for another minute.

• When the grain is cooked thoroughly, stir in the onion-corn mixture. Sprinkle on freshly ground pepper. Taste for salt and adjust if necessary.

• Use an ice-cream scoop or a 1/4-cup measuring cup to form 12 croquettes. Really press the mixture into the scoop or cup to make the croquettes firm. Arrange them on a parchment-covered baking sheet. Lightly brush the croquettes with oil and bake them for about 20 minutes, or until golden.

• Use a spatula to remove them from the baking sheet carefully so they don't crumble.

jalapeño-potato-tofu "cream"

The jalapeños give this "cream" a light bite and, along with the scallions, a pretty, pale green color. For the best texture, use a low-starch or medium-starch potato; avoid russets. This cream tastes delicious cool or warm, but heat only the portion you are going to use and heat it just until warmed through, without boiling.

1	large (8-ounce) potato
½	pound silken tofu
1	tablespoon fresh lemon juice
1	teaspoon rice vinegar
2	tablespoons extra-virgin olive oil
1	scallion, thinly sliced on the diagonal
2	jalapeños, stems removed and seeded
1	teaspoon salt

• Boil the potato in salted water until it is tender, 20 to 30 minutes. Remove the potato from the water and, holding it with a dish towel, peel it. Cut the potato into chunks, place in a food processor, and add the remaining ingredients. Process until smooth and creamy. Taste and add more salt if necessary.

olive tapenade

There are those who like olives and those who absolutely swoon over them. If you're one of the latter, as I am, you might be tempted to eat this by the spoonful, even though it's powerful. Tapenade is the ideal condiment; it lasts a long time, a little goes a long way, and it's a tasty complement to many foods. Make sure to use a delicious olive, not the bland canned Californian ones.

1	cup pitted black olives, preferably kalamata
1	tablespoon capers, drained
1	garlic clove
2	tablespoons fresh lemon juice
2	tablespoons extra-virgin olive oil
1	teaspoon grated orange zest

• Combine all the ingredients in a blender or food processor, and blend until smooth. A blender works best; if, however, you use a food processor, stop occasionally to scrape down the sides with a spoon or spatula.

Baked Tempeh with Creole Sauce

Cajun Sweet-Corn Relish

Rice with Parsley and Lemon

SERVES 4 TO 6

If you love your food with a little heat from the kitchen, this is a menu for you. Adapting new ingredients to traditional uses is a hallmark of both Creole and Cajun cooking, and this menu fits the bill perfectly, showcasing hot peppers and other fresh produce, a hallmark of both cuisines. You might not think that a typical New Orleans staple like crayfish has anything in common with a vegan staple like tempeh, but they do; they both taste delicious smothered in a fiery Creole sauce. A simple, light rice dish and sweet corn relish complement the fiery main dish..

Both Creole and Cajun cooking derive from European traditions, but they are quintessentially American cuisines that mirror the mixed ethnic history of New Orleans. Creole cooking was designed to please the palates of the wealthy. New Orleans switched back and forth between French and Spanish dominion, and when Europeans of aristocratic descent settled there in the mid-seventeenth century, entrenched African cooks had to adapt from one cuisine to another. Thus Creole cooking comprises a mixture of Spanish, French, and African elements as well as ingredients indigenous to Louisiana.

Cajun cooking has humbler roots. It originated in Louisiana in the mid-eighteenth century when French peasants who had been living in Acadia (Nova Scotia) were exiled by British colonialists. Some of the Cajuns ended up in Louisiana, where they resourcefully adapted their own techniques to a whole new set of ingredients.

Around the middle of the twentieth century, Creole and Cajun began to merge, and it is difficult at this point to tell where one ends and the other begins.

cook's notes

- Steam the tempeh and marinate it.
- Make the Creole sauce.
- Make the corn relish.
- Cook the rice 20 minutes before eating.
- To serve, use a ring mold or measuring cup to form ¾ cup of rice into a flat-topped tower. You can serve the corn relish on top. Arrange some of the Creole tempeh to one side with some greens such as mesclun or mizuna.

baked tempeh

When you marinate and bake tempeh, it develops enough bold flavor to hold its own when stirred into the Creole sauce. Eat this smothered in the sauce or simply on its own in a sandwich or accompanied by rice and a salad.

Tempeh is a high-protein fermented soy cake, made from whole soybeans. It has a meaty texture and absorbs flavors like a sponge. It's readily available in natural food stores.

SERVES 4 TO 6

1	pound tempeh
1	cup apple juice
¼	cup shoyu
2	tablespoons brown rice vinegar
¼	cup extra-virgin olive oil
2	tablespoons mirin (sweet Japanese sake)
2	tablespoons Chile Paste (page 56)
1	teaspoon hot red pepper sauce
2	garlic cloves, minced

• Cut the tempeh into 1-inch cubes. Place in a steamer over boiling water for 10 minutes. Meanwhile, prepare the marinade. Whisk the apple juice, shoyu, vinegar, oil, mirin, chile paste, hot pepper sauce, and garlic in a medium bowl. Add the tempeh, toss to coat, and marinate for at least 20 minutes.

• Preheat oven to 350° F. Arrange the tempeh cubes in a shallow baking dish in a single layer. Pour enough of the marinade over the tempeh to cover halfway. Bake for 30 to 40 minutes, or until most of the marinade has been absorbed and the tempeh is golden.

creole sauce

In New Orleans, you will find shops that sell nothing but hot pepper sauces. These incendiary condiments have names like Devil's Revenge, Triple Nuclear Explosion, and Burning Bayou. All these sauces are essentially hot peppers mixed with vinegar and salt, so choose your favorite or rely on the standard, Tabasco. The quantity specified here will make a medium-hot dish; if you want it very spicy, feel free to crank up the heat.

2 tablespoons extra-virgin olive oil
2 medium onions, thinly sliced
   (2 cups)
1 large green bell pepper, seeded
   and cut into thin strips
3 garlic cloves, peeled and thinly
   sliced
2 large tomatoes, peeled, seeded,
   and cut into small dice
1 teaspoon dried thyme
1 tablespoon paprika
1 bay leaf
2 6-ounce cans tomato juice
   (1½ cups)
2 tablespoons Chile Paste (page
   56)
1 teaspoon balsamic vinegar
1 tablespoon Sucanat
1 teaspoon salt
   Freshly ground black pepper
1 teaspoon arrowroot dissolved in
   3 tablespoons water
½ teaspoon Tabasco sauce
1 recipe Baked Tempeh (page 68)

AVAILABLE IN NATURAL FOOD STORES AND
MANY SUPERMARKETS, SUCANAT IS A NATURAL
SWEETENER MADE FROM DRIED GRANULATED
CANE JUICE. THE SMALL AMOUNT OF SWEETENER
IN THE RECIPE BALANCES THE ACIDITY OF THE
TOMATOES.

• Warm the oil in a large skillet. Add the onions, peppers, and garlic and sauté, stirring occasionally, for about 7 minutes, or until the onions and peppers are wilted. Add the tomatoes, thyme, paprika, and bay leaf. Cook 2 or 3 minutes, or until the tomatoes are softened. Add the tomato juice and chile paste and simmer 5 minutes. Add the balsamic vinegar, Sucanat, salt, and pepper to taste. Add the dissolved arrowroot and cook, stirring, until the sauce bubbles and thickens a bit. Turn off the heat and stir in the Tabasco. Taste and adjust salt if necessary. Stir in the baked tempeh and heat through.

cajun sweet-corn relish

A bit of sweetness is a welcome (and necessary) counterpoint to the heat of the Creole tempeh. Corn is very starchy and, when puréed, becomes a combination thickener and essence for the rest of the dish. Peppers and tomatoes round out the flavor.

3 cups fresh corn kernels (from 4 ears), or 3 cups frozen corn, thawed
1 tablespoon extra-virgin olive oil
1 medium onion, finely diced (1 cup)
½ green bell pepper, finely diced (½ cup)
2 tomatoes, peeled, seeded, and cut into small dice
¾ teaspoon salt
Freshly ground black pepper
Pinch of cayenne pepper

• Combine half of the corn kernels with ¼ cup water in a blender. Purée until smooth.

• Warm the oil in a medium skillet. Add the onions and bell peppers and sauté over medium-low heat for about 7 minutes. Add the tomatoes and cook a few minutes until the tomatoes are softened. Stir in the remaining corn kernels and the corn purée and cook for 5 minutes more over medium-low heat, stirring constantly. Season with the salt, pepper, and cayenne. Serve hot. To reheat, warm gently over medium-low heat. Add a little water if necessary to prevent sticking.

rice with parsley and lemon

The simple addition of parsley and lemon zest elevates rice to a significant savory dish in its own right.

SERVES 4 TO 6

1½ cups white basmati rice
1 tablespoon extra-virgin olive oil
3 cups water
½ teaspoon salt
2 tablespoons grated lemon zest
¼ cup finely chopped fresh flat-leaf parsley

• Wash the basmati rice well by immersing it in a bowl of cold water. Swish the rice around in the water with your fingers, then allow it to settle to the bottom so that any particles or husks rise to the surface. Tilt the bowl and drain off the water.

• Warm the oil in a medium pot. Add the drained rice and sauté over low heat until the grains are dry.

• Add the 3 cups of water, and stir once to dislodge any rice that might have stuck to the bottom. Add the salt and cover the pot. Bring the liquid to a boil, lower the heat to a simmer, and cook for 10 minutes, or until the water is absorbed and the surface is covered with steamy holes. Turn off the heat and let the rice sit for 5 minutes. Fluff the rice with a fork. Add the lemon zest and parsley and toss together.

African Groundnut Stew

Spicy Sautéed Spaghetti Squash

Ginger-Baked Tofu

Quinoa and Millet Pilaf

SERVES 4 TO 6

Suitable for company, this meal is one even kids will enjoy; in fact, you might be surprised by the enthusiasm with which they eat *these* vegetables. The centerpiece is a hearty stew, warmed with ginger and cayenne and enriched by a little peanut butter. It is accompanied by millet, which is indigenous to Africa, and by quinoa, a natural mate to millet that lightens the dish. A side of spicy sautéed spaghetti squash and gingery tofu triangles enhances the sweet, hot heart of the stew. If you don't feel like making the entire ensemble, make the essential parts, the stew and the baked tofu, and serve them over noodles or grain.

The part of the African continent that is south of the Sahara is roughly divided into Western, Eastern, and Southern Africa. The countries of these regions have their own culinary traditions, but many ingredients such as pumpkins, yams, sweet potatoes, peanuts, corn, cabbage, and coconuts are common to all of them. West Africa is the ancestral home to most African Americans: thus a lot of indigenous African ingredients found their way into Creole, Cajun, Southern, and Caribbean cooking. Earthy stews play a central role in the rich and fiery food of West Africa, with garlic, ginger, and chile as important flavors. Nutritious, starchy roots such as yucca (cassava) and yam are combined with peanuts and grains. Peanuts, a mainstay of the diet in many parts of Africa, were taken there by the Portuguese in the sixteenth century. In Africa they're called "groundnuts," and groundnut stews are common in Senegal, Mali, Ghana, and Zimbabwe.

cook's notes

- Press the tofu. Bake the spaghetti squash.

- Marinate the tofu. Remove the flesh of the spaghetti squash and set it aside to sauté at the last minute. These two steps can be done a day in advance.

- Make the stew. Roast the cauliflower while you prep the other vegetables and start cooking the stew.

- While the stew cooks, bake the tofu. After adding the root vegetables to the stew, put up the grain to cook.

- When the stew is ready, let it sit to absorb flavors while you sauté the spaghetti squash at the last minute.

- To serve, ladle stew into a wide bowl or soup plate. Arrange two tofu triangles, a small mound of spaghetti squash, and a small mound of pilaf off to one side. Arrange greens on the other side. Sprinkle with cilantro and chopped peanuts.

african groundnut stew

A small amount of peanut butter here lends that comforting childhood taste, and it thickens and enriches the broth. I'm sure you'll fall in love with the brown and crusty roasted cauliflower; likewise, you might be even tempted to intercept it on the way to the pot. The vegetables are most striking when cut into large pieces, and the skin should be kept on the squash to help retain its shape.

Yucca, also known as cassava or manioc, is a slender, elongated root that ranges from four inches to two feet in length. It has a smooth, barklike skin and white flesh with a sweet, bland flavor and buttery texture. Be sure, however, to remove its fibrous core before cooking. Look at Hispanic markets and other ethnic groceries for yucca—it's worth seeking out, although you could substitute turnip if necessary.

The spindly leaves and slightly bitter taste of mizuna make a great garnish for the stew. It's often sold in gourmet markets and at farm stands, but if it is not available, mizuna or other greens such as watercress, arugula, and dandelion will taste and look good, too.

SERVES 4 TO 6

½ large or 1 small head of cauliflower, cut into large florets (3 cups)

4 tablespoons extra-virgin olive oil
  Salt

1 onion, cut into small dice (1 cup)

2 garlic cloves, minced

1 tablespoon minced peeled ginger

¼ teaspoon hot red pepper flakes

½ pound yucca, cut in large chunks (see Note) (1 cup), or 1 medium turnip, peeled and cut into large chunks

2 medium carrots, peeled and roll cut (page 15) (1 cup)

1 celery stalk, cut on the diagonal into 2½-inch pieces

2 large tomatoes, peeled, seeded, and chopped into small chunks, or 1 14.5-ounce can diced tomatoes

2 tablespoons shoyu

2 cups water

1 small sweet potato, peeled and cut into large chunks (1½ cups)

- Preheat the oven to 375° F. Toss the cauliflower in a bowl with 2 tablespoons of the oil and sprinkle with salt. Spread on a parchment-covered baking sheet and roast in the oven for about 30 minutes, stirring after 15 minutes, until the cauliflower has begun to brown.

- Heat the remaining 2 tablespoons of oil in a large (6- to 8-quart) pot. Add the onions and cook over medium-low heat for about 5 minutes, or until the onions are translucent. Add the garlic, ginger, and red pepper flakes and cook another 5 minutes.

- Add the yucca (or turnips), carrots, celery, tomatoes, and shoyu and cook uncovered over medium heat, stirring from time to time, for about 5 minutes, or until the tomatoes are reduced and thickened.

- Add the water, cover the pot, and bring to a boil over high heat. Lower the heat and simmer, partially covered, for 10 minutes. Add the sweet potato, squash, and 1 teaspoon salt and cook for another 15 minutes, or until the vegetables are tender. Stir in the roasted cauliflower and the peanut butter mixture and cook for just a few minutes, stirring every so often to make sure nothing sticks to the bottom of the pot; once you add the peanut butter you have to be vigilant. Add the ginger juice, scallions, and cilantro, adjust salt to taste, and add a generous pinch of cayenne. If the stew is too

1 pound kabocha, red kuri, or delicata squash, halved, seeded, and cut into big chunks (about 4 cups)

¼ cup creamy peanut butter mixed with ½ cup warm water

2 tablespoons ginger juice (see page 197)

1 scallion, chopped into 1-inch pieces (¼ cup)

¼ cup chopped fresh cilantro, plus more for garnish
Pinch of cayenne pepper

½ cup chopped, roasted, unsalted peanuts, for garnish
Mizuna or other greens, for garnish

thick, add a bit more water. Serve with peanuts and chopped cilantro sprinkled on top and greens on the side.

☞ HAVE A BOWL OF WATER READY TO PUT CUT PIECES OF YUCCA IN TO PREVENT DISCOLORATION. TO PEEL YUCCA, CUT IT INTO 2-INCH SEGMENTS. STAND THE PIECES CUT-SIDE DOWN ON A CUTTING BOARD. CUT OFF THE SKIN WITH A PARING KNIFE USING DOWNWARD STROKES. CUT THE PEELED PIECES IN QUARTERS LENGTHWISE AND CUT THE MIDSECTION OF FIBROUS CORE OUT OF EACH QUARTER. CUT INTO 1-INCH PIECES AND PUT IN THE WATER.

spicy sautéed spaghetti squash

Mild-tasting spaghetti squash can sometimes be bland, so I rev it up with a boost of oil, garlic, and red pepper flakes.

SERVES 4 TO 6

1 medium spaghetti squash (2 pounds)

3 tablespoons extra-virgin olive oil

3 garlic cloves, minced

¼ teaspoon hot red pepper flakes
Salt

• Preheat the oven to 375°F.

• Place the whole squash on a baking sheet and bake for about 1 hour or until the squash is tender when pierced with a fork. Cool for 10 to 15 minutes.

• Halve the squash lengthwise and discard the seeds. Then use a fork to remove the stringy flesh.

• Heat the oil, garlic, and red pepper flakes together in a medium skillet. Cook over medium heat, stirring, until the garlic just begins to color, about 2 minutes. Add the squash flesh and salt and toss together until heated through.

ginger-baked tofu

Here tofu bakes in its marinade, for a chewy texture with a burst of ginger flavor. It makes a great leftover that can be eaten hot or cold, served over a bed of greens, or even in a sandwich.

SERVES 4 TO 6

1   pound firm tofu
2   tablespoons fresh lemon juice
2   tablespoons mirin (sweet Japanese sake)
2   tablespoons shoyu
2   tablespoons canola oil
1   teaspoon toasted sesame oil
1   tablespoon pure maple syrup
1   tablespoon minced peeled ginger
2   garlic cloves, minced
1   teaspoon dried thyme
    Pinch of cayenne

- Place the tofu on a pie plate and top with a second plate. Weight the plate with a heavy can or two and press for at least 30 minutes. Drain.

- Make the marinade by whisking together in a bowl the lemon juice, mirin, shoyu, canola oil, sesame oil, and maple syrup. Mix in the ginger, garlic, thyme, and cayenne.

- Place the tofu cake on its side and cut it into 3 thin slices. Place the cake flat again and cut diagonally through all 3 layers to make 6 triangles. Cut the triangles down the middle into smaller triangles. Arrange the triangles in an 8 X 8-inch baking dish in a single layer fitting the pieces together like a mosaic. Pour the marinade over the tofu. Let it sit for at least 30 minutes and up to overnight, turning once.

- Preheat the oven to 375° F.

- Bake the tofu in its marinade for about 40 minutes, or until the tofu is golden brown and the marinade is absorbed.

quinoa and millet pilaf

Tiny-grained quinoa lightens and lends textured dimension to a satisfying dish of millet. This makes about 3 cups of grain, enough for a small serving with the hearty stew. If you are serving big eaters, scale up proportionately.

SERVES 4 TO 6

½ cup quinoa
½ cup millet
¼ teaspoon salt

• Wash the grains (see page 4). Add the rinsed grains to a small saucepan over medium-low heat. Stir the grains with a wooden spoon until all of the water has evaporated. Continue stirring until the grains emit a faint, roasted aroma.

• Add 2 cups water and the salt. Stir once to dislodge any grains that might have stuck to the bottom. Cover, and bring to a boil. Lower the heat and simmer, covered, for about 10 minutes, or until the water is absorbed. Let the pilaf sit, covered, for 5 minutes before fluffing with a fork.

Chickpea Crepes with Wild Mushroom, Roasted Cauliflower, and Chickpea Filling

Balsamic Marinated Beets

Horseradish "Cream"

Maple-Roasted Squash

SERVES 6

This is an excellent meal for an autumn or winter soirée. Every element can be prepared in advance, so the menu requires very little last-minute fussing. For once you can spend your precious last minutes before the guests arrive fixing the flowers.

These eggless crepes make a great match for a wide range of flavors, so feel free to experiment with a great variety of fillings. The flavors of the delicate herbed crepe, the robust and earthy stew, the pungent horseradish "cream," and the sweet roasted squash and marinated beets make this menu one of my favorites.

cook's notes

- Make the crepe batter first thing, or even the day before.
- Make the stew.
- Put up the beets to cook while you prepare the horseradish "cream."
- Roast the squash just before you start to make the crepes.
- To serve, center two filled crepes on each serving plate. Spoon horseradish cream diagonally across the crepes and sprinkle with snipped dill. Arrange three pieces of marinated beets and three pieces of roasted squash around each serving. Tuck a few leaves of arugula under the crepes.

a word about crepes

The quality of a crepe depends on having just the right batter consistency. Too thick a batter will result in a heavy crepe; too thin and you'll have trouble making the crepe at all. The proper consistency is that of heavy cream; the batter should just coat your finger when you dip it in.

Start with two cups of water per two cups of flour and let the batter sit for at least twenty minutes so that the flour can absorb all the liquid. Make a test crepe to check the thickness, to adjust for seasoning, and to get the pan ready. Batters thicken as they sit, so if you find yours is getting harder to swirl around in the pan, add a few drops of water at a time and mix well until the batter again reaches the right creamy consistency.

A good crepe pan is usually made of cold rolled steel, also known as black steel. It is lightweight, and the long handle does not get too hot. In a pinch, I've used a cast-iron pan—its main downside is its weight—and a nonstick griddle. They both made good crepes, but not nearly as gracefully as the crepe pan.

A new crepe pan, or a pan that hasn't been used for a while, should be seasoned. Place a layer of salt over the entire pan and cover it with vegetable oil. Heat until the oil begins to smoke. Then discard the oil and wipe out the salt with a paper towel. The pan is now ready to use. If yours is properly seasoned, your first crepe will be the only crepe you will have to sacrifice. Between crepes, all you need to do is rub a little oil on the pan with a paper towel.

Another key to a good crepe is having your pan at the right temperature. You will quickly discover the right heat as you set about making your crepes; if the heat is too high, the crepes will burn, and if it's too low they will take too long to cook, resulting in a crepe that never browns.

If your pan gets too hot between crepes—you can tell this if the pan is smoking—simply remove it from the heat and let it sit for a moment or two. Sometimes I wave the pan in the air a bit to speed up the cooling. It does the trick. Do not put your crepe pan under running water. If a crepe sticks, clean your pan with salt and a paper towel—never with an abrasive scrub brush, which will damage the pan. A beautiful crepe turns a warm golden brown on the first side, so be sure to use that as the outside of the crepe.

chickpea crepes

These light, flavorful crepes are perfect with the mushroom filling in this menu and also with Grilled Spring Vegetables (see page 212). Chickpea flour has a distinctive, delicate flavor, and it does what eggs do in a conventional crepe: it binds. It is available at Indian specialty stores and at many natural food stores.

Crepes stack easily and can be made in advance and reheated. Reheat by wrapping them in foil and placing in a preheated 350°F. oven. This makes twelve 6- to 7-inch crepes.

SERVES 6

1 cup chickpea flour
1 cup unbleached white flour
1 teaspoon salt
2 tablespoons extra-virgin olive oil
2 cups warm water
2 tablespoons finely chopped chives

• In a medium bowl whisk together the flours and salt. Add the oil and water and whisk to combine, then transfer to a blender and thoroughly blend ingredients together. Alternatively, use an immersion blender to blend the batter in the bowl. Pour the batter back into a bowl and stir in the chives. Allow the batter to rest for at least 20 minutes. At this point, the batter can be refrigerated for up to a day.

• Heat a 6- to 7-inch crepe pan over medium heat. Lightly oil the pan using an oil-saturated paper towel. Pour ¼ cup batter onto the pan, tilting the pan in a circular motion so that the batter covers the entire surface. Cook until the surface bubbles and the crepe becomes golden around the edges, about 1 minute. Loosen the edges with a spatula, then with the spatula—or your hands—flip it. Cook the second side for about 30 seconds.

• Transfer the cooked crepe to a plate and continue making crepes, lightly oiling the pan between each, until the batter is finished.

chickpea crepes with wild mushroom, roasted cauliflower, and chickpea filling

Heady fall flavors are provided in the form of porcini mushrooms, roasted shiitakes, and roasted cauliflower, giving this stew a hearty presence. The stew is also delicious without the crepes. For a simpler meal, serve it with a dollop of horseradish "cream," some good bread, and a green salad.

SERVES 6

½ medium head of cauliflower, cut into florets (3 cups)

3 tablespoons extra-virgin olive oil
Salt

¼ pound fresh shiitake mushrooms, stems removed, sliced

1 tablespoon shoyu

½ ounce dried porcinis (about ½ cup)

2 medium onions, thinly sliced (2 cups)

1 tablespoon minced shallot

2 garlic cloves, minced

¼ green cabbage, thinly sliced (3 cups)

1 teaspoon ground cumin

1 teaspoon ground caraway seeds

1½ cups cooked chickpeas (page 136), or 1 15-ounce can of chickpeas, drained and rinsed

1 tablespoon fresh lemon juice
Freshly ground black pepper

¼ cup chopped dill, plus 2 tablespoons for garnish

12 Chickpea Crepes (page 80)
Arugula, for garnish

YOU CAN ROAST THE MUSHROOMS AND CAULIFLOWER ON THE SAME SHEET, EACH AT ITS OWN END, BUT MAKE SURE THE SHEET IS LARGE ENOUGH TO SPREAD THE VEGETABLES OUT. THE MUSHROOMS WILL COOK FASTER, SO REMOVE THEM WHEN DONE.

• Preheat the oven to 375° F. In a bowl, toss the cauliflower with 1 tablespoon of the oil and ¼ teaspoon salt. Place on a parchment-covered baking sheet and roast for 30 minutes, stirring every 10 minutes, until the tops are browned.

• Meanwhile, mix the sliced shiitake mushrooms with 1 tablespoon of the oil and add the shoyu. Place on a baking sheet and roast for about 20 minutes, stirring a couple of times, until the mushrooms have released their juices and become quite dry. Set aside the shiitakes and cauliflower.

• Rinse the dried porcinis. In a small bowl, pour 1 cup hot water over them and soak for 15 minutes.

• Warm the remaining tablespoon of oil in a medium saucepan and add the onions. Cook over low heat for 10 to 12 minutes, or until softened. Add the shallots, garlic, cabbage, cumin, and caraway, stir, and cook 5 minutes, or until the cabbage has completely wilted.

• Pour the porcinis and liquid through 2 layers of paper towels placed in a strainer. Reserve the soaking liquid. Rinse the porcinis to remove any remaining dirt and chop into small pieces. Add the chickpeas, shiitakes, cauliflower, and porcinis to the vegetable mixture. Combine the porcini soaking liquid with enough water to make 2 cups and add to vegetables.

• Simmer 10 minutes. Add the lemon juice, and salt and pepper to taste. Remove from the heat and stir in the dill.

• Fold each crepe around ½ cup of filling. Center two on a plate and sprinkle with dill. Tuck a few leaves of arugula under the crepes.

balsamic marinated beets

Beets, creamy mushrooms, and cabbage are a classic Eastern European combination. These beets could hardly be simpler, with just a dose of balsamic vinegar to heighten their natural sweetness. You can serve them right away, but if you let them marinate at least 30 minutes, you'll even get more intense beet flavor. Refrigerated, the beets stay good for several days.

SERVES 6

3 medium beets (¾ pound)
2 tablespoons balsamic vinegar
Pinch of sea salt

• Place the beets in a medium saucepan and cover with 1 inch of water. Cover the pot and simmer for about 1 hour or until the beets are tender.

• Drain the beets and rinse under cool water to slip off the skins. Cut the beets in half, then cut each half into 3 wedges. Place in a bowl, toss with the balsamic vinegar, and sprinkle with salt.

☞ THE BEETS CAN ALSO BE PREPARED IN A PRESSURE COOKER. COVER THE BEETS WITH WATER IN A PRESSURE COOKER AND BRING TO A BOIL OVER HIGH HEAT. LOCK THE LID IN PLACE AND COOK OVER HIGH PRESSURE FOR 9 TO 12 MINUTES, DEPENDING ON THE SIZE OF THE BEETS. LET THE PRESSURE RELEASE NATURALLY, AND CONTINUE AS ABOVE.

horseradish "cream"

As innocent-looking as it seems, this "cream" has so much zestiness you might want to double the recipe for extra slathering. You can always use the extra for a touch of high-protein pizzazz on vegetables and grains.

½ pound soft tofu
2 tablespoons fresh lemon juice
3 tablespoons canola oil
2 tablespoons brown rice vinegar
¾ teaspoon sea salt
¼ teaspoon white pepper
½ cup minced red onion
1 tablespoon chopped fresh dill
2 teaspoons prepared horseradish

• In a food processor fitted with a metal blade, combine the tofu, lemon juice, oil, vinegar, salt, and pepper and process until smooth. Transfer to a bowl and stir in the remaining ingredients.

maple-roasted squash

In this recipe, a small amount of maple syrup and a high roasting temperature intensify the squash's sweetness—I think of this as vegetable candy. I am fond of delicata squash, but you can use kabocha, red kuri, or any other squash with an edible skin.

SERVES 6

1 medium delicata squash
(¾ pound)
1 tablespoon canola oil
1 tablespoon pure maple syrup
Pinch of sea salt

• Preheat the oven to 375° F. Cut the squash in half lengthwise and use a teaspoon to remove the seeds. Cut the squash into triangular wedges, place in a bowl and toss with the oil, syrup, and salt. Spread on a parchment-lined baking sheet and roast until the squash is tender and lightly caramelized.

Mexicali Tamales with Seitan Picadillo

Black Beans with Epazote

Jicama, Radish, and Cucumber Salad

Maple-Glazed Squash

SERVES 4 TO 6

In Mexico, tamales are party or special-occasion food. In fact, preparing the tamales is often a communal event. So have a party and serve tamales, or have a party to make tamales; once you start the process going, you'll find it's loads of fun. And this meal is as interesting to look at as it is exciting to eat.

The main dish features tamales, which are both unusual and familiar. Although the Conquistadores' records show the Aztecs were making tamales long before the Spanish arrived in Mexico, the Conquistadores introduced *manteca,* or lard, into the traditional dish. My tamales won't weigh you down—they are much lighter on the fat than the usual kind— but they still have a rich flavor. In Mexico, tamales are most often wrapped in banana leaves; I've used corn husks here, which are much more accessible in the United States. The spicy black beans are flavored with epazote, an herb very common in Mexican cooking, and chile de árbol, a small, hot, dried chile. The sweet glazed squash and cool crunchy salad round out the menu.

cook's notes

- Soak the hominy and black beans overnight or use the quick-soak method (see page 8)

- Cook the hominy and beans.

- While the beans cook, make the seitan picadillo and the *masa* dough.

- Assemble the tamales and finish the beans.

- While the tamales are steaming, make the salad and prepare the squash.

- Cook the squash during the last 10 minutes of the tamales' cooking time.

- To serve, place two tamales on a plate. Open the tamales without untying the husk strings, and serve the beans so that they are spilling out of the husks onto the plate. Arrange the salad and squash on the side.

In small towns in Mexico, women soak fresh field corn (not to be confused with the sweet corn of corn-on-the-cob) overnight with slaked lime (or *cal,* as it is known in Mexico). In the morning they rub off the loosened husks, then take the husked corn to the neighborhood *molino,* or mill. They hold their baskets under the grinding machine as it spews forth the moist ground corn, which forms a dough known as *masa,* either of tamale (coarse) or tortilla (finer) grade. When the soaked and husked corn is dried whole, it is called hominy or *posole.* It is from the dried kernels that *masa harina,* or *masa* flour, is made.

It is difficult to find fresh *masa* in the United States, as *molinos* are few and far between, but dried hominy is readily available at ethnic markets and *masa harina* is so common that it can be found on many supermarket shelves. Whole hominy adds a wonderful chewy element to stews. I have found that by puréeing the reconstituted hominy with enough of its cooking liquid to make a very creamy purée, and then adding just enough *masa harina* to make a pliable dough, I can get a great texture with a lot of flavor, and much less fat than dough made the traditional way. This versatile dough works well when baked into a *masa* pie, steamed as tamales, or cooked on a griddle to make *arepas.*

Hominy comes in white, yellow, and the less common red or blue. I use the white or yellow when I'm going to purée, since they cook to a softer consistency.

I've had the unhappy experience of getting bits of skin caught in the release valve of my pressure cooker, so I prefer to cook hominy on the stovetop. Do take the time for this step, though, as the flavor of the canned variety pales in comparison.

mexicali tamales

Dried corn husks come tightly packed together, and you must soak them in water to make them pliable. Choose large, intact husks for your tamales. You can redry any corn husks that you do not use. Wrapped and stored in a dry place, husks stay good for at least a year.

To reheat the tamales, steam them until warmed through.

MAKES 12 TO 14 TAMALES

1 cup dried hominy, soaked overnight or use the quick-soak method (see page 8)
6 cups water
¼ cup plus 1 tablespoon canola oil
2 onions, halved and thinly sliced (2 cups)
1½ teaspoons salt
¼ cup *masa harina*
1 2-ounce package of corn husks
1 recipe Seitan Picadillo (page 88)

• Drain the hominy and place in a medium saucepan. Add the water and bring to a boil. Lower to a simmer and cook, partially covered, about 1½ hours, or until the hominy is just soft. Keep an eye on the water level, adding water if necessary to keep the hominy covered. Drain the hominy when soft, reserving the cooking liquid. Some of the hominy will open up like popcorn. Do not overcook it to the point where it becomes mushy.

• In a medium skillet, warm 1 tablespoon of the canola oil. Add the onions and cook over low heat for 15 to 20 minutes, or until the onions are very soft. Set aside.

• Meanwhile, soak the corn husks in warm water for 15 minutes. Pull them apart as they become supple and keep submerged.

• In a food processor fitted with a metal blade, combine the drained hominy, 1 cup of the reserved cooking liquid, the ¼ cup canola oil, and the salt. Process, scraping down the sides, until thick and creamy. You will have to run the processor for a good few minutes. Be sure to blend the ingredients while warm for the smoothest consistency. Then add the onions and process again, until they are well integrated into the purée.

• Transfer the purée into a mixing bowl. Add the *masa harina* and mix it thoroughly into the batter.

• Form the tamales (see Sidebar) and place 1 tablespoon of the Seitan Picadillo in each.

• Stack the tamales in a steamer or in a large pot with a steamer insert. Steam for 1 hour to 1 hour and 15 minutes. Check the water level in your steamer every 20 minutes and add water to the steamer if needed, making sure not to let the water evaporate.

• Open up a tamale to check it. Tamales should hold together in a solid form. Their surface should take on the striations of the husks. Let the tamales sit for a few minutes to firm up. You can reheat tamales by steaming them.

making tamales: a step-by-step guide

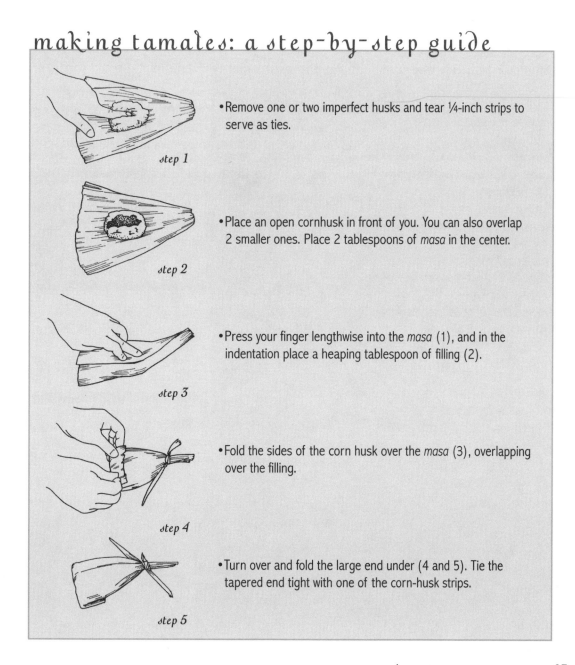

step 1

• Remove one or two imperfect husks and tear ¼-inch strips to serve as ties.

step 2

• Place an open cornhusk in front of you. You can also overlap 2 smaller ones. Place 2 tablespoons of *masa* in the center.

step 3

• Press your finger lengthwise into the *masa* (1), and in the indentation place a heaping tablespoon of filling (2).

step 4

• Fold the sides of the corn husk over the *masa* (3), overlapping over the filling.

step 5

• Turn over and fold the large end under (4 and 5). Tie the tapered end tight with one of the corn-husk strips.

seitan picadillo

This bold Seitan Picadillo filling was inspired by Susanna Trilling, who was my cooking teacher in Oaxaca, Mexico. In true Oaxacan Picadillo fashion, this one is full of tomatoes and sweet spices, and textured with raisins, capers, and almonds. *Picadillo* comes from the Spanish word *picar,* meaning to mince, so all of the ingredients need to be tiny. But after the chopping is done, the dish is fast and easy to put together.

SERVES 4 TO 6

6   whole almonds
1   tablespoon extra-virgin olive oil
1   onion, finely diced (1 cup)
2   garlic cloves, minced
1   medium tomato, finely diced
    (½ cup)
4   ounces seitan, minced (¾ cup)
8   green olives, pitted and minced
    (1 tablespoon)
1   tablespoon raisins
1   teaspoon capers, drained and
    minced if large
½   teaspoon fresh thyme leaves
    Salt and freshly ground black
    pepper
1   tablespoon chopped fresh flat-leaf
    parsley

• Toast the almonds in a dry medium skillet just until they start to darken, about 3 minutes. Remove to a cutting board and chop small.

• Warm the oil in the same skillet. Add the onions and garlic and cook over medium-low heat for about 10 minutes, until the onions are softened and beginning to brown. Add the tomatoes and cook 5 minutes more. Stir in the seitan, olives, raisins, capers, and thyme and cook just until heated through. Season to taste with salt and pepper. Remove from the heat and stir in chopped parsley.

black beans with epazote

These beans have genuine Mexican flavor, in part because of the *epazote,* a pungent-smelling, jagged-leafed herb. Increasingly available, especially in dried form, *epazote* is often used in Mexican cooking, especially with black beans. In Mexico, the anise-flavored avocado leaf would also be used, but the more easily available anise seeds make a good substitution.

SERVES 4 TO 6

1½ cups black beans, soaked
1   bay leaf
    Salt
2   teaspoons cumin seeds
½   teaspoon anise seeds
2   dried chiles de árbol
1   tablespoon extra-virgin olive oil
1   onion, finely chopped (1 cup)
3   garlic cloves, minced
1½ teaspoons dried epazote
¼   cup dry sherry
1   teaspoon fresh lemon juice

EPAZOTE SOMETIMES SHOWS UP FRESH IN FARMERS' MARKETS AND AMONG THE PRODUCE IN MEXICAN STORES. YOU CAN AIR-DRY IT SUCCESSFULLY. ONE TEASPOON OF DRIED EPAZOTE IS EQUIVALENT TO 7 DRIED CRUMBLED LEAVES.

CHILES DE ÁRBOL, "TREELIKE" CHILES, ARE BRIGHT RED, ABOUT 2 TO 3 INCHES LONG, AND ½ INCH WIDE. THIS HOT, SHARP, SEARING CHILE IS A CLOSE RELATIVE OF CAYENNE.

• Drain the black beans and put them in a medium-size saucepan. Cover with 6 cups of fresh water and the bay leaf and cook for 1 hour, or until the beans are soft. After 50 minutes, add 1½ teaspoons of salt. Cook until soft, then drain, reserving the cooking liquid.

• In a dry skillet over medium-low heat, toast the cumin and anise seeds until lightly darkened and fragrant, stirring constantly. Remove the stems and seeds from the chiles de árbol. Toast the chiles with the seeds until slightly darkened on either side, being careful not to burn them. Remove from the heat, and grind the chiles, cumin, and anise to a powder in a spice grinder or mortar and pestle.

• Warm the oil in a medium saucepan. Add the onion and garlic and sauté over medium-low heat for about 10 minutes, or until the onion is softened and lightly browned. Add the epazote and the ground spices and sauté a few more minutes.

• Add the sherry and scrape up any brown bits. Raise the heat and reduce the sherry until it's almost evaporated.

• Add the drained beans plus 2 cups of the reserved bean cooking liquid to the saucepan and simmer for 30 minutes to let the flavors marry and to thicken the beans. Add more liquid if necessary. Remove 1 cup of beans, purée, and add back into the bean pot to thicken. Alternatively, partially blend the sauce with an immersion blender.

• Add the lemon juice and adjust salt to taste. Since black beans thicken as they sit, adjust the consistency as needed with a little bean cooking liquid or water.

    ✍ AS AN ALTERNATE METHOD, PUT THE BEANS IN A PRESSURE COOKER. COVER WITH 5 CUPS OF LIQUID, BRING THE LIQUID TO A BOIL, LOCK THE LID INTO PLACE, AND COOK OVER HIGH PRESSURE FOR 11 MINUTES. ADD 1½ TEASPOONS SALT. LET THE BEANS SIT FOR A FEW MINUTES TO ABSORB THE SALT, THEN DRAIN, RESERVING THE LIQUID. PROCEED AS ABOVE.

jicama, radish, and cucumber salad

Three different crunchy textures and three distinct herbs make up this light, refreshing, oil-less salad.

SERVES 4 TO 6

½ medium jicama, peeled and cut into ¼-inch matchsticks (1 cup) (page 198)

5 medium radishes, sliced (½ cup)

½ medium cucumber, peeled, seeded, and diced (1 cup)

1 teaspoon finely chopped fresh mint

1 teaspoon finely chopped fresh flat-leaf parsley

1 teaspoon finely chopped fresh cilantro

¼ teaspoon salt

1 tablespoon mirin (sweet Japanese sake)

1 tablespoon fresh lemon juice

1 tablespoon brown rice vinegar

• In a bowl mix together the jicama, radishes, and cucumber. Toss with the herbs and sprinkle with the salt. Add the mirin, lemon juice, and vinegar. Toss again.

maple-glazed squash

The maple glaze coats the squash and complements the vegetable's natural sweetness. Use delicata, red kuri, kabocha, or any other squash with edible skin.

SERVES 4 TO 6

1   pound squash, seeded and cut
     into 1-inch pieces (3 cups)
¼   cup pure maple syrup
     Salt

TO PREP WINTER SQUASH FOR COOKING, CUT IN HALF AND BAKE FACEDOWN ON A BAKING SHEET UNTIL SOFT. REMOVE SEEDS AND SCOOP OUT THE FLESH.

IF YOU NEED TO PEEL THE SQUASH BEFORE COOKING IT, USE A KNIFE OR WIDE-MOUTHED PEELER. SCOOP OUT THE SEEDS AND CUT UP THE SQUASH ACCORDING TO THE RECIPE. BUTTERNUT SQUASH, WITH ITS PEAR SHAPE, SHOULD BE HANDLED AS TWO SEPARATE VEGETABLES. CUT THE SQUASH AT THE POINT WHERE THE SQUASH BECOMES ROUND AND BULBOUS, WHICH IS THE PART THAT CONTAINS THE SEEDS, AND TREAT THE 2 PIECES AS INDEPENDENT VEGETABLES.

- In a medium skillet, put squash in ½-inch water. Cook, covered, for 5 to 10 minutes, or until the squash is barely tender. Check after 5 minutes so as not to overcook.

- Uncover, add the maple syrup to the pan, and turn the heat up to high. Boil for a few minutes, until the syrup has reduced and thickened. Sprinkle with salt.

Red Kuri Squash and Bean Ragù

Arepas • Jalapeño "Sour Cream"

Sautéed Sweet Potatoes with Red Onions and Balsamic Vinegar

Caramelized Brussels Sprouts with Pecans

SERVES 4

This rich autumnal meal includes a variety of flavors and textures that packs each bite: garlic, caraway, chile powder, and paprika make for an unusual medley. In Algeria, this mixture is called a *charmoula*, but it is different from the more widely known Moroccan one. Its robust flavor mates perfectly with the corn-based *arepas,* the glazed Brussels sprouts, the balsamic-sautéed sweet potatoes, and the tofu "sour cream." Since the meal can be made in stages, it's ideal for a dinner party.

cook's notes

For advance preparation, you can make the "sour cream" up to two days in advance. You can make the sweet potatoes and form the *arepas* one day in advance.

• Soak and cook the beans and the hominy. Meanwhile, make the "sour cream" and the sweet potatoes.

• Form the *arepas* and set aside to cook at the last minute.

• Prep the vegetables for the stew, and start the stew while you are cooking the beans.

• Make the Brussels sprouts and cook the *arepas.*

• To serve, a wide soup plate makes for the most beautiful presentation. Ladle in the stew. Top with an *arepa* and squirt or drizzle everything with stripes of the cream. Mound sautéed sweet potatoes on top. Place Brussels sprouts, onions, and pecans around the sides. Sprinkle with fresh parsley.

red kuri squash and bean ragù

Many beans are suitable in this unusual stew. I like to use a mixture of baby lima, kidney beans, and anasazi because the colors and shapes are lovely together. This is also a good place to showcase "boutique beans," those unusual heirloom varieties that are increasingly available. The scarlet runner, a large red bean, is especially dramatic. Other interesting options include cranberry beans, flageolets, black beans, Swedish brown beans, or pinto beans. For the most pleasing result, look for contrasts of color and shape. Beans that do not cook at more or less the same rate, such as chickpeas and black beans, should be cooked separately, and do not use beans that would break down, such as split peas or red lentils.

Red kuri squash is a sweet, bright-orange squash whose cooked skin becomes tender enough to eat. The skin has many nutrients and helps the squash maintain its shape. Buttercup, ambercup, kabocha, hokaido, or delicata squash are all fine alternatives, as their skins also become soft enough to eat.

SERVES 4

⅓ cup dried kidney beans, soaked
⅓ cup dried anasazi beans, soaked
⅓ cup dried baby lima beans, soaked
1 bay leaf
5 cups water
  Salt
3 tablespoons extra-virgin olive oil
8 garlic cloves, peeled and quartered
2 teaspoons ground caraway seeds
1 teaspoon paprika
1 teaspoon chile powder, preferably New Mexican
1 onion, cut into small dice (1 cup)
1 pound red kuri squash, seeded and cut into 1½-inch squares or triangles
½ pound celery root, peeled and cut into 1-inch cubes (2 cups)
2 medium carrots, peeled and cut into large roll-cut chunks (page 15) (1 cup)
1 tablespoon fresh lime juice
⅓ cup chopped fresh flat-leaf parsley, plus more for garnish
1 tablespoon fresh thyme leaves

- Place the beans in a medium saucepan or Dutch oven with the bay leaf and the water. Cover and bring to a boil, then reduce the heat and simmer, partially covered, until the beans are tender, 1 to 1¼ hours. Check to make sure the beans are covered with water at all times, adding more if necessary. When the beans are done, add 1 teaspoon salt and let the beans sit for a few minutes. Drain, reserving the cooking liquid separately.

- In a large pot, combine the oil, garlic, caraway, paprika, chile powder, and onions. Cook slowly over low heat for 15 minutes, or until the garlic and onions are softened, stirring frequently so the spices don't stick. Add 1 cup water and cook over high heat, stirring to loosen anything sticking to the bottom of the pan. Continue to cook until the liquid has nearly evaporated. Add the squash, celery root, and carrots, and sauté for a few minutes.

- Add the cooked beans and 4 cups of the bean cooking liquid. (Add water if necessary to make 4 cups total.) Cover the pot and bring to a boil. Reduce the heat and simmer for about 20 minutes, or until the vegetables are cooked.

- Add the lime juice and salt to taste. Stir in the parsley and thyme. Turn off the heat and let the ragú sit for a few minutes before serving.

PREPARE THE KNOBBY CELERY ROOT BY PEELING OFF THE ROUGH SKIN WITH A WIDE PEELER OR KNIFE. CUT INTO PIECES AND KEEP THE CUT PIECES IN A BOWL WITH WATER AND A LITTLE LEMON JUICE TO PREVENT DISCOLORATION.

arepas

There are many variations on the basic *arepa,* a Colombian or Venezuelan flat corn pancake cooked on a griddle. Though usually made from *masa harina,* these are made with hominy that has been cooked until soft for a more intense corn flavor. The *arepas* can be formed in advance, covered with wax paper, and cooked the following day. Slathered with maple syrup, they make a great breakfast.

SERVES 4

½   cup dried white or yellow hominy, soaked (see Note)
5   cups water
¼   cup canola oil
1   teaspoon salt
¾   cup *masa harina*
¼   cup thinly sliced scallions

LIKE DRIED BEANS, HOMINY MUST BE SOAKED BEFORE COOKING. PLACE THE HOMINY IN A BOWL AND COVER WITH BOILING WATER. LET IT STAND FOR AT LEAST AN HOUR AND UP TO OVERNIGHT. THEN DRAIN, ADD FRESH WATER TO COVER, AND COOK AS YOU WOULD BEANS. PROCESSING THE HOMINY WHILE IT IS WARM YIELDS THE SMOOTHEST TEXTURE. IF YOU PRECOOK THE HOMINY, YOU CAN WARM IT UP IN THE COOKING LIQUID BEFORE PURÉEING.

• Drain the soaked hominy and place in a medium saucepan. Add the water, cover, and bring to a boil. Reduce the heat and simmer for 1½ to 2 hours, partially covered, until the hominy is soft and has started to open up like popcorn. Make sure the hominy is covered with at least 1 inch of water throughout the cooking time, adding more water if necessary. When the hominy is tender, remove it from the heat and drain, reserving the cooking liquid. Hominy expands a lot in the cooking process—you should have about 1¾ cups of cooked kernels.

• Place the hominy in a food processor fitted with a metal blade and purée, adding the oil, ¾ cup of the cooking liquid, and the salt. Run the processor for a few minutes until the mixture is very smooth and creamy.

• Pour the puréed hominy into a medium bowl. Add the *masa harina* and scallions and mix until you have a nicely pliable dough. Form into 5 equal balls.

• Flatten the balls into patties ½ inch thick and about 3 to 4 inches in diameter. Don't make them too thick or they won't cook through. Smooth the edges with your fingers so that the *arepa* is even all around. You can leave them on a plate, covered, until ready to cook, or wrap well in plastic and refrigerate for up to 48 hours.

• Heat a griddle or cast-iron pan over high heat until hot. Lightly oil the griddle, then turn the heat to medium and add the *arepas.* Cook them on the first side until golden, 5 to 10 minutes, then turn and cook on the other side 5 minutes longer. Keep them warm until ready to serve.

jalapeño "sour cream"

Chile-spiked "cream" adds an exciting spicy pop to the dish. The sum is so much greater than its parts—you have to try it to grasp how delicious it is.

½ pound silken tofu
2 tablespoons fresh lemon juice
3 tablespoons canola oil
2 teaspoons rice vinegar
¾ teaspoon salt
½ jalapeño, stem and seeds removed

• Combine the tofu, lemon juice, oil, vinegar, and salt in a food processor and process until very creamy. Add the jalapeño and process further, until the jalapeño is very finely chopped. Store the "cream" refrigerated for up to 4 days.

☞ THE OILS IN HOT CHILE PEPPERS, ESPECIALLY FRESH ONES, CAN BURN IF YOU TOUCH YOUR FACE OR RUB YOUR EYES AFTER HANDLING THEM. ALTHOUGH IT IS RECOMMENDED TO USE RUBBER GLOVES WHILE HANDLING THEM, I FIND IT EASIER SIMPLY TO MINIMIZE TOUCHING THE PEPPERS. I USE JUST TWO FINGERS OF MY LEFT HAND TO HOLD DOWN THE PEPPER WHILE I HAVE IT, THEN USE A SPOON TO SCRAPE OUT THE SEEDS. DO WASH YOUR HANDS WITH SOAPY WATER WHEN YOU'RE FINISHED.

sautéed sweet potatoes with red onions and balsamic vinegar

It takes patience and some facility with the knife to cut sweet potatoes into uniform ⅛-inch pieces, but it's key to both a beautiful presentation and delicate flavor. Review the information on page 14 for pointers on cutting.

These can be prepared earlier in the day, or the day before serving, and reheated in the oven.

SERVES 4 TO 6

2 tablespoons extra-virgin olive oil
½ cup minced red onion
1 small sweet potato, peeled and cut into ⅛-inch dice (1 cup)
Salt and freshly ground black pepper
A few drops balsamic vinegar

• Heat a skillet over high heat until your hand feels warm when held 3 inches above the surface.

• Add the oil and sauté the onions over high heat for 3 or 4 minutes, until brown. Add the sweet potatoes and cook, stirring constantly, for about 4 minutes, or until the sweet potatoes are cooked through and lightly browned. Remove from the heat and season with salt and pepper and a few drops of balsamic vinegar. Toss gently. Serve immediately or reheat, covered, in the oven.

caramelized brussels sprouts with pecans

Maple syrup and mustard give an autumn standby a burst of sweet and fragrant flavor. Brussels sprouts are really miniature cabbages, and assertive condiments like mustard that go well with cabbage also work with sprouts. In my experience, people who think they don't like Brussels sprouts really love them prepared this way. You can use larger sprouts and cut them in half, or tiny ones and keep them whole. You don't need to wash Brussels sprouts; just peel off the outer leaves and trim the stems, but don't cut too far up the stem or the sprouts will fall apart.

SERVES 4 TO 6

¼   cup pecan halves

¼   pound Brussels sprouts (20 small or 10 large)

2   ounces red or white pearl onions (12 to 16)

½   cup water

¼   cup pure maple syrup

1   teaspoon Dijon mustard

2   tablespoons extra-virgin olive oil
Salt and freshly ground black pepper

MANY PEOPLE CONSIDER PEARL ONIONS TOO "FIDDLY." THEY ARE NOT, IN FACT, THAT TIME-CONSUMING TO PREPARE UNLESS YOU'RE COOKING FOR A HUGE CROWD, AND THEY ARE SO FESTIVE-LOOKING THAT THEY ARE WORTH A BIT OF BOTHER NOW AND AGAIN. SIMPLY CUT OFF THE TIPS AND THE ROOTS AND BLANCH FOR A MINUTE IN BOILING WATER. THE OUTER SKINS PEEL OFF EASILY. LOOK FOR RED PEARL ONIONS, WHICH ARE PARTICULARLY PRETTY IN THIS MIX.

• Preheat the oven to 350° F. Arrange the pecan halves on a baking sheet and toast for 7 minutes, or until lightly golden. Set aside to cool.

• Remove the tough outer leaves of the Brussels sprouts and trim the stems. Cut in half if large. Set aside.

• Bring a small pot of water to a boil. Cut off the tip and root ends of the onions and blanch for 1 minute. Drain the onions and peel off the outer layer of skin from each.

• Whisk together the water, maple syrup, and mustard in a small bowl and set aside.

• Heat a medium skillet until it feels hot when you hold your hand 3 inches away. Add the oil, onions, and sprouts and sauté for a few minutes until the sprouts begin to brown. Add the syrup mixture to the pan, reduce the heat to low, and cover the pan. Cook until the sprouts are tender and the liquid is reduced to a glaze, 10 to 12 minutes. Stir in the pecans. Sprinkle with salt and pepper, and serve hot.

Moussaka

Sautéed Swiss Chard with Olives

SERVES 6

In Greek cuisine, moussaka is a layered eggplant casserole topped with a béchamel sauce. Unfortunately, to those used to the traditional version, vegetarian versions can seem bland. This one is anything but that. Layers of ground seitan, spiced in the traditional Greek way, along with portobello mushrooms, roasted eggplant, and zucchini make this dish rich and flavorful. Mashed potatoes and a soy béchamel with crispy breadcrumbs complete the indulgence. I just add a simple side of lemony Swiss chard with olives for a hearty meal perfect for when the weather starts to turn cold and crisp. You can make the casserole in advance, freeze it, and pull it out for a great luncheon.

cook's notes

- Make the moussaka according to directions. You can assemble the moussaka a day in advance and bake it the next, or freeze it for up to one month.

- Make the Swiss chard right before eating.

- Serve moussaka on a plate next to a mound of Swiss chard. Garnish with a few wedges of lemon and tomato.

moussaka

A deep 7 × 9-inch baking dish works perfectly for this casserole. I like to have the casserole assembled before I make the béchamel, so the sauce can come right off the heat and onto the casserole. Prepare the moussaka in steps: while the eggplant is salting, and then when the vegetables are cooking, you can begin to cook the potatoes and prepare the other ingredients. Skins stay on the potatoes while cooking—to give them a fuller taste—and are peeled off after.

SERVES 6

vegetable layer

1   medium eggplant (1¼ to
    1½ pounds), unpeeled
    Salt
2   small zucchini (about ½ pound)
    Extra-virgin olive oil for brushing
    Freshly ground black pepper
1   teaspoon dried thyme

SALTING LEACHES OUT BITTERNESS FROM MATURE EGGPLANTS AND KEEPS THEM FROM ABSORBING TOO MUCH OIL. (FRESHLY PICKED EGGPLANTS OR SLENDER ASIAN EGGPLANTS DO NOT NEED SALTING.) CUT THE EGGPLANT, PLACE IT ON A BAKING SHEET, SPRINKLE WITH SALT, AND SET IT ASIDE FOR 30 MINUTES. THEN USE A PAPER TOWEL TO BLOT THE JUICES THAT COME TO THE SURFACE.

ALTERNATIVELY, YOU CAN SALT THE EGGPLANT SLICES, PLACE THEM IN A COLANDER OVER A BOWL FOR 30 MINUTES, AND THEN QUICKLY RINSE AND BLOT THEM DRY. WHEN SEASONING THE EGGPLANT, USE A LIGHT TOUCH WITH THE SALT.

seitan layer

2   large portobello mushrooms
½   pound seitan
2   tablespoons extra-virgin olive oil
1   medium onion, finely chopped
     (1 cup)
3   garlic cloves, minced
1½   teaspoons ground cumin
¼   teaspoon ground cinnamon

(continued)

make the vegetable layer:

- Preheat the oven to 375° F. Slice the eggplant into ¼-inch rounds. (If your eggplants are small, cut into slabs lengthwise.) Arrange in one layer on a parchment-covered baking sheet, sprinkle with salt, and leave for 30 minutes to draw out the moisture. Blot dry with a paper towel.

- Cut the zucchini lengthwise into ¼-inch slices. Spread in a single layer on another parchment-covered baking sheet. (You might need to use an extra sheet for some of the eggplant and zucchini slices if your sheets are small.) Brush the eggplant and zucchini with olive oil, salt, and pepper and sprinkle the zucchini with ½ teaspoon of the dried thyme. Turn the vegetable slices and repeat on the other side.

- Bake for 20 minutes, or until the vegetables are softened. The eggplant will brown and shrivel at the edges. Remove from the oven, stack separately on a plate, and set aside.

make the seitan layer:

- Wipe any dirt off the mushrooms with a damp paper towel. Remove the stems. Quarter the mushrooms and place in a food processor fitted with a metal blade. Add the seitan and process until ground, scraping down the sides of the food processor with a spatula once or twice.

- Warm the oil in a medium skillet. Add the onions and cook over medium-low heat for 10 minutes, or until softened.

- Add the ground seitan–mushroom mixture to the skillet, raise the heat to medium, and sauté, stirring occasionally, for about 10 minutes, or until the mushrooms have released their juices and the pan is dry. Add the garlic, cumin, cinnamon, and tomatoes and cook for another 15 minutes or so, breaking up the tomatoes with a wooden spoon, until the mixture has dried out considerably. Add salt to taste and the lemon juice, and stir to combine. Set aside.

8   canned plum tomatoes, drained,
    or 2 large tomatoes, peeled and
    seeded
    Salt
1   teaspoon fresh lemon juice

mashed potato layer

2   pounds russet potatoes
    (3 medium or 5 small)
2   teaspoons salt, plus more to taste
2   tablespoons extra-virgin olive oil
½   cup unflavored soy milk
½   teaspoon fresh lemon juice
    White pepper

breadcrumbs

1   cup fresh breadcrumbs
1   garlic clove, minced
1   teaspoon fresh thyme
2   tablespoons extra-virgin olive oil
    Salt

THE BEST BREADCRUMBS ARE MADE FROM
BREAD (I LIKE TO USE SOURDOUGH) THAT IS A
BIT STALE. UNLESS THE CRUSTS ARE REALLY
HARD, THEY DON'T NEED TO BE CUT AWAY. SIM-
PLY PLACE THE BREAD IN A FOOD PROCESSOR
FITTED WITH A METAL BLADE, AND PROCESS
INTO CRUMBS. IF YOU'RE USING FROZEN BREAD,
TAKE IT OUT OF THE FREEZER AND PLACE IT IN
AN OVEN AT 250° F. FOR A FEW MINUTES JUST
TO WARM IT THROUGH. THEN PROCESS INTO
CRUMBS.

béchamel

1   tablespoon extra-virgin olive oil
4   teaspoons unbleached white flour
¾   cup unflavored soy milk
¼   teaspoon freshly ground nutmeg
    (about 20 swipes across a grater)
    Salt
    Freshly ground black pepper

make the mashed potato layer:

• Place the unpeeled potatoes in a medium pot with the salt and cold water to cover. Bring to a boil and cook for 15 to 30 minutes, depending on the size of the potatoes, until tender.

• Drain the potatoes and reserve the cooking liquid. Using a dish towel to protect your hands, peel the hot potatoes. Return them to the pot and mash them with a masher or a wooden spoon. Add the oil, soy milk, ¼ cup of the reserved cooking liquid, and the lemon juice and continue mashing, adding more cooking liquid if necessary to make the potatoes fluffy. Season to taste with salt and white pepper.

make the breadcrumbs:

• In a small bowl, toss the breadcrumbs with the garlic, thyme, oil, and a pinch of salt. Stir to combine thoroughly. Set aside.

assemble the dish:

• Preheat the oven to 350° F. In a deep 7 × 9-inch baking dish, layer the casserole as follows. Start with a layer of half of the cooked eggplant and top it with half of the seitan–mushroom mixture. Spread half of the mashed potatoes evenly over the mushrooms, then add another layer of eggplant. Arrange all of the zucchini slices over the eggplant, top with the remaining seitan–mushroom mixture, and finally, top with the remaining mashed potatoes. Set aside while you make the béchamel.

make the béchamel:

• Warm the oil in a small saucepan. Add the flour and, stirring constantly, cook over low heat for 6 to 8 minutes, or until the roux darkens slightly. Whisk in the soy milk, nutmeg, salt, and pepper. Continue to stir over low heat for another 2 minutes or so, until the mixture is hot and lightly thickened, but do not let it boil.

• Pour the béchamel evenly over the casserole and sprinkle it with the breadcrumbs. Bake for 30 minutes, until the béchamel is set and the breadcrumbs are golden. Remove from the oven and let the moussaka sit for 5 minutes before cutting into serving portions.

sautéed swiss chard with olives

Mashed garlic, lemon, and olive give assertive chard a tangy bite.

SERVES 6

4   garlic cloves
¾   teaspoon sea salt
3   tablespoons fresh lemon juice
4   tablespoons extra-virgin olive oil
2½ to 3 pounds Swiss chard, either
    red or green (2 bunches)
½   cup chopped olives

UNLIKE REGULAR SWISS CHARD, WHICH HAS
DARK GREEN LEAVES GROWING FROM WHITE
STEMS, RED CHARD HAS RUBY-RED STEMS. THE
RED STEMS AND VEINS GIVE FOOD A ROSY HUE,
WHICH IS LOVELY FOR THE DISH HERE. IT IS BEST
TO CUT THE LEAVES FROM THE STEMS BEFORE
COOKING. THE STEMS ARE DELICIOUS STEAMED
OR BOILED, AND THEY MAKE A VERY NICE ADDI-
TION TO A VEGETABLE STOCK.

• Mash the garlic and salt into a paste. (A mortar and pestle works very well for this, or mash the garlic with the back of a spoon into a small bowl.) Whisk in the lemon juice, and then drizzle and whisk in the oil.

• Use a sharp knife to cut the chard leaves off the stems. Cut the leaves into large bite-size pieces and place in a large bowl of cold water. Swish to loosen any dirt, then lift the chard out of the bowl, leaving the dirt and grit behind. Place the chard in a large pot or skillet and cook in the water cling-ing to the leaves over medium heat for 3 to 4 minutes, or until the chard is wilted and bright green. Stir frequently or toss with tongs to push the uncooked leaves to the bottom of the pot.

• Toss in the garlic mixture and the chopped olives and stir well to combine. Serve immediately.

Amaranth-Studded Cornbread

Cranberry Relish with Apples and Pears

Sweet Dumpling Squash with Chestnut Stuffing and Lima Bean Gravy

Sautéed Haricots Verts with Horseradish

Fennel, Orange, and Pomegranate Salad

SERVES 6 TO 8

Before we appropriated the term for our annual turkey and football orgy, Thanksgiving originally referred to the harvest festivals held by many Native American peoples, a feast rooted in long-standing traditions of reverence for the earth. Many components of the Thanksgiving dinner as we know it today are still characteristic of the Northeast autumn harvest, and the meal that follows offers all the flavors we've come to expect on that beloved holiday—though of course it would be a satisfying choice for any autumn evening.

To many people, the most exciting part of the traditional meal is the stuffing. Baked inside squash instead of turkey and paired with a smooth-as-silk lima bean gravy, the thyme- and sage-flavored cornbread, chestnut, and pecan stuffing is elevated to first-class status. If you're cooking for people with varying eating preferences, you can make the meal and serve it alongside the turkey.

- Make the cornbread a couple of days in advance.

- Make the cranberry relish next, up to three days in advance.

- One day ahead, soak the beans.

- Bake the squash and make the bean gravy. Marinate the fennel, orange, and pomegranate as you bake the squash. Make the stuffing and stuff the cooked squash.

- Make the haricots verts and toss the salad right before serving.

- To serve, ladle some of the gravy onto each plate. Cut the stuffed squash in half horizontally and open like a book. Spoon cranberry sauce before the open book. Put haricots verts to one side. Sprinkle with chopped parsley. Serve the salad on a separate plate.

amaranth–studded cornbread

Tiny amaranth grains give the cornbread flecks of texture. The moist cornbread will keep for days, and makes a very tasty accompaniment to soups and stews. If you are making the cornbread to use in the stuffing, make it at least one day in advance, and leave it uncovered to dry out slightly. Slightly stale cornbread is easier to toast than fresh cornbread.

SERVES 6

¼ cup amaranth
1½ cups yellow cornmeal
1 cup whole-wheat pastry flour
½ cup unbleached white flour
2 teaspoons baking powder
1 teaspoon baking soda
6 tablespoons canola oil, plus oil for oiling the pan
¼ cup pure maple syrup
1 cup original unflavored soy milk
¾ cup apple juice or apple cider
½ teaspoon salt

- Preheat the oven to 350° F. Oil a 9 × 11-inch glass baking dish.

- Place the amaranth in a heavy-bottomed skillet over medium heat. Stirring constantly, toast just until the grains start to pop, 2 to 3 minutes. Immediately transfer to a medium bowl and add the cornmeal, flours, baking powder, and baking soda. Mix well.

- In another bowl, whisk together the oil, syrup, soy milk, apple juice, and salt, until blended and emulsified. (This may also be done in a blender.)

- Pour the wet ingredients into the dry, stirring just until the dry ingredients are completely moistened. Pour the batter into the prepared baking dish and bake on the middle rack of the oven for 35 to 45 minutes, or until the cornbread is firm to the touch and a toothpick or cake tester comes out clean. Let cool before slicing.

cranberry relish
with apples and pears

This relish is on the tart side and is a good contrast to the sweet stuffed squash and the savory lima bean gravy.

1 medium apple, peeled and cut into ½-inch cubes

1 medium pear, peeled and cut into ½-inch cubes

1 12-ounce bag of fresh cranberries
Pinch of salt

½ teaspoon ground cardamom (substitute cinnamon if you prefer)

½ cup fresh orange juice

¼ cup currants

¼ cup pure maple syrup

1 tablespoon grated orange zest

• Combine all the ingredients in a medium saucepan. Cover and bring to a boil over medium heat, then lower the heat and simmer, uncovered, stirring occasionally, for about 20 minutes, or until the mixture thickens and the fruits are quite soft. Let cool to room temperature, then refrigerate until ready to serve.

sweet dumpling squash with chestnut stuffing

Flavorful sweet dumpling squashes make a beautiful container for cornbread stuffing; they look beautiful arranged like an open book on the plate. Sweet dumplings vary in size, so gauge the appetites of your guests as you decide which ones to buy.

You can cook the squashes, make the stuffing, and assemble the dish the night before eating. Just put it in the oven, covered, with a bit of water in the pan. If necessary, you can substitute store-bought cornbread in the stuffing, but either way, let it dry out for a day or two before using.

MAKES 5 TO 6 STUFFED SQUASHES

5   sweet dumpling squashes
1   tablespoon extra-virgin olive oil, plus more for oiling the squashes
½   cup dried chestnuts, soaked in 4 cups water (see Note)
½   cup pecans
4   cups Amaranth-Studded Cornbread (page 102), at least a day old
2   onions, cut into small dice (2 cups)
    Salt
1   tablespoon minced shallot
2   garlic cloves, minced
1   teaspoon dried thyme
2   medium carrots, finely diced (1 cup)
2   celery stalks, finely diced (1 cup)
1½ cups chestnut cooking liquid
1   tablespoon minced fresh sage
1   tablespoon fresh thyme
    Freshly ground black pepper
    Pinch of cayenne pepper
    Chopped fresh flat-leaf parsley for garnish

• Preheat the oven to 350° F.

• Slice off the stems of each squash and scoop out and discard the seeds. Also, if the squash is too round, slice a bit off the bottom so it can stand solidly upright. Lightly oil the flesh of the squashes and place facedown in a baking dish. Add ½ inch of water to the dish and bake until the squashes are tender, 30 to 40 minutes. Set aside.

• While the squashes bake, place the chestnuts with their soaking liquid in a small pot. Cover, bring to a boil over high heat, then lower the heat and simmer, partially covered, for 45 minutes to an hour, or until the chestnuts are soft. Make sure the chestnuts are covered with liquid as they cook, adding more water if necessary. Drain the chestnuts, reserving the cooking liquid. Go through the chestnuts, picking out and discarding any bits of skin. Break the chestnuts into quarters. Set aside.

• Spread the pecans on a baking sheet and toast lightly or until fragrant, 8 to 10 minutes. Remove and chop. Cut the cornbread into 1-inch cubes and spread on a baking sheet. Toast for about 20 minutes, or until the edges are crusty.

• Warm the tablespoon of oil in a medium skillet. Add the onions and salt to taste and sauté over medium-low heat for 5 minutes, or until the onions are translucent. Add the shallots, garlic, dried thyme, carrots, and celery and cook for 8 to 10 minutes, or until the vegetables are softened.

DRIED CHESTNUTS ARE READILY AVAILABLE IN NATURAL FOOD STORES, GOURMET MARKETS, AND BY MAIL ORDER ALL THROUGH AUTUMN AND EARLY WINTER. THEY ARE EASY TO USE AND LEND A DELIGHTFUL SMOKY QUALITY TO THE DISH.

CHESTNUTS SHOULD BE SOAKED LIKE BEANS, EITHER OVERNIGHT OR WITH A QUICK-SOAK METHOD. PLACE CHESTNUTS IN A POT COVERED WITH 5 CUPS WATER. BRING TO A BOIL. TURN OFF THE HEAT, AND LET SIT FOR 1 HOUR. REMOVE ANY BITS OF SKIN THAT ARE FLOATING TO THE TOP.

• Add the toasted cornbread cubes. Slowly add the chestnut cooking liquid, a bit at a time, mixing with the cornbread and vegetables. Scrape up any bits that have stuck to the bottom of the pan. Cook together, stirring constantly, until the liquid is absorbed. When the liquid has mostly evaporated, stir in the chestnuts, pecans, sage, and fresh thyme and remove from the heat. Add 1 teaspoon salt, pepper to taste, and cayenne. Taste and add more salt if necessary. The stuffing should be fairly moist.

• Tightly pack the cooked squashes with the cornbread stuffing, mounding it slightly in each. Place the stuffed squashes in a pan or glass baking dish with a little water. Cover, place in the oven, and heat just until heated through, about 15 minutes.

☞ SWEET DUMPLING SQUASH IS A SWEET, FLAVORFUL, FESTIVE-LOOKING VEGETABLE. CARNIVAL SQUASH, OR ANY TYPE OF SINGLE-SERVING-SIZE SQUASH, WOULD MAKE A SUITABLE SUBSTITUTION. IF THE SQUASH IS TOO LARGE FOR ONE PORTION, YOU COULD CUT IT IN HALF AND STUFF EACH HALF. SQUASH CAN BE STUFFED THE DAY BEFORE BAKING WITHOUT ANY LOSS OF FLAVOR OR MOISTURE.

lima bean gravy

Some people turn their noses up at lima beans; I'm sure they're remembering the mealy, frozen kind. In this savory gravy, the dried limas melt into the creamiest texture and develop a rich, bold flavor.

This sauce can be made on the stovetop, but it is quickest and easiest to make in a pressure cooker. I like to ladle a pool under the squash and pass extra around in a gravy boat.

2 tablespoons extra-virgin olive oil
2 medium onions, cut into small dice (2 cups)
¼ teaspoon hot red pepper flakes
1 tablespoon ground cumin
2 teaspoons ground caraway seeds
1½ cups dried lima beans, soaked and drained
4 cups water
8 garlic cloves, peeled
Bouquet garni of a few sprigs of fresh thyme, rosemary, 1 bay leaf, and 1 teaspoon black peppercorns
1½ teaspoons salt
1 tablespoon fresh lemon juice

• Warm the oil in a pressure cooker or medium saucepan. Sauté the onions over medium-low heat about 10 minutes, or until they are soft and just starting to brown. Add the red pepper flakes, cumin, and caraway seeds, and sauté a few minutes more.

• If you are using the pressure cooker, add the beans, 4 cups of water, garlic, and the bouquet garni. Bring the liquid to a boil, lock the lid into place, and bring it up to high pressure. Lower the heat and cook for 8 minutes. Allow the pressure to release naturally. The beans should be very soft. If they're still too hard, simmer until soft. Add the salt. If you are using the stovetop method, add to your pot 5 cups of water, the garlic, and bouquet garni, cover, and bring the liquid to a boil. Lower the heat and simmer the beans, partially covered, until tender, about 1 to 1¼ hours. Keep an eye on the liquid level and add more if needed to keep the beans from drying out. Stir in the salt.

• Remove the bouquet garni from the pot and purée the beans in a blender. Add water if necessary to achieve a gravy-like consistency. Add the lemon juice and simmer a few minutes to allow the flavors to marry. Taste again and add more salt if necessary.

sautéed haricots verts with horseradish

Haricots verts are the skinniest, tastiest, and most delicate French green beans. They add an elegant look to a holiday plate, but for everyday meals it's fine to use a larger green bean; simply cook them a bit longer in the initial stage. It is all right to blanch beans a couple of hours ahead of time before sautéing, but add the grated horseradish at the very end, as cooking will blunt its pungent flavor.

SERVES 6

Salt
1½ pounds haricots verts or green beans, trimmed and washed
3 garlic cloves, minced
2 tablespoons extra-virgin olive oil
1 teaspoon red wine vinegar
Freshly ground black pepper
1 tablespoon freshly grated horseradish (or prepared horseradish)

CUT THE HARD STEM ENDS OFF THE BEANS TO TRIM THEM. THE TAPERED TIPS USUALLY DO NOT NEED TRIMMING.

• Bring a large saucepan of lightly salted water to a boil. Add the beans and blanch for 3 to 5 minutes, or until they are cooked but still crisp. Drain and refresh with cold water. Drain again.

• In a medium skillet or sauté pan, heat the garlic and oil together until the garlic barely begins to color, about 3 minutes. Add the beans and toss to coat. Cook for about 4 minutes over medium-low heat until heated through, stirring constantly to prevent the garlic from sticking and burning. Add the vinegar, salt, and pepper, then turn off the heat and toss in the grated horseradish. Serve immediately.

fennel, orange, and pomegranate salad

In autumn, I make this salad as frequently as I can. I love how the tart, sweet, and licorice flavors of pomegranate, orange, and fennel play off one another. The vivid colors enliven any meal, especially those with earth-tone colors.

Slice the fennel as thin as possible for the best results. A plastic mandoline works well for this job.

SERVES 6

6   tablespoons fresh orange juice
2   tablespoons balsamic vinegar
¼   cup extra-virgin olive oil
     Salt and freshly ground black pepper
½   medium fennel bulb, cored and very thinly sliced (see drawing on page 147)
¼   cup pomegranate seeds
2   navel oranges cut into segments
2   bunches of watercress, well washed and tough stems removed

• Make the dressing by whisking together the orange juice, vinegar, and oil. Add a pinch of salt and a sprinkle of black pepper.

• Combine the fennel, pomegranate seeds, and orange sections in a bowl. Pour half of the dressing over them and marinate at room temperature for 30 minutes. Drain, reserving the marinated fennel, orange, and pomegranate separately. Stir the strained dressing back into the rest of the dressing.

• When ready to serve, toss the watercress with the dressing. Arrange the fennel, orange, and pomegranate on top of individual portions of the watercress.

Mushroom Filo Triangles with Delicata-Porcini Sauce

Frisée Salad with Lemon-Miso Dressing

Sautéed Broccoli with Roasted Peppers

SERVES 4 OR 5

Here's a treat for mushroom lovers: crisp pastry packets filled with savory mushrooms and paired with an earthy porcini-accented sauce. It just about screams fall. Easy to make, the filo triangles taste as impressive as they look. They are accompanied by a lemony frisée salad and sautéed broccoli with roasted red peppers. When all the elements are combined, this makes for a lively, balanced, and colorful meal.

cook's notes

- Defrost the filo. Press the tofu.
- Put the squash in to roast. Meanwhile, soak the porcini mushrooms and roast the peppers for the broccoli.
- Finish the sauce.
- Make the filling, fold the triangles, and put them in to bake.
- Make the dressing for the frisée salad while the triangles bake.
- Sauté the broccoli right before serving.
- To serve, pool the sauce at one side of each plate, and place a filo triangle in the middle of the sauce. Sprinkle with chopped hazelnuts. Arrange a mound of salad and broccoli on either side.

mushroom filo triangles
with delicata-porcini sauce

This is a good dish to prepare for people who think they don't like tofu; they'll devour it without guessing what's in the filling. The triangles freeze well without losing their flavor or texture—just put them on a baking sheet in the freezer for a couple of hours until frozen. Then stack and wrap well, separating the layers of triangles with plastic wrap. When you're ready to serve, just spread them out on a baking sheet and bake, adding about 5 minutes to the cooking time.

These also make great appetizers. Simply make them half the size by using one sheet of filo and folding it twice.

SERVES 6

½ pound firm tofu, pressed for at least 30 minutes (see page 76)

1 pound fresh spinach

1 large portobello mushroom (½ pound)

2 teaspoons umeboshi paste

2 teaspoons light miso

1½ teaspoons fresh lemon juice

1½ teaspoons balsamic vinegar

2 tablespoons mirin or dry sherry

3 tablespoons extra-virgin olive oil, plus more for brushing the filo

2 onions, finely chopped (2 cups)

1 tablespoon chopped fresh sage

4 garlic cloves, minced

½ teaspoon salt
Freshly ground black pepper

¾ pound filo dough (if frozen, defrost)

½ cup breadcrumbs (optional)
Delicata-Porcini Sauce (recipe follows)

½ cup toasted hazelnuts, chopped (see page 112)

• In a small bowl, mash the tofu with a fork or crumble it by hand into small pieces, with no large lumps.

• Cut the stems off the spinach and discard. Wash the spinach thoroughly, using several changes of water, and put it in a large pot with just the water clinging to the leaves. Cook over medium heat, stirring frequently or tossing with tongs to push the uncooked leaves to the bottom of the pot. When it is wilted, remove it from the pot, cool slightly, and squeeze out any excess liquid. Chop fine. You should have about 2 cups of chopped greens. Set aside.

• Wipe the portobello mushroom with a damp paper towel to remove dirt and discard the stem. Cut the mushroom into large chunks. Place in a food processor fitted with a metal blade, and whir until the mushroom is ground into small pieces.

• In a small bowl, combine the umeboshi paste and the miso with a small rubber spatula. Add the lemon juice, vinegar, and mirin and mix well.

• Warm 1 tablespoon of the oil in a large skillet. Sauté the onions over medium heat until softened, about 7 minutes. Add the ground mushrooms and chopped sage and cook

(continued on page 112)

Adding fried garlic at the end lends a garlicky lift to food that is very different from the flavor you get by adding the garlic early and slow-cooking it. This is a great technique for adding pizzazz to a soup or sauce.

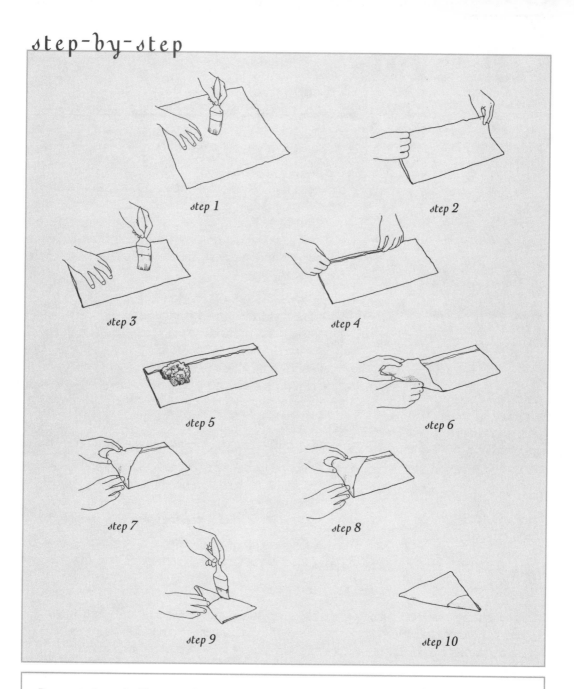

step 1

step 2

step 3

step 4

step 5

step 6

step 7

step 8

step 9

step 10

Be sure to keep the filo covered at all times as you work with it. Spread out a layer of plastic wrap, butcher paper, or a dish towel. Unroll the filo and spread it out. Lay a damp dish towel or several paper towels on top. Peel off the piece you are using and cover the remaining stack as you work with that piece. Filo can be refrozen if it hasn't been exposed to air. It can be refrigerated for a week or so and frozen for a couple of months. If you can get bakery-made filo, please do! It's so much better and easier to use than commercial brands.

until the mixture is almost dry, about 5 minutes. Add the tofu and spinach to the pan and stir. Add the umeboshi mixture to the pan. Stir well and cook for about 5 minutes longer, or until the filling is almost dry. Turn off the heat.

- In a small pan, heat the remaining 2 tablespoons of oil with the minced garlic. Cook over medium heat just until the garlic starts to turn golden, about 3 minutes. Remove from the heat and immediately pour the garlic into the filling mixture. Season with the salt and a generous sprinkle of freshly ground black pepper and mix well. Set the mixture aside to cool to room temperature.

- Preheat the oven to 375° F. Arrange 1 sheet of filo on a work surface, keeping the remainder covered with a damp kitchen towel as you work. Dip a pastry brush in the oil and lightly brush the entire surface. Lightly sprinkle the surface with breadcrumbs, if using. Lay another sheet of filo on top of the first one and brush it with oil. Fold in half lengthwise. Turn the edges in 1 inch. Oil the top.

- Place ½ cup of filling at one end of the strip. Fold up from the corner into a triangle, then continue folding as illustrated.

- Fold down the last edge and brush the entire triangle with oil. Transfer the triangle to a parchment-covered baking sheet. Repeat with the remaining filo and filling. Bake for 15 to 20 minutes, or until the triangles are golden brown.

- To serve, spoon some of the Delicata-Porcini Sauce onto each plate, top with a triangle, and sprinkle with hazelnuts.

To toast hazelnuts, spread out on a cookie sheet and bake in a preheated 350° oven for 6 to 12 minutes (fresher nuts will toast quicker), until skins begin to blister and crack. Remove from oven. Lay a dish towel on your counter, and pour the nuts onto the towel. Fold up the towel around the nuts and rub, removing the skins.

The breadcrumbs (you can use dry or fresh) are optional, but I like to use them to separate the pastry leaves so that the filo stays especially crispy when it bakes. You can also sprinkle finely chopped nuts between the layers for a similar result.

delicata-porcini sauce

A quick porcini stock orchestrates this sweet squash sauce with bold bass notes of mushroom.

2 pounds delicata squash
3 tablespoons extra-virgin olive oil
2 tablespoons pure maple syrup
Salt
½ cup dried porcini mushrooms
5 cups water
2 onions, finely diced (2 cups)
1 teaspoon fresh lemon juice
1 tablespoon chopped fresh sage
Pinch of cayenne pepper

DELICATA SQUASH IS MY FAVORITE FOR THIS
RECIPE, BUT IT IS AVAILABLE FEWER MONTHS
THAN SOME OF THE OTHER WINTER SQUASHES.
MY SECOND CHOICE IS KABOCHA, WHICH IS
AVAILABLE MUCH LONGER AND ALSO WORKS
WELL. IN A PINCH YOU COULD SUBSTITUTE THE
READILY AVAILABLE OLD STANDBY—BUTTERNUT
SQUASH.

- Preheat the oven to 400° F. Peel the delicata squash and cut in 2-inch chunks. Toss with 2 tablespoons of the oil, the maple syrup, and salt. Place the squash pieces on parchment-covered baking sheets and roast them for about 20 minutes, or until tender.

- Place the porcinis in a small saucepan with the water and simmer, partially covered, for 20 minutes. Line a strainer with paper towels or cheesecloth and strain the mushrooms, reserving the stock.

- Heat the remaining 1 tablespoon of oil in a medium saucepan. Add the onions and sauté over medium-low heat for 10 minutes, or until the onions are softened. Add the roasted squash pieces and 4 cups of the porcini stock and simmer together gently, uncovered, for 10 minutes. Transfer to a blender and purée. (This is a perfect instance in which to use an immersion blender.)

- Add the lemon juice, sage, cayenne, and salt to taste. Keep the sauce warm until ready to serve.

frisée salad with lemon-miso dressing

Frisée is a delicate, raggedy-edged green in the chicory family, which includes endive, escarole, dandelion, and radicchio. All of these greens have a degree of bitterness ranging from slight to pronounced, frisée weighing in at the milder end of the scale.

This bright, pungent dressing stands up well to the assertive frisée, as well as to endive and radicchio.

SERVES 4 OR 5

¾ pound frisée (1 large head)
4   red radishes, thinly sliced
1   teaspoon light miso
½ teaspoon Dijon mustard
1   tablespoon fresh lemon juice
1   tablespoon balsamic vinegar
¼ cup extra-virgin olive oil
    Salt

LIGHT MISO, SOMETIMES CALLED CHICKPEA MISO, IS THE MOST DELICATE-TASTING OF ALL THE MISOS, AND IT WORKS WELL IN SALAD DRESSINGS.

• Gently tear the frisée into bite-size pieces. Wash the greens by gently swishing them around in a bowl of cold water. Lift the greens out, leaving the dirt behind. (Frisée and other chicories can be gritty at the base, so make sure the leaves are really clean.) Dry well, then place the greens in a bowl and toss with the radishes.

• In a small bowl, combine the miso and mustard. Work in the lemon juice with a small rubber spatula until the miso and mustard are completely dissolved. Whisk in the balsamic vinegar. Slowly add the oil in a steady stream, whisking constantly until well combined. Add salt to taste.

• Pour the dressing over the salad and serve.

sautéed broccoli with roasted peppers

With preroasted peppers, this colorful side dish is ready in minutes. It's a perfect weeknight preparation for a familiar standby.

SERVES 4 OR 5

1 small bunch of broccoli or ½ large (¾ pound)
Salt
2 tablespoons extra-virgin olive oil
½ roasted red bell pepper, cut into thin strips (see page 188)
½ teaspoon dried oregano
1 garlic clove, minced
Freshly ground black pepper
Juice of ½ lemon
1 tablespoon finely chopped fresh flat-leaf parsley

• Cut the broccoli into medium florets. (Reserve the stems for another use.) Bring a pot of salted water to a boil, add the broccoli, and blanch for 3 minutes, or until cooked to your liking. (You can also steam the broccoli if you prefer.)

• Warm the olive oil in a medium skillet. Add the broccoli, peppers, oregano, and garlic and sauté over medium heat until heated through, 2 to 3 minutes. Sprinkle with salt and pepper. Stir in the lemon juice and parsley, and serve hot.

Curried Chickpea Tart with Fennel-Cauliflower Sauce

Herbed Coconut Chutney

Wilted Spinach

Cucumber Raita

Roasted Chickpea Nuts

Cardamom-Spiced Basmati

SERVES 6

Chickpeas in various forms—roasted and ground to a flour—star in this menu, which I think of as Indian fusion food. The curried tart, made from chickpea flour, is akin to the Provençal *panisse*, a thick creamy chickpea crepe baked in a large black steel pan. The tart's subtle flavor and smooth texture blend nicely with a creamy cauliflower and fennel sauce and are brightened by a spicy mint-cilantro-coconut chutney. I like to serve it over fluffy cardamom-spiced basmati rice and wilted spinach and sprinkle some roasted chickpea "nuts" on top.

While the whole menu is a veritable feast, when I'm pressed for time I make only the tart with the rice, chutney, and spinach. Every dish on this menu can stand either on its own or as an accompaniment to other meals, and every dish but the spinach makes a delicious leftover.

cook's notes

Everything can be made ahead and reheated, except the rice and spinach.

- Make the chickpea tart first. While it sets in the refrigerator, make the sauce.

- Put the coconut in the oven to crack and the chickpeas to roast.

- Make the chutney and finish the sauce.

- Make the raita. This can be made up to two days in advance.

- Twenty minutes before serving, oil the tart and put it in the oven to bake.

- Make the rice. Wilt the spinach right before serving.

- To serve, place a mound of basmati rice on the plate. Top with a wedge of tart. Pour sauce so that it drapes over the tart. Place a dollop of chutney on top, and sprinkle with chickpeas. Serve the wilted spinach surrounding the dish. Sprinkle with cilantro. Serve the raita off to one side.

curried chickpea tart

The texture of this tart is so luscious your guests may not guess what it's made of; it has a custardy, quiche-like consistency. The basis is a polenta-like porridge of chickpea flour and water that cooks slowly; once the "polenta" reaches a boil, it starts to thicken fast, so be sure to stir frequently with a wooden spoon. The mix is ready when it pulls away from the side of the pot as you draw your spoon through it. Be sure to cut the tart into serving-size portions, and brush it with oil before placing it in the oven.

SERVES 6

4   tablespoons canola oil, plus more for oiling the pan and brushing the tart
1   onion, finely chopped (1 cup)
1   tablespoon curry powder
4¾ cups cold water
1½ cups chickpea flour
2   teaspoons sea salt

CHICKPEA FLOUR IS AVAILABLE IN INDIAN STORES, GOURMET MARKETS, AND MANY NATURAL FOOD STORES. ALWAYS ADD COLD LIQUIDS TO POLENTA, NEVER HOT, AND BEAT THOROUGHLY BEFORE HEATING TO AVOID LUMPS.

- Oil a 9-inch tart pan and set aside.

- Warm 1 tablespoon of the oil in a medium skillet. Add the onions and sauté over medium heat until the onions start to brown, about 7 minutes. Add the curry powder and ¼ cup of the water and cook for a few minutes, stirring occasionally, until the water has evaporated. Set aside.

- Place the chickpea flour, the remaining 4½ cups of water, and the remaining 3 tablespoons of oil in a blender and blend until smooth. Pour into a medium pot or saucepan and cook over medium heat, stirring occasionally, until the mixture reaches a boil; do not cover.

- Add the salt. Continue to cook, stirring constantly. When the mixture begins to thicken, turn the heat down to medium-low. The heat should be just high enough that the "polenta" bubbles like molten lava. Continue cooking for 20 to 30 minutes, uncovered, stirring to prevent sticking, until the mixture loses its raw taste.

- When the polenta is ready, turn off the heat and stir in the curried onions. Pour into the oiled tart pan and spread evenly with a metal spatula. Let sit for an hour or so in the refrigerator to firm. (At this point, you could refrigerate the tart for up to 2 days.)

- Preheat the oven to 350° F. Cut the tart into serving portions and brush each with oil. Bake for 20 minutes, or until the tart is heated through and the top has formed a crust.

fennel-cauliflower sauce

A chickpea roux makes this flavorful sauce super creamy. This recipe makes enough sauce to assure a generous amount for each serving.

4 teaspoons plus 1 tablespoon canola oil
2 tablespoons chickpea flour
2 teaspoons fennel seeds
½ large fennel bulb, or 1 small bulb
1 onion, finely chopped (1 cup)
½ small head of cauliflower, cut into florets (2 cups)
4 cups water
Salt
1 tablespoon fresh lemon juice
1 tablespoon ginger juice (see page 197)
Pinch of cayenne pepper

• Warm 4 teaspoons of the oil in a small saucepan. Add the chickpea flour and cook over low heat, stirring constantly, for about 5 minutes, or until the roux darkens slightly, turning a nutty golden color. Transfer to a small bowl to cool.

• Toast the fennel seeds in a dry medium skillet until fragrant. Immediately transfer them to a mortal and pestle or a spice grinder and grind to a powder.

• Trim off the stalks and any discolored parts of the fennel bulb. Cut it in half and cut out the hard core. Slice it thin lengthwise; you should have about 2 cups.

• Warm the remaining tablespoon of oil in a large saucepan or pot. Add the onions and sliced fennel and sauté over medium heat for 7 minutes, or until the onions start to brown. Add the ground fennel seeds and sauté for a couple of minutes more. Add the cauliflower and the water. Cover and bring to a boil, then lower the heat to a simmer. Remove ½ cup or so of the hot liquid and pour it into the bowl with the reserved roux. Whisk vigorously to dissolve the roux in the hot water, then pour the dissolved roux back into the pot. Simmer, partially covered, stirring from time to time to prevent sticking, for about 20 minutes, or until the cauliflower is soft.

• Purée the mixture, using an immersion blender, or purée in small batches in a regular blender. (Hold a towel over the top and do not fill the blender more than half full if you are puréeing while the liquid is hot.)

• Return the sauce to the pot and add salt to taste. Let the sauce sit for a couple of minutes to absorb the salt, then add the lemon juice, ginger juice, and cayenne. Adjust salt if necessary.

herbed coconut chutney

The fresh tastes of coconut, mint, and cilantro sparkle in every bite of this vibrant chutney. You could use unsweetened dried coconut (look for "desiccated" on the label) if you can't find fresh, but the fresh is much better. Coconut freezes well; if you go to the trouble of cracking one, you'll have about 3 cups of grated coconut meat.

Chutney keeps well refrigerated for several days.

Juice of 1 lemon
2 tablespoons water
½ cup fresh grated coconut (see page 125)
½ cup packed fresh cilantro leaves
½ cup packed fresh mint leaves
1 garlic clove, peeled
1 1-inch piece of peeled ginger, roughly chopped
1 jalapeño, stem and seeds removed
½ teaspoon salt

• Place all ingredients in a blender in the order listed and blend until smooth. Be patient; allow the ingredients a few minutes to descend into the blender while blending. Taste and adjust salt if necessary.

wilted spinach

This is the simplest dish, but it rounds out the meal perfectly, and the bright green leaves are pretty surrounding the plate. Don't be daunted by the quantity of spinach, as it reduces significantly when wilted.

SERVES 6

1½ pounds spinach, tough stems removed
Salt

• Wash the spinach thoroughly in several changes of cold water.

• Transfer the spinach to a large pot and cook over medium heat in just the water clinging to the leaves, stirring frequently or tossing with tongs to push the uncooked leaves to the bottom of the pot. Cook until the leaves have wilted and shrunk and are bright green. Sprinkle with salt and serve immediately.

cucumber raita

Although raita traditionally is made with a yogurt base, this recipe here is so full-flavored you won't miss the dairy. It serves as a cooling dish for the more assertive flavors in the meal and tastes great with just about any Indian food.

1   medium cucumber
½   teaspoon whole cumin seeds
1   pound silken tofu
⅓   cup canola oil
¼   cup fresh lemon juice
1   tablespoon plus 1 teaspoon brown rice vinegar
1½ teaspoons sea salt
¼   teaspoon white pepper
    Pinch of cayenne pepper
3   tablespoons chopped fresh mint leaves

• Peel and cut the cucumber lengthwise down the center and scoop out the seeds. Slice into ¼-inch half moons and place in a medium bowl.

• Toast the cumin seeds in a small skillet for a couple of minutes over medium heat, until fragrant, stirring constantly. Grind to a powder in a mortar and pestle or spice grinder.

• In a food processor, combine the tofu, oil, lemon juice, vinegar, salt, pepper, cayenne, and cumin and process until smooth.

• Stir the mixture into the cucumbers along with the chopped mint. Cover and refrigerate until cool.

roasted chickpea nuts

Roasted chickpea "nuts" have a sneaky way of disappearing off the baking tray, so you may want to make some extra of this delightful snack to keep on hand. The chickpeas become crisp and nutty in the oven, shrinking almost to their precooked size. This is one instance where I like to use canned chickpeas for a shortcut. Make sure to roast them for 45 minutes, so they develop the desired flavor.

1½ cups cooked chickpeas, or 1 15-ounce can, drained and rinsed
2   tablespoon canola or coconut oil
    Salt
1   tablespoon fresh lemon juice
1   tablespoon minced peeled ginger
    Generous sprinkle of cayenne pepper

• Preheat the oven to 375° F. In a medium bowl, toss the chickpeas with the oil, a sprinkle of salt, and the lemon juice, ginger, and cayenne. Spread on a parchment-covered baking sheet and roast for about 45 minutes, stirring 2 or 3 times, until the chickpeas are shrunken and browned. They can be eaten hot, warm, or at room temperature. If you make them in advance, put them in a baking dish and reheat before serving.

cardamom-spiced basmati

Fragrant and delicate, white basmati rice is considered by Indians to be the finest rice in the world—possibly the only rice worth eating. I asked a proprietor of an Indian grocery what he thought of the other long-grain white rice he was selling, and he had one word on the subject: a vehement "Garbage!"

You definitely need to wash basmati before cooking it. Washing removes the starch that makes the rice gummy. There are those who say you have to soak basmati for at least 30 minutes and wash it five or six times, and those who say washing it once is good enough and that no soaking is necessary. I don't generally soak basmati, but I do wash the rice and sauté it in a little oil to dry out and coat the grains. This produces a long, fluffy, pilaf-like rice, perfect every time.

SERVES 4

1¼ cups white basmati rice
1   tablespoon canola or coconut oil
2½ cups water
     Salt
1   cinnamon stick
1   teaspoon cardamom pods
1   bay leaf

• Wash the rice well in a bowl with cold water. Swish the rice around in the water with your fingers, then let the rice settle to the bottom. Any particles or husks will rise to the surface. Tilt the bowl and drain off the water. Repeat once or twice until the water is clear.

• Warm the oil in a medium saucepan. Add the rice and sauté over low heat, stirring constantly, until the grains are dry.

• Add the water and stir once to dislodge any rice that might have stuck to the bottom. Add a pinch of salt and the cinnamon stick, cardamom pods, and bay leaf. Cover the pot. Bring to a boil, then lower the heat to a simmer and cook for 15 minutes. Turn off the heat and let sit for 5 minutes. Fluff the rice with a fork. Discard the bay leaf, cinnamon stick, and cardamom pods.

Thai Vegetable Stew with Baked Tofu Triangles

Jasmine Rice with Coconut

Mint, Orange, and Red Onion Salad

SERVES 4

Thai cooking is one of the most distinctive Southeast Asian cuisines, perhaps because, unlike neighboring countries, Thailand was never colonized. Thai cuisine is characterized by certain predominant flavors: coconut, garlic, chiles, fish sauce, and citrus from lemongrass and kaffir lime leaves. Also significant are ginger and its cousin galangal. Mint, basil, and cilantro add important green accents. Coconut milk offsets the pungent quality of other strong and spicy ingredients.

This savory and fiery stew hits most of the requisite Thai flavors, and is paired with coconut Jasmine rice and baked tofu triangles. A refreshing salad of mint, orange, and red onion fills out the meal.

cook's notes

Up to one day in advance:

- Press the tofu. Prepare the marinade. Preheat the oven to 375° F. and place the coconut in the oven to "crack" (see page 125). Marinate the tofu.

- Make the orange and red onion salad. Hammer open the coconut and grate the coconut meat.

- Prep the vegetables for the stew. Put the tofu in to bake. Make the stew and put up the rice.

- To serve, ladle the stew into a wide soup plate or bowl. Place a scoop of rice on one end and lean a couple of tofu triangles against the rice. Sprinkle chopped peanuts over the whole bowl. Serve the salad on the side.

thai vegetable stew

Impress your guests with this authentic-tasting Thai stew. It is worth the effort to seek out an Asian grocery store, but you can substitute for the exotic ingredients and still come out with a good dish. Don't be put off by the long list of ingredients; this recipe goes together easily.

The sugar snap peas are brightest if cooked only for a minute or two, so add those at the end. If you are making the stew in advance, add the sugar snaps when you reheat it.

SERVES 4

2 tablespoons canola oil
2 scallions, cut into 1-inch pieces
1 medium red bell pepper, cut into 1-inch squares
1 small eggplant or Japanese eggplant, peeled and cut into 1½-inch cubes (1½ cups)
8 tiny Thai chiles, stems removed, or 2 serranos
3 medium garlic cloves, peeled
1 3-inch piece of fresh galangal, or peeled fresh ginger
2 lemongrass stalks
1 14-ounce can coconut milk
¼ cup shoyu
2 cups water
1 small head of cauliflower or ½ medium head, broken into florets (2 cups)
1 medium zucchini, or 2 slender zucchinis, cut into large roll chunks (see page 15)
1 tablespoon minced kaffir lime leaves (8 leaves), or 1 tablespoon lime zest and the juice of 1 lime
2 medium carrots, peeled and cut into thin matchsticks
¼ pound sugar snap peas
Salt
¼ cup roughly chopped fresh cilantro
¼ cup basil chiffonade
¼ cup dry-roasted chopped peanuts

• Warm the oil in a medium-large pot, Dutch oven, or saucepan. Add the scallions, red pepper, and eggplant, and sauté over medium heat for 7 minutes, or until the pepper is softened.

• Meanwhile, place the chiles and garlic in a food processor fitted with a metal blade. Cut the galangal into small chunks and add. Cut off the lemongrass stalks just above the fat part of the bulbs and discard. Slit the bulbs and remove the hard outer layer, then cut the bulbs into 3 or 4 pieces. Add to the food processor. Process until the mixture is finely chopped. (You can also mince everything together by hand or pound it together in a mortar and pestle.) Add the chile mixture to the pot and cook for a few minutes with the pepper and eggplant.

• Add the coconut milk, shoyu, and water to the pot, and cover. When the liquid reaches a boil, reduce the heat to a simmer and add the cauliflower. Partially cover and cook for 7 minutes, or until the cauliflower is almost tender. Add the zucchini and cook for about 5 minutes more.

• Remove the lid, add the lime leaves, carrots, and snap peas, and cook for just a minute. Season with salt to taste, then stir in the cilantro and basil. Sprinkle with the peanuts just before serving.

☞ KAFFIR LIME LEAVES HAVE A HARD CENTER SPINE THAT SHOULD BE REMOVED. IT'S EASIEST TO FOLD THE LEAF IN HALF BEFORE CUTTING AWAY THE SPINE.

Galangal looks a lot like a thin-skinned ginger, but has a distinctive flavor. Widely used in Thailand and Malaysia, it is found in Asian grocery stores, often frozen, and is sometimes sold under the name of Khan or Lengkuas. Its delicate floral bouquet resembles a mix of ginger, pepper, and sour lemon. It can be chopped or puréed unpeeled because its skin is so thin. In a pinch, substitute ginger—but be sure to peel the ginger first.

If you have dried galangal, still include the ginger. Add minced ginger and 5 or 6 galangal chips to the cooking liquid. Wrap them in cheesecloth first to make it easy to remove them at the end of cooking.

Lemongrass can be frozen or bought waterpacked, but never substitute with dried.

baked tofu triangles

Thai chiles and lemongrass lift these golden triangles out of the ordinary into the unexpected.

SERVES 4

1 pound firm tofu
3 garlic cloves, peeled
1 1-inch piece of fresh galangal (or peeled fresh ginger)
1 lemongrass stalk (page 31)
¼ cup apple juice or apple cider
2 tablespoons pure maple syrup
¼ cup shoyu
2 tablespoons fresh lemon juice
¼ cup canola oil
4 Thai chiles, stems removed and cut in half lengthwise, or 2 serrano chiles
½ cup roughly chopped fresh cilantro

• Place the tofu on a pie plate and top with a second plate. Weight the plate with a heavy can or two and press for at least 30 minutes. By hand, or in a food processor, finely chop the garlic, galangal, and lemongrass. Set aside.

• To make the marinade, in a medium bowl whisk together the apple juice, maple syrup, shoyu, lemon juice, and oil until thoroughly blended. Add the chopped lemongrass mixture.

• Place the tofu cake on its side and cut into 3 thin slabs. Cut the slabs diagonally into triangles, the triangles in half to make smaller triangles. Place the tofu pieces in an 8 × 8-inch baking dish in a single layer, fitting the pieces together like a mosaic. Pour the marinade over the tofu, add the chiles, and sprinkle with the cilantro. Marinate for at least 30 minutes, turning once.

• Preheat the oven to 350° F.

• Pour off about ½ cup of the marinade; it should reach about halfway up the sides of the tofu. Bake the tofu for 40 to 45 minutes, or until the tofu is golden brown and most of the marinade has been absorbed.

jasmine rice with coconut

Jasmine rice, available at natural food markets and specialty stores, is a long-grain white rice not unlike basmati, but with a more floral essence and a smooth, silky texture. Fresh coconut gives a lovely light coconut flavor, and the citrus leaves lend a delicate citrus note. In a pinch you could substitute lime zest for the lime leaves and desiccated coconut for the fresh.

SERVES 4

1 cup jasmine rice
2 cups water
½ teaspoon salt
⅓ cup fresh grated coconut (see Note)
8 kaffir lime leaves

• Place the rice in a medium bowl and cover with cold water. Swish the rice until the water runs clear. Drain.

• In a small saucepan or pot, bring the water to a boil. Add the rice, salt, coconut, and lime leaves. Reduce the heat to a simmer and cover. Cook for 20 minutes, or until all the liquid is absorbed.

troubleshooting rice

If all the water is absorbed but your rice is not tender, add a bit more water to the pot and continue cooking. If you have a lot of excess water, drain your rice. If there is just a little water, don't worry; it will absorb into the rice as it sits.

cracking a coconut

When choosing a coconut, shake it to listen for the sound of the liquid sloshing inside it. The freshest ones are the heaviest because they contain the most liquid. You can open a coconut by banging it against concrete or whacking it with a hammer until it cracks but cookbook author Julie Sahni recommends a safer and easier way:

"Preheat an oven to 375° F. Pierce the 'eyes' of the coconut (the 3 indented marks at one end of the coconut) with a sharp object such as a screwdriver and drain the liquid. Place the coconut in the oven for 25 minutes or until the shell cracks. Remove the coconut from the oven and tap it all around with a hammer to release the meat from the shell, then whack it hard to crack the shell." Peel the brown skin off the coconut meat with a knife and cut the meat into pieces. Grate the coconut by hand or in a food processor or blender. One coconut yields about 3 cups of meat. Since coconut can go rancid quickly once opened, store it for up to 3 days in the refrigerator or freeze it.

mint, orange, and red onion salad

The salad has a refreshing citrus lift, and is an excellent partner for any spicy entrées, especially Mexican or Moroccan meals.

SERVES 4

2 navel oranges
⅓ cup minced red onion
2 tablespoons finely chopped fresh mint leaves
1 tablespoon brown rice vinegar
 Salt

• Cut a disk off the top and bottom of each orange, slicing through the colored peel and white pith to expose the flesh. Set each orange on one cut end and cut downward, following the contours of the fruit, to remove all the skin and the pith, exposing the orange flesh. Cut the orange crosswise into ½-inch-thick rings. (A serrated knife does this easily.) Cut into quarters by cutting between sections. Place in a medium bowl.

• Add the minced onion and the mint and mix gently. Toss with the vinegar and sprinkle with salt to taste.

Spaghetti Squash with Sofrito

Chili and Corn-Biscuit Casserole

Guacasalsa

Garlic-Braised Broccoli

SERVES 6

This variation on a classic Texas chili is tucked into a double-corn biscuit crust. It makes timeless Super Bowl party fare, and it's a good spicy mouthful for those who are "wild at heart." Baked in a casserole, it makes a perfect dish to bring to a potluck. It's also a lot of fun to eat in individual ramekins. Moreover, you can make the chili on its own and bake the biscuit alongside of it, or bake some Amaranth-Studded Cornbread (page 102) instead. Whichever way you like it, be sure to make plenty of guacasalsa to pass around.

cook's notes

- Soak the beans for the chili.
- Up to a day in advance: Cook the beans and make the chili. Bake the spaghetti squash and scoop out the flesh.
- Mix together the biscuit, layer the casserole, and place in the oven to bake.
- Make the guacasalsa.
- Sauté the spaghetti squash.
- Cook the broccoli right before serving.
- To serve, place a portion of chili casserole in the middle of the plate. Or place an individual ramekin in the middle of each plate. Top with a dollop of the guacasalsa. Serve on either side a little mound of spaghetti squash and a stalk of broccoli.

spaghetti squash with sofrito

The delicate strands of this mild squash marry joyfully with a combination of sautéed tomatoes, bell peppers, garlic, and scallions, a combination known in Latin America as "sofrito." Achiote, or annatto, seeds infuse the oil with their color, giving the dish its beautiful red-orange glow.

SERVES 6

1½ pounds spaghetti squash (½ large or 1 small)

½ large red bell pepper, stem, seeds, and membrane removed

2 tablespoons extra-virgin olive oil

1 tablespoon achiote seeds (optional)

½ pound plum tomatoes (3 to 4), peeled and seeded, or 4 canned plum tomatoes, roughly chopped

1 garlic clove, minced
Salt and freshly ground black pepper

2 scallions, thinly sliced on the diagonal

• Preheat the oven to 375°F.

• Place the whole squash on a parchment-covered baking sheet and bake for 50 minutes to 1 hour, or until the squash is tender when pricked with a fork. Remove the squash from the oven, halve it lengthwise, and discard the seeds. (If using only half, rub the flesh with oil and place facedown on a parchment-covered baking sheet. Bake for 50 minutes to 1 hour or until the squash is tender.) Use a fork to scrape the flesh from the squash (it comes out in strands). Put it in a bowl and set aside.

• Slice the red pepper into thin lengthwise strips and then cut the strips into 1-inch pieces.

• Combine the oil and achiote seeds in a small skillet and heat gently over low heat. As soon as the oil is warm and infused with orange color, pour it through a strainer. Discard the seeds. Return the oil to the skillet, add the tomatoes, peppers, and garlic, and sauté over medium heat for 5 to 7 minutes, or until the tomatoes are broken up and the peppers are softened. Add the spaghetti squash and cook for another 5 minutes, stirring occasionally, until warmed through and stewed together. Add salt and pepper. Stir in the scallions.

chili and corn-biscuit casserole

This hearty vegetarian chili has a good kick. Here it's sandwiched between two layers of biscuit batter and baked until golden and fluffy—you get chili and biscuit in every bite. Topped with guacasalsa, every mouthful is scrumptious.

Besides the combination of anasazi beans and pinto beans suggested here, other quick-cooking beans that work well are kidney beans, purple Appaloosa, Swedish brown beans, or even black beans. The chili can be made one day and baked into the casserole the next, but don't mix the wet and dry ingredients of the biscuit until you are ready to put the whole casserole together.

SERVES 6

chili

¾ cup anasazi beans, soaked, or
    1 15-ounce can
¾ cup pinto beans, soaked, or
    1 15-ounce can
    Salt
1 tablespoon extra-virgin olive oil
2 onions, cut into fine dice (2 cups)
3 garlic cloves, minced
2 teaspoons ground cumin
1 teaspoon dried oregano
1 chipotle chile
1 pasilla chile
1 ancho or guajillo chile
½ cup sun-dried tomatoes
6 ounces seitan
1 tablespoon mirin or dry sherry
1 tablespoon fresh lemon juice

THE CHILI, SANDWICHED BETWEEN LAYERS OF CORN BISCUIT, SHOULD BE VERY THICK—NOT DRY, JUST THICK. SIMMER UNCOVERED AT THE END OF COOKING TO EVAPORATE ANY EXCESS LIQUID.

CHIPOTLE CHILES ARE HOT AND SMOKY; ANCHO AND GUAJILLO ARE MEDIUM-HOT CHILES, AND PASILLA IS MILDER. THEY ALL COMBINE HERE TO MAKE A MEDIUM-HOT CHILI. IF YOU WANT IT HOTTER, ADD ANOTHER CHIPOTLE.

make the chili:

• Cover the beans with 7 cups water and simmer, partially covered, for about 1 hour or until the beans are softened. Add salt to taste. (Alternatively, put the beans in a pressure cooker with 4 cups water. Bring to a boil, covered, then lock on the lid and pressure-cook for 6 minutes. Let the pressure come down naturally. Remove the lid and salt the beans.) For canned beans, drain the liquid and add to a pot covered with 1½ cups water. Don't add more salt at this stage, since canned beans are already salted.

• Warm the olive oil in a medium skillet. Add the onions and cook over medium-low heat for 10 minutes. Add the garlic, cumin, and oregano and cook 5 minutes more.

• Cut off the stems of the dried chiles and shake out the seeds. Place the chiles and sun-dried tomatoes together in a bowl. Cover with boiling water and let soak for 15 minutes, until soft. Drain, reserving the soaking liquid. Put the sun-dried tomatoes in the blender with the chiles and ¼ cup of the soaking liquid and blend until smooth.

• Place the seitan in a food processor fitted with a metal blade and process until ground. Transfer the ground seitan to a skillet with the chile-tomato purée and cook for 5 minutes, stirring constantly.

• Add the contents of the skillet to the bean pot. Add the mirin and lemon juice to the pot and simmer for 15 to 20 minutes, uncovered, to evaporate any excess liquid and allow the chili to thicken. (If you are using canned beans, add the salt now.) Stir from time to time to prevent the chile from sticking. Adjust salt to taste.

corn biscuit

1 cup unbleached white flour
1 cup cornmeal
½ teaspoon baking soda
1½ teaspoons baking powder
½ teaspoon salt
½ teaspoon chile powder, preferably New Mexican
¼ cup apple cider vinegar
½ cup soy milk
6 tablespoons canola oil
¼ cup water
½ cup tortilla chips, crushed

make the corn biscuit:

• Preheat the oven to 350°F. Oil a deep 7 × 9-inch baking dish.

• In a medium bowl, whisk together the flour, cornmeal, baking soda, baking powder, salt, and chile powder. In another medium bowl, mix the vinegar, soy milk, oil, and water. Whisk together until thoroughly blended and emulsified. (You can use a blender for this.) Add the wet ingredients to the dry ingredients and mix together with a spatula just until the ingredients are fully moist; do not overmix.

• Spread a thin layer of batter on the bottom of the baking dish. Spoon the chili on top and finish with the rest of the batter. With a spatula (a small metal offset spatula works best here), smooth the batter evenly. Sprinkle with the crushed tortilla chips.

• Bake for 45 minutes, or until the casserole is cooked through, and a toothpick inserted in the biscuit comes out clean. Let the casserole stand for 5 minutes before cutting it into squares to serve.

The crushed tortilla chips give the biscuit a crunchy top crust. Any kind of good-quality tortilla chip will work, but I prefer to use baked tortilla chips.

guacasalsa

This avocado salsa combines the best of salsa and guacamole and is great in most instances where you would serve guacamole. The avocado retains a good shape because it's diced, not smashed, before it's tossed with the other ingredients. Mince the other ingredients first so that they are ready to mix with the avocado as soon as it's cut. The lime juice adds tangy flavor and helps the avocado keep its green color. Guacasalsa can be covered with plastic wrap, pressed directly onto the surface, and refrigerated for up to one day.

2   scallions, thinly sliced on the diagonal (¼ cup)
1   jalapeño, stem and seeds removed, minced
1   medium cucumber, peeled, seeded, and cut into ¼-inch cubes (1 cup)
½   cup minced red onion
2   garlic cloves, minced
½   cup chopped fresh cilantro
2   ripe avocados
2   tablespoons fresh lime juice
    Salt

THE BEST AVOCADOS ARE THE SMALL, ROUGH-SKINNED HASS AVOCADOS. UNRIPE AVOCADOS TAKE 2 TO 5 DAYS TO RIPEN OUTSIDE THE REFRIGERATOR.

• Combine the scallions, jalapeño, cucumber, red onion, garlic, and cilantro in a medium bowl.

• Cut the avocados in half and remove the pits. Holding each avocado half in one hand, make ¼-inch crosshatch cuts through the flesh with a table knife, cutting down to the skin. Separate the diced flesh from the skin by gently scooping out the avocado cubes with a spoon. Add these to the bowl with the lime juice and mix gently. Season with salt to taste.

garlic-braised broccoli

The combination of sautéing and steaming is a quick and flavorful way to cook broccoli that allows it to keep its great color.

SERVES 6

2 tablespoon extra-virgin olive oil
3 garlic cloves, minced
½ pound broccoli (½ large head or 1 small head), cut into florets
  Salt

- Warm the oil and garlic in a medium skillet over medium heat until the oil is shimmering and the garlic barely starts to color. Add the broccoli and stir for a minute or two until it is heated through.

- Add ¼ cup water to the skillet. Cover the skillet and cook for about 2 minutes, until the broccoli is crisp-tender and bright green. Sprinkle with salt.

Rosemary Aïoli

Provençal Stew

Roasted Potato Batons

Basic Couscous

Citrus and Cucumber Salad

SERVES 4

Provence is memorable for its strikingly intense colors and equally vivid tastes, as well as for people who are passionate about good food. With all the excellent raw ingredients available, it's no wonder so many brilliant and familiar dishes originated there. When I created this menu, I was inspired by the exceptional flavor of the bouillabaisse, "golden soup." Bouillabaisse originated as a simple stew that included whatever the fisherman brought home that day, which was then quickly boiled with saffron, herbs, and garlic. Like a good bouillabaisse, this stew has complex harmonious flavors and textures. It includes a creamy rosemary aïoli as the finishing touch, and it is piled with roasted potato batons—as crispy and satisfying as French fries, but lighter on the belly. For me, bouillabaisse signals a sense of inviting abundance, so invite some friends over, and be sure to make extra potato batons.

- Put the garlic in to roast for the aïoli.

- Prep the vegetables for the stew and finish the aïoli.

- Cook the stew.

- Roast the potatoes while you make the salad dressing and cut the citrus pieces.

- Cook the couscous and toss the salad right before serving.

- To serve, ladle stew into a wide soup plate or pasta bowl. On one side, serve a small amount of couscous. Arrange potatoes on another side with a large spoonful of aïoli in the center. Sprinkle with parsley. Serve the salad on its own plate.

rosemary aïoli

In Holland and Belgium, mayonnaise is the preferred dipping sauce for *pommes frites,* or French fries. In this version, the tofu does a real disappearing act with magical results. What you have is a flavor-packed dip with a fraction of the oil of standard mayonnaise. You might be as tempted as I am to put dollops of the aïoli on practically everything, especially simple vegetables and baked potatoes.

    The aïoli improves as it sits, so allow at least 20 minutes for the flavors to marry.

1	small head of garlic or ½ medium head
2	tablespoons plus 1 teaspoon extra-virgin olive oil
½	pound silken tofu
1	teaspoon mustard powder
1	teaspoon fresh lemon juice
1	teaspoon salt
	Pinch of white pepper
1	teaspoon finely chopped fresh rosemary

- Preheat the oven to 375°F. Remove the papery outer skin of the garlic and cut off the top fifth. Place the garlic on aluminum foil and drizzle with 1 teaspoon of the oil. Wrap the garlic completely in the foil and place on an oven rack to roast about for about 30 minutes, or until soft. Squeeze the softened garlic cloves out from their skins.

- In a food processor fitted with a metal blade, combine the garlic, the remaining 2 tablespoons of oil, the tofu, mustard powder, lemon juice, salt, and pepper. Process until smooth. Add the rosemary and pulse to combine. Pour into a bowl and let sit for 20 minutes or so before using.

provençal stew

Saffron, herbs, fennel, wine, and vegetables—all contribute to the medley of flavors and textures in this stew. It's neither a difficult nor time-consuming recipe, especially when you use cooked or canned beans. If you're not making the whole meal, prepare the stew with toasted baguette croutons floating on top, and don't forget a hearty spoonful of rosemary aïoli.

SERVES 4

1	tablespoon extra-virgin olive oil
2	cups chopped cleaned leeks (about 1 medium leek, white part only)
2	medium portobello mushrooms, cleaned and cut into 1-inch squares (½ pound)
½	cup dry white wine
1	14.5-ounce can diced tomatoes Pinch of saffron
2	teaspoons ground fennel seeds
2	medium carrots, roll cut (see page 15)
1	small head of cauliflower, cut into florets (3 cups)
2	celery stalks, cut on the diagonal into 2-inch chunks (1 cup) Bouquet garni of 2 rosemary sprigs, 4 thyme sprigs, a handful of parsley stems, and ¼ teaspoon black peppercorns
3	cups water
1½	cups cooked chickpeas (see box), or 1 14.5-ounce can, drained
1	teaspoon fresh lemon juice Salt and freshly ground black pepper
¼	cup chopped fresh flat-leaf parsley

• Warm the oil in a pot or Dutch oven over medium heat. Add the leeks and mushrooms and sauté for 10 minutes, or until the leeks are softened, but not browned. Add the wine, turn the heat up to high, and cook until the liquid is reduced by half, about 5 minutes.

• Add the tomatoes, saffron, and fennel seeds to the pot and cook for 5 minutes, stirring once or twice.

• Add the carrots, cauliflower, celery, bouquet garni, and the water. Cover and bring to a boil, then lower the heat, partially cover, and simmer for 15 minutes. Add the chickpeas, and cook another 10 minutes.

• Add the lemon juice and season with salt and pepper. Remove the bouquet garni and stir in the chopped parsley.

Because the dried, thread-like stigmas of the saffron crocus are so light and have to be handpicked, saffron is very expensive. Fortunately, its flavor is so strong that a small amount—a pinch, in fact—will flavor a whole dish and color it a brilliant gold.

The stigmas are about an inch long, are very light, and range in color from vibrant red-orange to fiery yellow. The deeper their color, the better their quality. Do be sure to buy threads instead of ground saffron, as the ground is sometimes adulterated with an extender.

To cook chickpeas: For 1½ cups cooked chickpeas, start with ¾ cup dried chickpeas. Follow the directions on pages 7–8 for sorting, soaking, and cooking beans. For the stovetop method, chickpeas should be cooked for 1½ to 2 hours, or until tender. For the pressure-cooker method, they should be cooked for 10 to 12 minutes.

roasted potato batons

When potatoes are cooked this simply, the particular way they are cut and treated has everything to do with the way they taste. I cut them into batons, and wash the starch off to make the surface brown better. These potatoes are a lot like French fries but are less messy to make, with a fraction of the oil. They can be quite addictive.

SERVES 4

2 pounds russet potatoes
(3 medium)
¼ cup extra-virgin olive oil
Salt

- Preheat the oven to 375°F.

- Peel the potatoes and cut lengthwise into ¼-inch slabs. Stack a few slices at a time and cut lengthwise again into ¼-inch batons. Rinse the potatoes under running water to remove surface starch. Drain on paper towels and pat lightly to dry. Place in a medium bowl and toss with the oil and salt to taste.

- Spread the potatoes on a parchment-covered baking sheet and roast for about 45 minutes, tossing every 10 minutes, until the potatoes are lightly golden and cooked through.

basic couscous

Most markets in the United States carry the instant kind of couscous, which cooks up to be quite fluffy. This is a basic recipe, good for when you're preparing couscous for salads or side dishes. The couscous here acts as a garnish for the stew and aïoli. Reheat over hot water in a double boiler if necessary.

SERVES 4

¾ cup couscous
1 cup water
2 teaspoons extra-virgin olive oil
¼ teaspoon salt

- Pour the couscous into a shallow baking dish. Combine the water, oil, and salt in a saucepan and bring to a boil. Pour over the couscous and and stir to mix. Cover the dish and let stand for 10 minutes or so. Fluff with a fork or with your fingers.

citrus and cucumber salad

Citrus supremes—citrus segments cut free from their membranes—are a colorful and elegant addition to many preparations. Here, tart lime contrasts with the sweet orange and crunchy cucumber for a very satisfying salad.

SERVES 4

¼ cup fresh orange juice
2 tablespoons red wine vinegar
¼ cup extra-virgin olive oil
1 teaspoon grated orange zest
1 teaspoon fresh thyme leaves
  Salt and freshly ground black pepper
1 red grapefruit
1 navel orange
1 lime
½ medium cucumber
6 cups red-leaf and green-leaf lettuce, torn into bite-size pieces

• To make the dressing, whisk together the orange juice, vinegar, and oil. Stir in the orange zest, thyme, salt, and pepper.

• Supreme the grapefruit, orange, and lime. (See Sidebar.)

• Peel the cucumber and cut in half lengthwise. Seed it, then cut crosswise into thin half-moons. Place the cucumber in a bowl with the lettuce and toss with the dressing.

• Arrange the salad on individual plates, and arrange 2 grapefruit, orange, and lime segments on each.

how to supreme oranges and other citrus fruits

1. Cut a disk off the top and bottom of each orange, slicing through the colored peel and white pith to expose the flesh. Stand the fruit on one of its cut ends and cut downward, following the contours of the fruit, to remove the skin and pith, exposing the orange flesh.
2. Holding the fruit over a bowl to catch the juices, use a paring knife to separate the segments from the inner membranes by slicing down to the core on either side of each segment.

Potato Latkes with Rosy Applesauce and Shallot "Sour Cream"

Red Cabbage Braised with Beer and Mustard

Carrots, Daikon, and Mustard Greens

SERVES 4

Generally associated with Hanukkah dinners or Eastern European fare, potato pancakes are my idea of the perfect comfort food. Here, the latkes, topped with shallot "sour cream" and rosy applesauce, are married with earthy, slow-cooked red cabbage and a mix of sweet roots and bitter mustard greens. This combination makes for a surprisingly nongreasy meal that won't weigh you down.

cook's notes

- Make the shallot "sour cream" and the applesauce.
- Braise the cabbage. The first two steps can be done a day or two in advance.
- Make the potato pancakes. (These can be cooked earlier the same day and reheated in the oven. They can even be frozen and reheated.)
- Make the vegetables right before serving.
- To serve, place three latkes on one side of the plate. Serve the applesauce and shallot "sour cream" on either side of the latkes. Put a mound of cabbage in the middle of the plate, and vegetables on the other side.

potato latkes

No need to save this recipe for holiday dinners; latkes are great anytime, especially for breakfast or brunch. And you're not going to miss the eggs one bit: a little baking powder gives the batter a lift, and stirring the potato starch back into the batter helps the ingredients bind. (Make sure to use the starchy russet variety.) Half of the potatoes are finely chopped and half are grated for great textures.

MAKES TWELVE TO FIFTEEN 4-INCH LATKES

1½ pounds russet potatoes (2 large)
½ cup unbleached white flour
½ teaspoon baking powder
1½ teaspoons sea salt
    Freshly ground black pepper
1 cup minced onion
½ cup grated carrot
½ cup thinly sliced scallions
2 tablespoons unflavored soy milk
    Canola oil for shallow frying

• Peel the potatoes. In a food processor fitted with a metal blade, process half of the potatoes until they are finely chopped. Change the blade to the grater and grate the remaining potatoes or grate them by hand. Combined, you should have about 4 cups of potatoes.

• Transfer the potatoes to a strainer placed over a bowl and let them drain for about 10 minutes. Squeeze the potatoes with your hands to extract any remaining liquid. Let the liquid sit for a few minutes to allow the starch to settle to the bottom of the bowl, then pour off the liquid, leaving the starch behind. Add the potatoes and stir to combine. Add the flour, baking powder, salt, pepper to taste, onion, carrot, scallions and soy milk to the potatoes and mix thoroughly.

• Heat ½ inch of canola oil in a medium or large skillet until very hot. (Do not let the oil get so hot that it smokes, however.) Press a heaping tablespoon of potato mixture flat between your hands, round the edges, flatten and smooth again, then gently drop into the hot oil. Make 3 or 4 more latkes the same way and add to the pan, taking care not to crowd them. Fry for 3 to 4 minutes, or until the edges are golden, then turn and fry for 2 to 3 minutes on the other side.

• Preheat the oven to 275°F. Remove the pancakes onto a plate lined with paper towels or a brown paper bag to absorb the extra oil. Repeat with the remaining latke mixture, keeping each batch of latkes hot until ready to serve. Serve hot.

Latkes can be reheated but they should never be refrigerated. You can make them a few hours in advance and keep them covered at room temperature. To reheat, set them on a baking sheet and put in the oven at 350°F. for about 5 minutes, or until they are heated through. Latkes can, however, be frozen. To freeze, spread them on a tray and freeze for a couple of hours. After they are frozen individually, you can stack them and place them in a covered container. To reheat, spread them on a baking sheet and bake at 350°F. until heated through.

rosy applesauce

Cooking apples with their peel on and passing them through a food mill gives applesauce a beautiful blushing color. Rome apples are especially good prepared this way. If you don't want to take the extra step of using the food mill, or if you don't have one, just peel the apples first and let them cook until they are broken down and saucy.

Applesauce is a good place to use those apples that are less than crisp.

2 pounds red apples (4 to 5 apples)
½ cup apple cider or apple juice
1 teaspoon ground cinnamon
¼ teaspoon ground allspice
10 gratings of fresh nutmeg on a
    grater, or a pinch of ground
    nutmeg
    Pinch of salt

• Halve and core the apples, then roughly chop. Place them in a saucepan with the remaining ingredients.

• Cover and bring to a boil, then simmer, uncovered, for 20 minutes, or until the apples are very soft. Pass the sauce through a food mill, discarding the skin. Serve warm or at room temperature.

shallot "sour cream"

I like to slather this spread, which tastes like sour-cream-and-onion dip, on top of the potato pancakes. Your guests will be amazed to discover that *this* is tofu. Serve the "sour cream" on crudite or any type of prepared potato.

½ pound silken tofu
3 tablespoons canola oil
2 tablespoons fresh lemon juice
2 teaspoons brown rice vinegar
¾ teaspoon salt
1 tablespoon minced shallots

• Combine all ingredients except the shallots in a food processor and process until creamy. Add the shallots and pulse to combine.

red cabbage braised with beer and mustard

Beer gives this Alsatian-inspired side dish its earthy depth. The alcohol evaporates, leaving only its flavor to mix with the rest of the braise. The vinegar restores some of the vibrant color that gets cooked out of the cabbage during braising, for an appealing deep-purple result. Pair this side dish with any hearty winter entrée.

SERVES 4

½ medium head of red cabbage, outer leaves and core removed (6 cups)
1 tablespoon extra-virgin olive oil
1 onion, cut in half and sliced thin
1 teaspoon ground caraway seeds
1 12-ounce bottle of beer
½ cup apple juice or apple cider
2 tablespoons whole-grain mustard
3 tablespoons umeboshi vinegar
Salt and freshly ground black pepper

UMEBOSHI VINEGAR IS THE BRINE IN WHICH JAPANESE UMEBOSHI PLUMS ARE PICKLED. ITS CHARACTERISTIC COLOR COMES FROM THE PURPLE SHISO LEAVES ADDED TO THE BRINE. ALTHOUGH IT'S NOT TECHNICALLY A VINEGAR, IT DOES GIVE FOOD A SOUR-SALTY BOOST OF FLAVOR. FIND IT IN MOST NATURAL FOOD STORES.

- Slice the cabbage very thin.

- Warm the oil in a medium saucepan over medium heat. Add the onions and sauté for 7 minutes, or until the onions are softened.

- Add the caraway and cook for 2 to 3 minutes more. Add the cabbage, beer, and apple juice, cover, and bring to a boil. Reduce the heat to a simmer and cook for 5 minutes, covered. Uncover and simmer, stirring occasionally, for 15 more minutes, or until the cabbage is tender and the braising liquid has reduced by half.

- Add the mustard, umeboshi vinegar, salt, and pepper. Cook for 5 minutes more, stirring occasionally. Serve hot.

carrots, daikon, and mustard greens

Apple cider mellows the taste of the pungent, peppery mustard greens, the most intensely flavored of all greens. When very small, mustard greens are mild tasting and are often found in salad mixes. The larger the greens, the more intense the flavor. Prepare mustard greens by stripping off any tough stems; chop the leaves roughly; then immerse the greens in water to wash. Like spinach and chard, they reduce dramatically when cooked.

SERVES 4

1 pound mustard greens, stems removed, cut into 1-inch pieces
1 tablespoon extra-virgin olive oil
2 garlic cloves, minced
1 1-inch piece of ginger, peeled and minced
½ cup apple cider or apple juice
3 medium carrots, peeled and cut in roll-cut chunks (page 15) (2 cups)
½ pound daikon, peeled and cut into roll-cut chunks (page 15) (2 cups)
Salt

• Wash the greens by immersing them in a large bowl or sink full of cold water. Swish well to loosen dirt, then lift the greens out and set aside.

• Warm the oil, garlic, and ginger together in a medium skillet over medium heat and cook, stirring, until the garlic is just starting to brown lightly, about 2 minutes.

• Add the cider, carrots, and daikon, cover, and cook for about 5 minutes, stirring occasionally. Then add the greens and cook, stirring occasionally, for another 4 minutes, or until the carrots and daikon are cooked through and the greens are tender. Season with salt to taste.

Broccoli Rabe Polenta

Beet, Daikon, and Carrot Salad over Arugula

Mediterranean Braised Fennel

Mushroom, French Lentil, and Chestnut Ragù

SERVES 4

The flavors in this menu are rich and mysterious. I've catered this meal for one hundred guests, so I know it scales up well and gets applause. Serve this on a romantic occasion or a special night; you can prepare most of the dishes a day in advance. Polenta, anything but dull when emboldened by savory broccoli rabe, pairs wonderfully with a wild mushroom ragù. The fennel braise sports flecks of sun-dried tomatoes and black olives, and slivers of fresh basil. The salad, both sharp and sweet, balances the rich flavors of the menu.

cook's notes

Everything on this menu can be made a day in advance and reheated.

- Soak the chestnuts.
- Make the polenta first. Put up the beets to cook if you are using the stovetop method for them.
- Put the fennel and leeks in to roast.
- Make the ragù.
- Then finish the braised fennel dish. Bake the polenta while you make the salad.
- To serve, pour ragù over most of a large serving plate. Place polenta triangles on top, overlapping with a serving of braised fennel on one side. Serve salad on a separate plate.

broccoli rabe polenta

When cooked and then cooled, polenta becomes firm and sturdy enough to cut into shapes. Baked or fried, these polenta shapes make a wonderful foundation for any number of stews or sauces. Here the broccoli rabe speckles this polenta with green flecks and lends a tangy flavor.

You can make the polenta up to several days in advance and then bake it, pan fry it, grill it, or deep fry it just before serving. Polenta traditionally needs vigilant attention while it's cooking—that is, constant stirring for 40 to 50 minutes. Substituting quick-cooking corn grits for half of the cornmeal here allows the polenta to cook in a fraction of the time, and the corn grits give the polenta texture, too.

Polenta scales up well, but it is helpful to have an immersion blender handy when you make polenta in large amounts, to blend out any lumps quickly.

SERVES 4

½ pound broccoli rabe
Salt
3 cups water
1 tablespoon extra-virgin olive oil, plus more for brushing the polenta
½ cup quick-cooking corn grits
½ cup stone-ground yellow cornmeal

BROCCOLI RAPE IS A GREEN WITH A PRO-
NOUNCED, SOMEWHAT BITTER FLAVOR. ITS
LEAVES LOOK LIKE THOSE OF A TURNIP, WITH LIT-
TLE BROCCOLI-LIKE FLORETS INTERSPERSED
AMONG THE GREENS. ALL PARTS ARE EDIBLE. IT
IS EATEN WIDELY IN ITALY AND IS AVAILABLE IN
ITALIAN STORES AND MOST SUPERMARKETS.

- Oil an 8 × 8-inch baking dish and bring a large pot of salted water to a boil. Cut off any tough stems from the broccoli rabe. Blanch the broccoli rabe, uncovered, for about 5 minutes, or until it is bright green and tender. Drain, and when it is cool enough to handle, chop it fine. You should have about 1 cup.

- Bring the 3 cups of water to a boil in a medium saucepan. Add ½ teaspoon salt and the oil. Gradually whisk in the corn grits and cornmeal in a slow, steady stream, whisking constantly to prevent the polenta from becoming lumpy. Crush any lumps you do encounter against the side of the pot with a wooden spoon. When the polenta is bubbling gently, reduce the heat and cook for 15 to 20 minutes, stirring often with a wooden spoon to prevent sticking. When the polenta is cooked, it will pull away from the side of the pot when drawn with a wooden spoon. Turn off the heat and taste for salt.

- Add the chopped broccoli rabe to the polenta, stirring in thoroughly. Pour the polenta into the baking dish and spread it evenly with a spatula. Cool the polenta for at least 45 minutes or cover and refrigerate for up to 3 days.

- Preheat the oven to 375°F. Cut the cooled polenta into 4 squares and cut each square into 2 triangles. Set the triangles on a parchment-covered baking sheet and brush the surface of each triangle with olive oil. Bake for 30 to 40 minutes or until the polenta is golden.

beet, daikon, and carrot salad over arugula

This pungent dressing with the pronounced flavor of walnut oil, plus the sharpness of arugula and daikon, contrast with the sweet taste of the colorful beets, whose bright red color stands out and nicely dyes the adjacent carrots.

The beet can be cooked in a pressure cooker: Cover the beet with water and cook at high pressure for about 10 minutes.

SERVES 4

1   medium to large beet (about ¾ pound)
2   medium carrots, peeled and thinly sliced on the diagonal (1 cup)
¼   pound daikon, peeled and thinly sliced on the diagonal (1 cup)
2   bunches of arugula
½   cup walnut pieces
3   tablespoons red wine vinegar
1   teaspoon Dijon mustard
1   garlic clove, minced
½   cup walnut oil
    Salt and freshly ground black pepper

• Place the beet in a small pot with water to cover. Bring to a boil and cook for about 45 minutes, or until the beet is tender when pierced with the tip of a knife. Remove the beet from the water and let it cool a bit, then remove the skin from the beet while it is still warm. It will slip off easily. Slice the beet into ½-inch wedges. Place in a small bowl. Place the carrots and daikon in a medium bowl with the arugula.

• Preheat the oven to 350°F. Place the walnuts on a baking sheet and lightly toast them for 10 minutes. Remove the walnuts from the oven and place them in a strainer while still warm. Holding them over the sink, rub the walnuts against the strainer to loosen the skins. Remove the walnuts from the strainer (discard the papery skins left in the strainer) and hand chop into small (¼-inch) pieces. Set aside.

• In a small bowl, whisk together the vinegar, mustard, and garlic. Add the oil in a steady stream, whisking constantly to emulsify. Stir in salt and pepper to taste.

• Toss the beets with 2 tablespoons of the dressing. Pour the remaining dressing over the arugula, carrots, and daikon and toss to coat. Divide the salad among individual salad plates and arrange some of the beets on each portion. Sprinkle with walnuts and serve.

mediterranean braised fennel

Roasting and then braising the leeks and fennel may seem like an unnecessary step, but it concentrates their flavors in a wonderful way. Flavorful flecks of sun-dried tomato, basil, and chopped olives make this an especially lively braise.

SERVES 4

½ medium fennel bulb or 1 small bulb

2 leeks, white part only

2 tablespoons extra-virgin olive oil
Salt and freshly ground black pepper

6 sun-dried tomatoes (not oil-packed)

3 tablespoons pitted black olives, preferably kalamata, slivered

12 fresh basil leaves, cut into thin strips (2 tablespoons chiffonade)

• Preheat the oven to 375°F.

• Cut away any discolored or soft spots from the outside of the fennel. Cut the fennel in half (if using a small bulb), and remove the fibrous core. Thinly slice the fennel lengthwise and place it in a mixing bowl.

• Cut the white part of the leeks into 2-inch pieces, then slice lengthwise into thin strips. Immerse the strips in a large bowl of water, swishing around to loosen dirt. Lift the leeks from the bowl, leaving the dirt behind, pat them dry, and add them to the fennel pieces.

• Toss the leeks and fennel with the oil and add salt and pepper to taste. Spread on a parchment-covered baking sheet and roast, stirring every 5 minutes, for about 20 minutes, or until the vegetables have started to brown.

• Remove the vegetables from the oven and transfer them to a 9 × 11-inch baking dish. Add ½ cup water, or enough to fill the baking dish to a depth of ½ inch. Cover with foil and bake for another 20 minutes, or until the fennel and leeks are tender.

• Meanwhile, soak the sun-dried tomatoes in hot water for 15 to 20 minutes or until softened. Drain and thinly slice.

• Remove the fennel and leeks from oven, uncover, and let cool to warm. They should be juicy and tender. Stir in the olives, sliced tomatoes, and basil. Adjust seasonings to taste.

mushroom, french lentil, and chestnut ragù

Smoky dried chestnuts, roasted mushrooms, and fresh herbs give their rich tastes to this satisfying dish. French lentils, known as lentilles du Puy, keep their shape, look elegant, and cook quickly. You can substitute any combination of oyster mushrooms, chanterelles, or other meaty wild mushrooms for the shiitakes and portobello, but you should have a total of three quarters of a pound. Cultivated mushrooms are the least interesting here.

½ cup dried chestnuts (see Glossary), soaked in 5 cups water

¾ cup French lentils
   Bouquet garni of 3 rosemary sprigs, 3 thyme sprigs, and 1 bay leaf tied in a square of cheesecloth or between 2 celery stalks

6 ounces fresh shiitake mushrooms

1 large portobello mushroom (6 ounces)

3 tablespoons extra-virgin olive oil

2 tablespoons shoyu

1 onion, cut into small dice (1 cup)

2 garlic cloves, minced

2 celery stalks, cut into large pieces on the diagonal
   Salt and freshly ground black pepper

2 teaspoons fresh lemon juice

1 teaspoon minced fresh rosemary

1 teaspoon minced fresh thyme

• Preheat the oven to 375°F.

• Skim off any chestnut skin that has floated to the top as they soaked, then transfer the chestnuts in their soaking liquid to a saucepan or pot. Bring to a boil, then reduce the heat and simmer, partially covered, for about 45 minutes, or until the chestnuts are tender. Drain, reserving the cooking liquids.

• Meanwhile, cover the lentils with 4 cups water in a medium saucepan. Add the bouquet garni, cover, and bring to a boil. Reduce the heat and simmer, partially covered, for 30 to 35 minutes, or until the lentils are soft. Keep an eye on the water level and add just enough water, if necessary, to prevent the lentils from sticking

• Remove the stems from the portobello and shiitake mushrooms. Quarter the shiitakes and cut the portobello into chunks, and place them in a medium bowl. Toss with 2 tablespoons of the olive oil and the shoyu and place in a shallow baking pan. Roast for about 30 minutes, or until the mushrooms have released their juices and shrunk.

• Warm the remaining tablespoon of oil in a medium skillet. Add the onion, garlic, and celery and sauté for 10 minutes, or until the onions have started to color and the celery is tender. Add the vegetables to the cooked lentils. When the mushrooms are ready, add them to the lentils as well, along with any juices that might have accumulated.

• Add the cooked chestnuts to the lentils along with ½ cup of their cooking liquid. Season with salt and pepper to taste and simmer for a few minutes to allow the flavors to marry. Add more chestnut cooking liquid if necessary for a thick sauce consistency. Stir in the lemon juice, rosemary, and thyme and serve.

Shepherd's Pie with Horseradish Glaze

Sautéed Brussels Sprouts and Carrots

SERVES 6

The gourmet status of shepherd's pie in restaurants today belies its colorful history. At one time, this dish was available at any number of establishments, from boarding schools to seaside pubs. English cooks used the shepherd's pie as a glorified repository for leftovers, which were ground, then covered with a layer of mashed potatoes. The hallmark of the dish is still a top crust of potatoes, but the fillings have evolved to something a bit more refined. The possibilities are limited only by the imagination of the chef. The pie can be made in elegant, individualized servings, or as a larger casserole. It also makes a great leftover that can be reheated in the oven for 20 minutes or frozen in individual portions.

This version consists of layers of vegetables, spiced tempeh, and mashed potatoes with horseradish—a new "comfort food" classic.

cook's notes

Up to one day in advance, assemble the pie.

• Put the zucchini in to roast.

• Put up the potatoes in a pot of water to boil.

• Next, make the tempeh and cook the spinach. Meanwhile, start reducing the glaze.

• Mash the potatoes.

• Layer the casserole.

• Finish the glaze while you bake the casserole.

• Blanch the vegetables and sauté them right before serving.

• To serve, surround the pie with a stream of glaze. Arrange pieces of carrot and Brussels sprouts around the pie. Sprinkle with dill.

shepherd's pie

Without meat or sticky cream sauce, this layered pie is surprisingly light. It's ideal for company, as it can be assembled one day and baked the next. It's also delicious reheated. I like to make it in a deep 7 × 9-inch Pyrex baking dish (my favorite size for casseroles). The tempeh has a strong, vibrant flavor that holds its own against the mashed potatoes and vegetables.

SERVES 6

zucchini

1   pound zucchini (2 medium)
    Extra-virgin olive oil for brushing the zucchini
    Salt and freshly ground black pepper
1   teaspoon dried thyme

mashed potatoes

2   pounds russet potatoes (3 medium)
3   cloves garlic, peeled
    Salt
2   tablespoons extra-virgin olive oil
½   cup original flavored soy milk
    White pepper
1   tablespoon freshly grated horseradish

HORSERADISH CAN BE PUNGENT WHEN BAKED, SO IT'S BETTER TO BE JUDICIOUS HERE. WHEN IT IS STIRRED INTO THE HOT GLAZE (SEE PAGE 152), HOWEVER, IT LOSES ITS POTENCY.

make the zucchini:

- Preheat the oven to 350°F.

- Slice the zucchini lengthwise into thin (¼- to ⅜-inch) slices. Arrange on a parchment-covered baking sheet and brush with oil. Sprinkle with salt and pepper and half of the thyme. Turn the slices and repeat. Bake the zucchini for 20 minutes, or until it is softened. Set aside. Keep the oven on if you're baking the pie afterward.

make the mashed potatoes:

- Place the unpeeled potatoes in a medium pot with the whole peeled garlic cloves. Cover with cold water and 2 teaspoons salt and bring to a boil, then reduce to a simmer and cook until the potatoes are tender, 15 to 30 minutes, depending on their size. Drain, reserving the cooking liquid and garlic.

- Holding each hot potato in a dish towel, use a peeler to peel off the skin. Discard the skin. Return the potatoes to the pot with the garlic and add the oil, soy milk, salt, and white pepper to taste. Mash the potatoes with a hand masher, adding about ¼ cup of the cooking liquid a little at a time, until the potatoes are smooth and have the desired moistness. (You want them a little on the moist side; they're still going to bake.) Stir in the horseradish.

make the tempeh:

- Steam the tempeh over boiling water for 7 minutes. Transfer to a food processor and process until finely chopped.

For a beautiful presentation, use 3- or 4-inch bottomless round metal ring molds to make individual pies. (They should be at least 3 inches deep.) Place the molds on a baking sheet. Layer the ingredients in each mold as above, cutting the zucchini to fit. After baking, use a spatula to place the individual pie in the center of the plate, then lift off the ring mold with tongs.

Potatoes taste better when cooked with the skin on, so I cook them whole. I look for medium potatoes so that the cooking time is not too long. Yukon Gold and Yellow Finn potatoes are creamy when mashed. Russet, or Idaho, my favorite for mashed potatoes, are the fluffiest.

Mashed potatoes should never be put in a food processor—unless you want a bowl of glue. For good results, they can be hand-mashed or passed through a food mill, a ricer, or a sieve.

tempeh

½ pound tempeh
2 tablespoons extra-virgin olive oil
2 onions, minced (2 cups)
3 garlic cloves, minced
1 tablespoon ground fennel seeds
1 teaspoon dried thyme
1 teaspoon dried savory
½ teaspoon dried sage
1½ teaspoons paprika
3 tablespoons shoyu
½ cup water
1 tablespoon fresh lemon juice
   Freshly ground black pepper
   Cayenne pepper
   Salt

spinach

1 pound spinach, stems removed
   and well washed
   Salt

THE FLAVOR OF TEMPEH IS GREATLY ENHANCED BY STEAMING IT FIRST. (FOR AN EXPLANATION OF TEMPEH, SEE THE GLOSSARY.)

- Warm the oil in a medium skillet. Add the onions and cook over medium-low heat for about 7 minutes, or until the onions are sweated and juicy. Add the garlic, fennel, thyme, savory, sage, and paprika and cook for another 5 minutes.

- Add the shoyu, scraping up any brown bits that might have stuck to the bottom of the pan, then add the chopped tempeh and ¼ cup of the water. Cook, stirring, until the tempeh has absorbed the water, then add the remaining ¼ cup of water. Cook for about 10 minutes more, or until all of the water is absorbed and the flavor has developed.

- Add lemon juice, a generous sprinkling of pepper, and a large pinch of cayenne. Season with salt to taste. (Even though it already has a lot of flavor, the salt will add the finishing touch and pop all the other flavors forward, so don't be timid!)

make the spinach:

- In a large pot, cook the spinach over medium heat, stirring frequently or tossing with tongs to push the uncooked leaves to the bottom of the pot. You don't have to add water to the pot, because the water clinging to the leaves from washing is enough to cook them. Cook until the leaves have wilted and are bright green. Sprinkle with salt.

- Remove the spinach from the pot and squeeze out any excess liquid. Finely chop. Salt again to taste and set aside.

assemble the pie:

- Oil a deep 7 × 9-inch baking dish. Layer the zucchini side by side, and cover that with a second layer of zucchini laid at a right angle to the first. Cover that with a layer of spinach. Next add the cooked tempeh, making sure to spread it completely over the spinach. Cover that with the mashed potatoes. Brush the top surface of the mashed potatoes with olive oil. If you want, you can run fork lines through the top for a decorative, textured surface. Bake for 45 minutes, or refrigerate the pie until ready to bake. Let the baked pie sit a few minutes before cutting and serving.

horseradish glaze

This vibrant sauce, studded with little red beet squares, has a lot of horseradish, but the bite mellows considerably when cooked this way. Make sure to use strained carrot juice, so that you don't have unsightly shreds floating in the sauce.

3   cups strained carrot juice
1   4-ounce beet, peeled and cut into ¼-inch cubes (1 cup)
2   tablespoons fresh lemon juice
2   tablespoons brown rice vinegar
    Salt and freshly ground black pepper
1   tablespoon kudzu or 1 heaping tablespoon arrowroot, dissolved in 2 tablespoons cold water (page 273)
2   tablespoons grated fresh horseradish
2   tablespoons chopped dill

• Combine the carrot juice and beet cubes in a small saucepan and bring to a boil over high heat. Lower the heat just enough so that the liquid doesn't boil over and cooks uncovered for 40 to 45 minutes, or until the liquid is reduced by half. There is no need to stir. Add the lemon juice and vinegar and a pinch of salt and pepper.

• Pour in the dissolved kudzu and stir until the mixture begins to bubble. (Stop stirring now and then to check if it's bubbling.) Turn off the heat and stir in the horseradish and dill. If it is necessary to reheat this sauce, do so gently without boiling it.

sautéed brussels sprouts and carrots

A dish of simple sautéed fall vegetables is a good addition to nearly any menu. Blanch the vegetables ahead, if you like, and have them ready to sauté at the last minute.

SERVES 6

½ pound Brussels sprouts
Salt
½ pound carrots (2 medium or 4 small, or ½ pound baby carrots), cut in thin roll-cut pieces (2 cups)
2 tablespoons extra-virgin olive oil
Freshly ground black pepper
Chopped fresh dill

• Peel the outer leaves off the Brussels sprouts. Trim the stems, leaving enough to keep the heads intact. Cut the sprouts in half.

• Fill a bowl with ice water and set aside. In a pot of boiling, salted water, blanch the carrots until they are cooked but crisp, about 2 minutes. Remove with a slotted spoon and refresh in the ice water to stop the cooking. Add the Brussels sprouts to the boiling water and blanch until crisp-tender, about 3 minutes. Add to the bowl of ice water to cool. Drain and set aside.

• Heat a medium skillet until very hot. Add the oil to coat the bottom of the pan. Immediately add the Brussels sprouts and carrots and sauté until lightly browned. Sprinkle with salt and pepper. Remove from the heat and sprinkle with chopped dill.

Anise-Scented Brown Rice and Barley

Oden Stew

Sweet and Hot Sesame Nori Strips

SERVES 4 TO 6

It's easy to understand why the belly-warming stew called oden is a national favorite in Japan. Although this dish varies much from region to region, oden generally has fried (agé) tofu and a wide range of ingredients, including root vegetables, along with a quick-cooking stock (a *dashi*). It is served as a favorite accompaniment to hot sake, which is how I recommend serving *this* oden. My cold-weather version features a potpourri of vegetables, most easy to find, especially if you have access to a local Chinatown, but feel free to substitute at will. It is complemented by anise-flavored rice and barley and garnished with sweet and hot sesame-crusted nori strips.

cook's notes

- Press the tofu.
- Fry the tofu. Then make the stew.
- Put the rice and barley up to cook. While that is cooking, make the sesame strips.
- To serve, ladle oden into a wide bowl or soup plate. Place a mound of rice and barley off to the side. Arrange a few nori pieces poking out of the grains. Garnish with some greens.

anise-scented brown rice and barley

The star anise in this mix of rice and barley invigorates it with a lovely fragrance. Short-grain brown rice, together with small, round, compact barley grains, are natural accompaniments to the winter root vegetables in the oden stew. This combination of grains also works as a great side dish for any cold-weather meal.

Barley absorbs more water than rice, so you need a generous quantity of cooking liquid. You can use hulled barley, from which only the hulls are removed, or pearled barley, from which the hulls and most of the bran have been removed; both are available in natural food stores. I prefer the chewy texture of the hulled barley over the softer texture of pearled. If using hulled, soak it first with the rice for a couple of hours. If there is no time to soak it, cook it longer, adding water as needed.

SERVES 4 TO 6

½ cup short-grain brown rice
½ cup hulled or pearled barley
4   cups water
3   star anise
¼   teaspoon salt

GROWN IN SOUTHERN CHINA AND VIETNAM, STAR ANISE IS A HARD, REDDISH-BROWN SPICE SHAPED LIKE A STAR. (ITS CHINESE NAME MEANS EIGHT POINTS.) IT HAS A SWEET, PUNGENT LICORICE-LIKE FLAVOR. I LIKE TO PUT A FEW STARS INTO THE LIQUID WHEN I COOK GRAINS SO THEY CAN INFUSE THE GRAINS WITH THEIR SUBTLE BUT DISTINCTIVE FLAVOR.

• Cover the rice and barley with water in a bowl, stirring and swishing around the submerged grains with your hand, then let the water settle for a moment. Pour off the water, catching the grains at the last moment with a strainer. Transfer to a medium pot and stir over medium heat for a few minutes, until the grains are toasted and dry.

• Add the water, star anise, and salt. Bring to a boil, then reduce the heat and simmer, uncovered, for about 30 minutes, until the liquid is almost absorbed. The barley should be quite tender; if not, add ½ cup more water and simmer until it is almost absorbed and the grain is tender. Cover the pot, lower the heat, and cook for 5 minutes longer, until the liquid is fully absorbed.

oden stew

Deep-fried tofu, the centerpiece of this warming stew, is surprisingly not greasy. Frying gives the tofu a deep brown crust that stays intact in the stew; the tofu absorbs the flavors of the stew and has a pleasing, chewy texture. I've used some of my favorite Asian root vegetables here, but other vegetables that would go well include taro root, rutabaga, squash, cabbage, and bamboo shoots. The hot-pepper sesame oil, available in Asian stores and natural food markets, is optional—but I love the special dimension it adds.

SERVES 4 TO 6

1 pound firm tofu

2 tablespoons canola oil, plus more for deep-frying

2 cups chopped, cleaned leeks, white part only

½ cup mirin (sweet Japanese sake) or sherry

2 ounces burdock (1 thin stalk; 2 ounces), scrubbed and cut into a thin roll cut (½ cup)

2 medium carrots, peeled and roll cut (1¼ cups)

1 cup lotus root (optional), peeled and cut into ¼-inch slices

5 cups water

1 6-inch piece of kombu and 8 dried shiitake mushrooms, tied in a cheesecloth

1 medium parsnip (¼ pound), peeled and roll cut (1 cup)

¼ pound daikon, peeled and roll cut (1 cup)

1 small knob of kohlrabi (¼ pound), peeled and cut into 1-inch cubes

¼ pound celery root, peeled and cut into 1-inch squares (1 cup)

1 small sweet potato, peeled and cut into 1-inch cubes

½ small cauliflower (½ pound), cut into florets (1½ cups)

• Press the tofu for at least 30 minutes (see page 76).

• In a small, deep pot, heat 1½ inches of oil to 350°F. If you don't have a thermometer, test the temperature by dropping in a piece of tofu. When it turns golden after just a few minutes, the oil is hot enough to fry. Gently drop several tofu pieces into the oil with a slotted spoon and cook for a few minutes, until golden brown. Move the tofu cubes around occasionally so they don't stick to the bottom. Drain on paper towels.

• In a large pot or saucepan, warm the 2 tablespoons of oil. Add the leeks and sauté over medium heat for 10 minutes, or until they are until soft. Add the mirin, scraping up any brown bits, and simmer, uncovered, for about 5 minutes, or until the liquid is reduced by half.

• Add the burdock, carrots, and lotus root (if using) to the pot and cook for 5 minutes. Add the 5 cups of water, the kombu and shiitake bouquet, and the parsnip, daikon, kohlrabi, and celery root. Cover the pot, bring to a boil, then reduce to a simmer and cook the vegetables, partially covered, for 10 minutes. Add the sweet potato, cauliflower and agé tofu and simmer, partially covered, for 15 more minutes. Remove the bouquet from the stew, and cool the bouquet for a few minutes. Remove and discard the shiitake stems and thinly slice the caps. Chop the kombu into small pieces and return to the pot along with the shiitakes.

• While the stew simmers, first grate the unpeeled ginger. Wrap the grated ginger in a piece of cheesecloth and squeeze out the juice. (Or, just pick up a handful and squeeze.) You should have about 3 tablespoons.

1 4-inch piece of ginger (to make
 3 tablespoons of ginger juice)
3 tablespoons shoyu
1 tablespoon brown rice vinegar
2 tablespoons kudzu dissolved in
 ¼ cup cold water
1 scallion, cut into 1-inch pieces
 (¼ cup)
½ teaspoon hot-pepper sesame oil
 (optional)
 Salt

BURDOCK IS A ROOT VEGETABLE THAT IS AVAIL-
ABLE IN NATURAL FOOD STORES OR ASIAN MAR-
KETS. IT HAS A DEEP, EARTHY TASTE AND ADDS
SO MUCH DIMENSION TO THE STEW THAT IT IS
WORTH SEEKING OUT. NO NEED TO PEEL BUR-
DOCK—JUST SCRUB AND CUT IT. LOTUS ROOT IS
ANOTHER UNUSUAL VEGETABLE WORTH THE
SEARCH. IT CAN BE FOUND FRESH IN ASIAN GRO-
CERIES AND DRIED IN NATURAL FOOD STORES.
LOTUS ROOT IS EXOTIC AND BEAUTIFUL LOOKING,
AND IS SHAPED LIKE A WHEEL WITH SPOKES.
FRESH LOTUS ROOT IS BEST, BUT IF YOU'RE
USING DRIED, SOAK 6 PIECES IN WATER FOR
2 HOURS.

• Add the shoyu, vinegar, and ginger juice to the stew. Add the kudzu mixture and stir until the liquid has turned from cloudy to clear and has thickened. Turn off the heat and stir in the scallions and hot-pepper sesame oil, if using. Sprinkle with a little salt if necessary.

☞ WITH ITS LONG, SPINDLY RED OR GREEN STEMS COMING OUT OF A SMALL
 KNOB, KOHLRABI LOOKS A LOT STRANGER THAN IT TASTES. IT HAS THE
 SWEET FLAVOR OF A YOUNG TURNIP AND IS AVAILABLE FROM SUMMER
 THROUGH WINTER. PEEL IT AND PREPARE IT ANY WAY YOU WOULD A TURNIP.

sweet and hot sesame nori strips

Mild nori is the ideal sea vegetable wrapping for sushi rolls, but it is far more versatile than that. Spread with a syrupy oil, cayenne, and sesame, it has a sweet, salty, and spicy crunch. It's a great snack with hot sake or beer.

¼ cup brown rice syrup
¼ cup canola oil
　 Pinch of cayenne pepper
½ cup sesame seeds
3 nori sheets
　 Salt

BUY NORI SHEETS AT NATURAL FOOD STORES OR ASIAN MARKETS. NORI COMES EITHER UNTOASTED, OR AS "SUSHI NORI," WHICH IS PRE-TOASTED, EITHER OF WHICH IS FINE FOR THIS RECIPE.

• Preheat oven to 350°F.

• Whisk together the rice syrup and canola oil in a small bowl, then stir in the cayenne.

• Place the sesame seeds in a small bowl, with water to cover. Swish to rinse and pour off any floaters (they are rancid). Drain the seeds in a strainer, then transfer to a dry skillet and toast until fragrant.

• Tear each nori sheet into three strips. Use a pastry brush to paint each strip with a thick coat of the syrup mixture. Sprinkle evenly with toasted sesame seeds and sprinkle liberally with salt.

• Place the nori strips on a parchment-covered baking sheet and bake for 10 minutes. Remove from the oven, let sit for a few minutes to allow the coating to set, then turn the strips over and paint the other sides with the syrup mixture. Sprinkle as before with sesame seeds and salt. Return to the oven for 10 minutes, then set aside for 20 minutes to crisp. Break each strip in two pieces.

Seitan Pot Pie

Cranberry-Pecan Sauce

Collard Greens and Kale with Garlic Chips

Daikon Pickles

SERVES 6

The pot pie—savory ingredients encased in a pastry crust—is a British tradition that goes back at least to the Middle Ages. The crust was originally a device for keeping the filling moist, but it developed into a refined element in its own right. Here it is the centerpiece of a meal dainty enough to set before a king. While the pie does not contain four and twenty blackbirds, it does boast a host of good things, including spiced green beans, sweet potatoes, and seitan, all bathed in a béchamel sauce. Collards and kale tossed with coins of fried garlic, and luminous yellow daikon pickle ducats, complete an autumnal meal worth a king's ransom.

cook's notes

- Pickle the daikon a day or two in advance if possible, or earlier the same day. If you can't do either, make the pickles first.

- Put the oil in the freezer while you make the filling for the pie. Make the crust, roll it out, and assemble and bake the pie.

- While the pie is baking, make the cranberry sauce and prep the greens.

- Cook the greens as soon as the pie comes out of the oven.

- To serve, this works best as a straightforward presentation. Place a wedge of pie (or an individual pie) on the plate with some cranberry sauce next to it. Serve a mound of collard greens with a few pickles on the side.

seitan pot pie

This old-fashioned pie makes great comfort food. You can bake all the filling in a single pie, but I like to make individual pot pies in 10-ounce ceramic ramekins. It is a little more work with the dough, but it's not hard, and it's a real treat for everyone to have an individual pie. With just the addition of a simple green salad, the pie makes a good cozy dinner. Be sure to make the accompanying cranberry sauce, however; it's an ideal mate for the pie.

SERVES 4 TO 6

vegetables

2   tablespoons toasted sesame oil
½   pound seitan, cut into ½-inch cubes
1   tablespoon extra-virgin olive oil
2   onions, finely chopped (2 cups)
3   garlic cloves, minced
¼   pound green beans, cut diagonally into 1-inch pieces (1½ cups)
1   small sweet potato, peeled and cut into ½-inch cubes (1 cup)
1   medium carrot, peeled, sliced in half lengthwise, then cut into ½-inch pieces (1 cup)
2   teaspoons ground cumin
1½   teaspoons dried thyme
1   teaspoon dried savory
½   teaspoon dried marjoram
1   cup fresh or frozen peas
     Salt and freshly ground black pepper

make the vegetables:

• Warm the sesame oil in a skillet over medium heat. Add the seitan cubes and sauté for about 10 minutes, or until they are browned on all sides. Remove from the heat and set aside.

• Warm the olive oil in a medium (4-quart) pot. Add the onions and garlic and sauté over medium heat for 8 minutes, or until the onions are starting to brown. Add the green beans, sweet potatoes, carrots, cumin, thyme, savory, and marjoram, and sauté for 2 minutes more.

• Add ½ cup of water and bring to a simmer, using a wooden spoon to scrape up the brown bits on the bottom. Cover and cook over medium-low heat for 5 minutes. Add the seitan and peas and add up to ½ cup more water if necessary. Cover and cook for an additional 5 minutes. Uncover and season with salt and pepper to taste. Transfer to a bowl and cool to room temperature.

make the béchamel:

• Combine the soy milk and mustard in a measuring cup.

• Warm the olive oil in a small saucepan. Add the flour and cook over low heat, stirring constantly, for 4 to 5 minutes, or until the roux is fragrant and light brown. Whisk in the soy milk and mustard all at once and bring to a boil over medium heat. Lower the heat and simmer gently for 5 minutes, stirring with a wooden spoon to prevent the sauce from sticking or burning. When it is quite thick, season with salt and pepper to taste.

béchamel

1½ cups unflavored soy milk
2 teaspoons Dijon mustard
2 tablespoons extra-virgin olive oil
2 tablespoons plus 2 teaspoons
  unbleached white flour
  Salt and freshly ground black
  pepper
1 recipe Savory Oil-Based Pie Crust
  (page 162)
1 tablespoon barley malt mixed with
  1 tablespoon water, for glazing

assemble the pot pie:

• Preheat the oven to 350°F. Oil a 9-inch pie plate—preferably Pyrex—or 6 individual ramekins.

• Divide the dough in 2 pieces and place one on a large square of parchment or wax paper. Press it into a flat disk, then roll it out, starting from the center and moving outward, until it is as thin as possible (about 1/16 inch). Lift the parchment paper and invert it over the pie plate, then peel away the parchment, lifting the sides as you lightly press the crust into the pie pan.

• Spoon all of the filling into the crust in a smooth mound. Pour the béchamel over the vegetables. Roll out the second crust in the same way as the first and center it over the pie. Trim the two crusts together at the edge of the pie plate, using a small knife or kitchen scissors, and pinch to seal. Flute the edge decoratively, if desired. Make 5 or 6 slashes in the top crust to allow steam to escape while baking.

• Place the pie on a rack in the middle of the oven and bake for 50 minutes or until the crust is beginning to brown. Paint the crust with the barley malt and bake for an additional 10 minutes, or until the crust is brown and has a shiny glaze. Remove the pie from the oven and let it sit for a few minutes before cutting.

savory oil-based pie crust

This is the flakiest oil crust I've ever tasted. It's made from a blend of unbleached flour and whole wheat pastry flour, with an added touch of vinegar for tenderness. The dough is ready to roll and bake as soon as it's made—and it rolls out very easily on parchment paper.

MAKES ONE DOUBLE-CRUSTED PIE

2 cups unbleached white flour, chilled

1 cup whole wheat pastry flour, chilled

1 teaspoon baking powder

½ teaspoon salt

½ cup very cold canola oil

1 tablespoon cider vinegar

½ cup ice water

TO ENSURE THE FLAKIEST CRUST, HAVE ALL YOUR INGREDIENTS VERY COLD. PLACE THE CANOLA OIL AND WATER IN THE FREEZER 30 MINUTES BEFORE USING. CANOLA OIL IS FULL OF MONOUNSATURATES, WHICH BEGIN TO SOLIDIFY WHEN COLD. THUS, THE CONSISTENCY OF THE CANOLA OIL CHANGES QUITE A BIT—IT BECOMES THICK AND VISCOUS. THIS ALLOWS THE OIL TO CLUMP IN SOME PARTS AND NOT OTHERS—MUCH THE SAME WAY BUTTER D[...] THE FLOUR ALSO WORKS BEST IF IT IS QUITE COLD, SO I STORE MY FLOURS IN THE FREEZER.

• Toss the flours, baking powder, and salt together in a bowl. Drizzle in the oil, a little at a time, tossing lightly with your fingers or a wooden spoon. The flour should lump in different-size pebbles, from very small to ¾-inch lumps. Don't attempt to distribute the oil more evenly than that.

• Combine the vinegar and ice water. Drizzle this mixture over the flour a little at a time as you did with the oil, just until the dough starts to hold together when pinched. Do not add all of the water if you don't need to, but add a little more if necessary. Be careful not to overhandle the dough.

• Separate the dough into two balls if not rolling immediately. Wrap one in plastic wrap or roll immediately.

cranberry–pecan sauce

Pecans give this sweet cranberry sauce extra flavor and texture. Madeira is my favorite choice for the wine, but I've used other sweet dessert wines, such as Marsala. The alchohol cooks off, leaving a lovely lingering flavor. It's a good idea to buy extra cranberries in December to freeze, since they are sometimes difficult to find after the holidays, and this meal is good to make all through the winter months. If you prefer your cranberries on the tart side, use just ½ cup of the maple syrup.

½   cup pecan halves
½   cup Madeira
½ to ¾ cup maple syrup
1   teaspoon ground cinnamon
3   cups cranberries, fresh or frozen
    Pinch of salt

• Preheat the oven to 350°F. Spread the pecans on a baking sheet and toast for 8 to10 minutes, or until fragrant. Remove, let cool for a few minutes, and roughly chop by hand.

• In a medium saucepan, combine the madeira, maple syrup, cinnamon, cranberries, and salt. Cook and bring to a boil, watching carefully to make sure it does not boil over. Uncover and cook at a rapid simmer for 15 to 20 minutes, stirring every so often, until the cranberries have burst and the liquid has reduced enough to become saucy.

• Stir in the pecans and pour into a bowl. Refrigerate until cool. Serve cold or at room temperature.

collard greens and kale with garlic chips

Garlicky oil infuses greens with rich flavor. The garlic chips make a delightfully crisp addition to salads and cooked vegetables as well as to these greens. After making the chips, be sure to let the oil cool down for a few minutes before adding the greens, or else they'll hiss and splatter when they hit the hot oil.

SERVES 4 TO 6

1 pound collard greens
1 pound kale
3 tablespoons extra-virgin olive oil
3 garlic cloves, thinly sliced
   Salt
½ cup water
1 tablespoon fresh lemon juice

CURLY-HEADED KALE AND FLAT-LEAFED COL-
LARDS ARE BOTH HEARTY WINTER GREENS THAT
CAN REQUIRE UP TO 15 MINUTES TO COOK,
DEPENDING ON HOW TOUGH THEY ARE. THEY
BOTH NEED THEIR STEMS REMOVED BEFORE
COOKING.

• Remove the stems from the collard greens and kale and coarsely chop the greens. Wash the greens well in a large bowl of cold water. Lift the greens out of the water and drain in a colander; do not spin dry.

• Warm the oil and garlic together in a large skillet over medium heat for about 3 minutes, just until the garlic is lightly browned. Remove the garlic from the oil with a slotted spoon and set aside.

• Turn off the heat for 2 minutes to let the oil cool. Add enough collard greens and kale to make one layer in the pan. Turn the heat back on and cook, uncovered, over medium heat. As the greens wilt, turn with metal tongs and add more greens to the pan. Keep adding more greens and turning the wilted greens until all the greens are in the pan. Add salt, the browned garlic chips, and the water. Cover the pan and turn the heat to low. Cook for 5 to 15 minutes, depending on the greens, until they are tender. Uncover, sprinkle with the lemon juice, and toss.

daikon pickles

These mild pickles can be eaten after a few hours, but they taste best after sitting for a couple of days. The thinly sliced daikon is not parboiled, as the boiling liquid poured over it is enough to cook it. It takes on a beautiful yellow glow from the turmeric. Sometimes I like to mix in thinly sliced cauliflower florets, which also soak up the yellow coloring. You might double the vegetables and the brine, since these last very well refrigerated for up to a month.

1   pound daikon, peeled
3   medium garlic cloves, sliced thin
2   teaspoons coriander seeds, slightly crushed
1   teaspoon black peppercorns, slightly crushed
1   cup roughly chopped fresh dill
2   cups cold water
¼   cup apple cider vinegar
1   tablespoon salt
1   teaspoon turmeric

• Slice the daikon into ¼-inch rounds. Place the rounds in a heatproof bowl. Add the garlic, coriander seeds, peppercorns, and dill.

• Place the water, vinegar, salt, and turmeric in a small saucepan and bring to a boil. Pour the liquid over the vegetables and let the pickles cool to room temperature.

• Transfer the pickles to a covered container, refrigerate, and let develop for 24 to 48 hours before eating.

Mesclun with Raspberry Vinaigrette

Seitan Bourguignonne

Mashed Potatoes with Parsnips

SERVES 4 TO 6

Here's a great menu to warm the body and soul through a cold winter's night. With its rich and sophisticated flavor, the menu is ideal for entertaining, yet it's much easier to prepare than it looks. "Meat and potatoes" lovers will adore this one.

Technically, "bourguignonne" or "bourguignon" means a dish that comes from Burgundy, land of red wine. But the term has come to signal any dish cooked with red wine. The recipe here features seitan, a chewy "wheat-meat" made from wheat gluten. Its texture resembles that of meat yet it is easier to digest and has its own distinct taste, texture, and lightness. Seitan absorbs nicely the flavor of other ingredients with which it is cooked. The mashed potato–parsnip combination, amazingly enough, makes the whole meal seem almost delicate.

cook's notes

- Marinate the seitan.
- Prep the vegetables for the stew while you roast the seitan, peppers, and onions.
- Put up the potatoes and parsnips to cook.
- Finish the stew and make the salad dressing.
- Mash the potatoes and parsnips.
- To serve, a wide soup bowl or pasta plate is ideal for this dish. Ladle the bourguignonne into the bowl. Place a mound of mashed parsnips and potatoes in the middle. Serve the salad on the side.

mesclun with raspberry vinaigrette

There are several kinds of raspberry vinegars on the market, but my favorite is a balsamic made with crushed whole raspberries. This assertive dressing will not overpower the taste of delicate greens. It is also delicious over cooked greens.

SERVES 4 TO 6

3   tablespoons raspberry vinegar
¼   teaspoon Dijon mustard
1   garlic clove, minced
½   cup extra-virgin olive oil
    Salt and freshly ground black
    pepper
½   pound mesclun, or mixed baby
    greens

• In a small bowl, whisk together the vinegar, mustard, and garlic. Drizzle in the oil, whisking constantly until emulsified. Season to taste with salt and pepper.

• Toss the mesclun with the dressing and serve immediately.

Mesclun mixes usually come prewashed and ready to use. They cost more per pound than other lettuces, but you get a lot of volume and there is virtually no waste.

Mesclun mixes can include as many as 15 to 20 varieties of lettuces and greens, all in the tender baby phase. They can include green, red, and oak leaf lettuces, romaine, mâche, radicchio, mustard greens, mizuna, chard, broccoli rabe, frisée, and herbs such as chervil and sorrel. Edible flowers such as nasturtiums are sometimes included.

seitan bourguignonne

This dish gets its voluptuous flavor from seitan and vegetables that are first roasted in a rich marinade and then stewed with wine and tomatoes. It also makes a great leftover to serve over rice. You can freeze the bourguignonne for a couple of months, and it will taste just as delicious as the day it was made.

Prep the vegetables while the seitan is marinating. Then roast the seitan, mushrooms, and peppers at the same time. You may prefer to substitute tempeh for the seitan, but remember to steam it for 7 minutes before marinating if you do.

SERVES 4 TO 6

½ cup shoyu

2 teaspoons mellow barley miso

2½ cups dry red wine, such as Cabernet Sauvignon

½ cup mirin (sweet Japanese sake)

¼ cup balsamic vinegar

½ cup canola oil

3 garlic cloves, minced

1 bay leaf

¾ pound seitan or steamed tempeh, cut into ¾-inch cubes

½ ounce (½ cup) dried porcini mushrooms

3 cups boiling water

2 medium red bell peppers, stems, seeds, and membranes removed, cut into 1-inch pieces

¾ pound fresh mushrooms, preferably shiitakes

1 tablespoon extra-virgin olive oil

2 onions, halved and thinly sliced (2 cups)

1 28-ounce can plum tomatoes, drained

2 tablespoons tomato paste

1 cup fresh or frozen peas
   Salt and freshly ground pepper
   Cayenne pepper
   Chopped fresh chives, for garnish

- Pour the shoyu into a medium bowl. Add the miso and beat it with a spoon until it is evenly blended. Add ½ cup of the wine, the mirin, vinegar, canola oil, and garlic and whisk together until well combined, then stir in the bay leaf. Immediately set aside ¾ cup of the marinade, and pour the remainder over the seitan cubes. Marinate for 30 minutes.

- Preheat the oven to 375°F.

- Place the porcinis in a bowl and cover with the boiling water. Set aside for 20 minutes.

- Remove the seitan from the marinade and arrange it in a shallow baking dish in a single layer. Pour enough marinade over the seitan to cover halfway. (Save the rest of the marinade, refrigerated, for another use.) Bake for 30 to 40 minutes, or until most of the marinade has been absorbed.

- Meanwhile, in a bowl, toss the red peppers with 2 tablespoons of the reserved marinade. Spread on a parchment-covered baking sheet and roast for 40 minutes, turning every 10 minutes.

- While the peppers roast, remove the stems from the shiitakes and cut into 1-inch chunks. Place the shiitakes in a bowl and toss with ½ cup of the reserved marinade. Put on a parchment-covered baking sheet and roast for 30 minutes, turning after 15 minutes.

- Pour the porcinis and liquid through 2 layers of paper towels placed in a strainer. Reserve the liquid. Rinse the porcinis to remove any remaining dirt and chop them into small pieces.

- Warm the olive oil in a large (6- to 8-quart) heavy-bottomed pot. Add the onions and cook over medium-low heat, stirring occasionally, for 12 to 15 minutes or until the onions have sweated and softened.

- Add the 2 remaining cups of wine, turn the heat to high, and cook until the liquid is reduced by half, about 15 minutes. Turn the heat to medium and add the tomatoes, breaking them up with a spoon. Stir in the tomato paste and cook for 5 minutes.

- Add the roasted peppers and shiitakes. Stir in the seitan with 2 tablespoons of marinade from the baking dish. (If you have less than 2 tablespoons, add all of it.) Add the chopped porcinis and 2 cups of the porcini soaking liquid. Cover and bring the liquid to a boil, then lower the heat to a simmer.

- Add the peas, salt to taste, a generous sprinkle of pepper, and a generous sprinkle of cayenne. Simmer gently, uncovered, for 10 minutes to cook the peas and let the flavors marry. Garnish with chives.

mashed potatoes with parsnips

The combination of mashed parsnips with the potatoes makes this whole ensemble exquisite. The parsnips lightly sweeten the mashed potatoes and give them a distinctive taste. I love to mash potatoes with other vegetables like rutabaga and celery root. Why not try a combination?

SERVES 4 TO 6

2 pounds russet potatoes
(3 medium or 6 small)
1 pound parsnips, peeled and cut
into 3-inch chunks (2 large)
Salt
3 tablespoons extra-virgin olive oil
½ cup unflavored soy milk, warmed
White pepper

MASHED POTATOES ARE BEST EATEN RIGHT AWAY, BUT YOU CAN HOLD THEM IN A DOUBLE BOILER. SET THE MASHED POTATOES IN A HEAT-PROOF BOWL AND SET THE BOWL IN A POT THAT CONTAINS A COUPLE OF INCHES OF WATER. COVER THE POT AND KEEP THE WATER AT A LOW SIMMER.

- Wash the potatoes and place them, without peeling, in a pot along with the parsnips. Cover with cold water and add 2 teaspoons of salt. Bring to a boil, then reduce to a simmer and cook until the potatoes are cooked through, 15 to 30 minutes, depending on their size. Check with a fork to see if they're done. If the potato is softened to the core, it's done.

- Drain the vegetables, reserving the cooking liquid. Hold each hot potato in a dish towel and remove the skin with a peeler. Return the potatoes and parsnips to the pot.

- Add the oil, soy milk, and ¼ cup of the cooking liquid, and mash with a hand-masher. Add more cooking liquid if necessary until you reach the desired texture. Add salt and white pepper to taste.

Cooking the potatoes with the skin on makes them more flavorful than cooking them peeled.

Orange-Ginger Tofu Triangles

Arame Salsa

Citrus-Scented Basmati Rice with Cinnamon and Cumin

Teriyaki Vegetables

SERVES 4

This meal elevates tofu, brown rice, and seaweed to a whole new level. Combining elements from the southwest United States and Japan, this meal is easy, but there are some unexpected elements that make the meal. Tofu triangles, baked in an orange marinade, are spiked with chiles and crowned with cilantro and scallions. The salsa has traditional ingredients, with the quirkiness of sweet arame at the center. The basmati is enlivened with toasted cumin and orange zest, and the teriyaki vegetables make a succulent side. This is great luncheon or Sunday supper fare.

cook's notes

The tofu can be marinated up to a day in advance.

• Press the tofu. Meanwhile, make the marinade.

• Soak the arame. Prep the ingredients for the salsa and make it.

• Marinate the tofu while you prep the teriyaki vegetables.

• Bake the tofu while you make the rice.

• Cook the teriyaki vegetables last.

• To serve, place a mound of rice in the center of the plate. Put one tofu triangle over the rice and the other balanced upright against it on a right angle. Place a small mound of the salsa where the two pieces of tofu meet. Serve the teriyaki vegetables on the side.

orange-ginger tofu triangles

When the flavorful marinade works its magic, the tofu changes into chewy, succulent morsels. You could serve the tofu with the rice and a green salad for a simple meal, or serve it hot or cold in a sandwich, or cut into cubes on top of a salad. It keeps well for days.

Cut the tofu before you press it, but don't separate the pieces until after pressing because it is easier to press the tofu when it's in a block.

SERVES 4

1	pound firm tofu
1	cup fresh orange juice
¼	cup rice vinegar
⅓	cup shoyu
⅓	cup canola oil
4	teaspoons dark sesame oil
3	garlic cloves, minced
1	tablespoon minced peeled fresh ginger
¼	teaspoon hot red pepper flakes
1	scallion, chopped into 1-inch pieces
¼	cup roughly chopped fresh cilantro
2	dried chipotle chiles (optional)

STRAIN THE JUICE OF CITRUS TO GET RID OF PULP AND SEEDS BEFORE MEASURING.

• Turn the tofu on its side and cut it into 4 thin slices. Lay the tofu flat again and cut the block diagonally to make 8 triangles. Without separating the pieces, press the tofu for at least 30 minutes (see page 76).

• In a medium bowl, whisk together the orange juice, vinegar, shoyu, oils, garlic, ginger, and red pepper flakes.

• Separate the pressed tofu pieces and place them in a baking dish in a single layer. Cover with the marinade and sprinkle with the scallions and cilantro. Cut the stems off the chiles, remove the seeds, and place the chiles in the baking dish. Marinate for at least 30 minutes, and up to overnight. Preheat the oven to 350°F.

• Pour off some of the marinade so the tofu is covered halfway. Bake for 40 to 45 minutes, without turning, until the tofu is golden and most of the marinade has been absorbed.

arame salsa

Arame is a very mild sea vegetable, made sweet in this recipe with apple juice or cider. So there's nothing fishy about this salsa; even the kids will like it. The sweet arame is combined with traditional salsa ingredients for a sour and spicy accompaniment. The black arame contrasts strikingly with the reds and greens of the other ingredients in this twist on a classic.

1   cup dried arame (1 ounce)
1   cup apple cider or apple juice
½   medium cucumber, peeled,
    seeded, and cut into small cubes
    (1 cup)
2   tablespoons fresh lemon juice
1   scallion, finely sliced (¼ cup)
½   cup minced red onion
1   small jalapeño, minced
    (1 tablespoon)
¼   cup chopped fresh cilantro
1   garlic clove, minced
    Salt

• Soak the arame in water for 20 minutes. Drain, then place the arame in a medium skillet with the apple cider. Simmer, uncovered, until the cider has completely evaporated, about 10 minutes. Transfer the arame to a bowl and let it sit for a few minutes to cool.

• Add the cucumber, lemon juice, scallions, onions, jalapeño, cilantro, and garlic. Mix thoroughly to combine and season with salt to taste.

citrus-scented basmati rice with cinnamon and cumin

This simple recipe will fill your kitchen with rich and exotic aromas. The addition of toasted cumin seed and orange zest gives this simple rice dish a tasty spark.

SERVES 4

2 cups brown basmati rice
6 cups water
¼ teaspoon salt
2 whole cinnamon sticks
2 teaspoons whole cumin seeds
Grated zest of 1 orange

ZEST IS THE OUTER SKIN OF A CITRUS FRUIT. IT IS USED TO GIVE COLOR, TEXTURE, AND FLAVOR TO VARIOUS PREPARATIONS. THE ZEST INCLUDES ONLY THE SKIN'S BRIGHTLY COLORED PART, WHICH CONTAINS FLAVORFUL AND GOOD-SMELLING VOLATILE OILS. ZEST DOES *NOT* INCLUDE THE UNDERLYING PITH, WHICH HAS A BITTER TASTE. USE A SWIVEL-BLADED PEELER (YOUR BASIC METAL POTATO PEELER) OR ZESTER TO REMOVE ONLY THE PEEL'S COLORED SUR-FACE. IF JULIENNE OR GRATED ZEST IS CALLED FOR, USE A CHEF'S KNIFE TO CUT OR MINCE THE ZEST.

A BEAUTIFUL KIND OF ZESTER IS MODELED AFTER A CARPENTER'S RASP. THIS LONG METAL TOOL GRATES VERY EASILY AND QUICKLY. THE SMALL TEETH ARE DESIGNED TO GRATE ONLY DEEP ENOUGH TO GET THE ZEST AND ONLY THE ZEST, YIELDING CURLS OF NICE, LIGHT ZEST LIKE HAIR.

• Place the rice in a bowl and add water to cover. Swish the submerged grains with your hand, then let the water settle for a moment. Pour off the water, catching the grains at the last moment with a strainer. Transfer the rice to a medium saucepan and toast it over medium heat. Add the 6 cups of water, salt, and cinnamon sticks. When the water reaches a boil, reduce the heat and simmer, uncovered, for about 20 to 25 minutes, or until most of the water has been absorbed. Cover, lower the heat, and cook 5 minutes more.

• Meanwhile, in a medium skillet, toast the cumin seeds for a few minutes until fragrant, stirring continuously to make sure the seeds don't burn. Alternatively, place the seeds in a baking dish and toast for 10 minutes in a 350°F oven. Set aside until the rice is cooked.

• When the rice is tender, remove the cinnamon sticks from the rice and discard. Stir in the cumin seeds and orange zest.

teriyaki vegetables

Teriyaki is such a basic sauce, it's a good one to have in your repertoire to whip up at a moment's notice. Some natural food enthusiasts sing the praises of burdock for its blood-strengthening capacity; I love it for its singularly earthy flavor. It combines perfectly with carrots and daikon. Burdock is the hardest of the vegetables, so you need to cook it 5 minutes longer than the other two. If you can't find burdock, or you don't enjoy its particular taste, parsnip makes a tasty substitution. Cook the parsnip with the carrots and daikon.

SERVES 4

1   burdock root (4 ounces)
¼   cup shoyu
¼   cup mirin
2   cups apple cider or juice
1   2-inch piece of fresh peeled ginger
2   medium carrots (8 ounces)
1   medium daikon (6 ounces)
2   tablespoons kudzu

THESE ARE APPROXIMATE WEIGHTS ON THE VEGETABLES. THE IMPORTANT THING IS TO HAVE 1 POUND OF VEGETABLES WHEN WEIGHED TOGETHER—WHETHER IT'S ONE, TWO, OR THREE DIFFERENT ROOTS.

• Peel the vegetables and cut in a roll cut (see page 15 for directions).

• Place the burdock in a medium skillet with the shoyu, mirin, and 1½ cups of the apple cider. Cut the ginger into 3 pieces and add it to the pot, cover, and bring to a boil over medium heat.

• Lower the heat and simmer for 5 minutes. Add the carrots and daikon and cook for about 10 minutes, or until the vegetables are tender.

• In a small bowl, mix the kudzu with the reserved ½ cup of apple cider. Stir the slurry into the skillet and cook, stirring constantly, until the mixture goes from cloudy to clear and the liquid just starts to bubble. Turn off the heat. The vegetables can be gently reheated if necessary.

Pumpkin, Sage, and Pecan Ravioli

White Bean and Garlic Sauce

Sautéed Arugula

Frizzled Leeks

SERVES 6

This is one of my absolute favorites. Vegetable purées make perfect ravioli fillings, and this one is no exception. Paired with the savory white bean sauce, the sweet pumpkin, sage, and pecan filling makes each mouthful a delight. A little pile of crispy leeks and a garnish of sautéed arugula complete the sensuous experience.

Cozy yet elegant, this meal is perfect for a candlelight dinner; the presentation is quite striking, too. This dish is suitable when you need to make a meal for someone you want to impress, even if it's just yourself.

cook's notes

You can make the raviolis long in advance and freeze them. Otherwise:

- Put the squash in to bake first and start the beans cooking while you make the dough. Let the dough rest while you prepare the filling and get everything prepared for the beans.

- Make the bean sauce.

- Slice the leeks and roast them while you roll out the dough and make the ravioli. Put up water to cook the ravioli.

- Sauté the arugula right before serving.

- To serve, in a wide pasta plate, or even on a flat plate, ladle bean sauce in a circle around the plate. Add 6 to 8 ravioli on top of the bean sauce. Place the sautéed arugula in the middle with a mound of frizzled leeks on top.

a word about pasta

Making pasta dough is not at all difficult, although the directions are involved and detailed. Pasta dough is, in fact, a good place to start for those unfamiliar with dough. Within a short while, it is easy to recognize if your dough has been kneaded properly, or if enough flour has been worked in. A good dough is firm, elastic, pliant, and easy to work with. Traditional pasta dough usually includes eggs as a binder, but the doughs here use a small amount of firm silken tofu as a binder. It works so well that it is virtually impossible to detect a difference in the finished product. While I usually do not advocate using the boxed tofu, in this instance it is my tofu of choice; its consistency is ideal for pasta dough. You can get silken in a firm texture in a box. It comes in 12-ounce packages, which is enough for 3 recipes of dough. The dough handles very well and goes easily through the pasta machine. The dough also freezes beautifully, and it takes only a couple of hours to defrost.

Although you can roll out the dough by hand, a small, inexpensive hand-cranked pasta machine is more than worth the investment as a time-saver. Also, it's just fun to use. A pasta machine rolls out dough evenly and readily.

A ravioli mold, which is a tray with indentations (not unlike an ice cube tray, except with each mold shaped like a ravioli), is another inexpensive and useful tool. Without requiring a lot of effort on your part, it makes uniform ravioli. The half-moon agnolotti shapes and triangles, made by hand, are worth that little extra time.

Stuffed, boiled dough is an important element in most cuisines of the world. Perhaps it is the surprise of discovering something delectable inside each little package that brings out the child in us. Maybe it's that stuffed shapes inherently mean a variety of textures and tastes. Filled shapes are fun to make and can involve a whole pasta-making party or an assembly-line event in which kids can enjoy helping. Stuffed pasta is also the ideal food for an intimate dinner party. You can make the ravioli a week in advance and freeze them without any sacrifice of quality. They are guaranteed to impress your guests. Just follow these steps:

Tear off an egg-size piece of dough and cover the rest with plastic wrap. Flatten the piece of dough into a patty, then square it off into a rectangle. Feed this through the pasta machine on the lowest setting. Fold the dough in half, and send it through again. Repeat several times until the dough is smooth and regular-shaped. Run it through the first setting one more time and then move on to the next setting.

Run through one setting after another, lowering it each time (do not fold the dough any more) so that the sheet gets thinner, wider, and longer each time it goes through. Make sure to catch it and draw it away when it comes through the machine, so it doesn't fold on itself. If the dough becomes too unwieldy, cut it in half and send through half at a time. Or if you have another person to help you, one can feed and catch the dough while the other cranks. When the dough has gone through the next to last setting (or is as thin as you can comfortably work with), it is ready to be stuffed.

If you have a ravioli mold, place the sheet of dough over the mold and gently press it into the indentations. Add the filling and press it in. Add just enough, and press just enough, so that it is flush with the surface of the mold. Lay another sheet of dough on top and press the two sheets together with your fingers to remove any air pockets. Lightly roll over the top surface with the rolling pin that comes with the ravioli mold so that the two sheets stick together at all points where they meet. Turn the mold upside down and carefully peel out the strip of raviolis. If the raviolis have not separated, score the edges with a fluted pastry cutter and peel away the scrap. Separate the raviolis and lay them on a tray. Repeat with the remaining dough and filling. Place the raviolis on a lightly floured tray.

Alternatively, if you don't have a ravioli mold, you can roll sheets of dough and score a grid of 2-inch squares with a ruler and a pastry cutter. Put an equal, well-rounded amount of stuffing on each of the squares. Brush a little water along the edges of the squares in case the dough starts to dry out. Lay the second sheet over the first and press down around the mounds to seal the edges. Cut out the squares with a pastry wheel using a ruler to help guide you. Lay the raviolis on a lightly floured tray.

You can make tortelloni by cutting the sheets of dough with a fluted cutter into disks about three inches in diameter. Put 1 teaspoon of stuffing in the center of each disk of dough. Brush the edge with water, fold each disk over into a thickened half-moon shape, and firmly press the edges together to seal.

You can make pansotti, which are triangles, in much the same way. Cut out 2-inch squares of pasta, place 1 teaspoon of stuffing in the middle, brush the edges with water, and fold over into triangles, pressing the edges together firmly to seal. Or you can cut out rectangles and place filling on one half of the rectangle, fold the other half over, and press the edges together.

At this point you can freeze the ravioli, tortelloni, pansotti, or whatever shape you have made. Spread them flat (separated so they don't touch) on a tray. When they are frozen solid, about 2 hours later, you can stack them. I like to store them in resealable plastic bags. If you have some dough left over, wrap it in plastic and pop it in the freezer to use another time.

Cook the raviolis in a large skillet filled with a 2-inch depth of simmering water for 3 to 5 minutes, depending on the dryness of your pasta and whether or not they were frozen.

Use a slotted spoon to gently lift the raviolis out of the water. It is a good idea to put all of the raviolis on a platter for a moment, before serving, to allow liquid to drain off. Do this without delay so that the raviolis do not get cold.

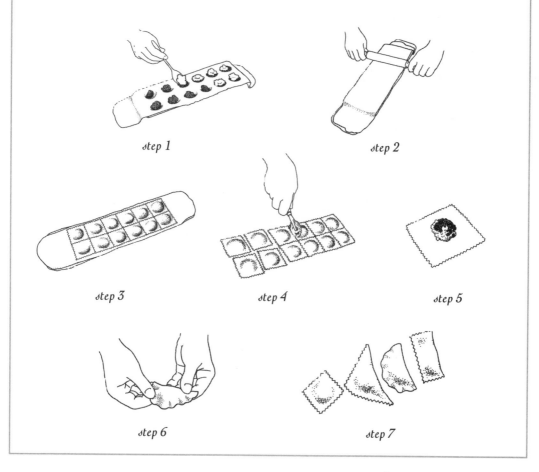

step 1

step 2

step 3

step 4

step 5

step 6

step 7

pumpkin, sage, and pecan ravioli

What a way to eat orange squash! Toasted pecan, fried onion, and sage add so much to the dish—my mouth waters just thinking about it.

You can use most types of winter squash here, but my favorite is kabocha for its bright orange, super-sweet flesh. The filling works best when it is on the dry side.

SERVES 6

1 medium winter squash (2 to 2½ pounds) such as kabocha, butternut, or hokaido (you will need 2 cups cooked squash)
3 tablespoons extra-virgin olive oil
1 onion, finely chopped (1 cup)
½ cup chopped pecans
2 tablespoons minced fresh sage
Salt and freshly ground black pepper
Red Chile Pasta Dough (page 181)

- Preheat the oven to 350° F. Cut the squash in half from stem to bottom and place cut-side down on a parchment-covered baking sheet. Bake for about 45 minutes, or until tender. Let the squash cool for a few minutes, then remove and discard the seeds. Scoop the flesh into a bowl, and mash with a fork. Measure out 2 cups of mashed squash, reserving any extra.

- Warm the oil in a medium skillet. Add the onions and sauté until they are browned, about 10 minutes. Add the pecans and sauté for a few minutes more. Add the squash, mixing until it is heated through. Stir in the sage, and season with salt and pepper to taste. Remove from the heat.

- Roll out the dough and fill and form raviolis as directed on page 178.

- Bring a large skillet filled with 2 inches of water to a simmer. Add the raviolis and cook for 3 to 5 minutes, depending on the dryness of your pasta and whether or not they were frozen.

- Use a slotted spoon to gently lift the raviolis out of the water. Drain briefly for a moment, then serve immediately.

red chile pasta dough

The lovely burnt-orange color of this dough comes from the dried chiles and annatto seeds. Any mild dried chiles work well. The annatto seeds are optional; they intensify the color.

SERVES 6

1   ancho or guajillo chile
1   pasilla or New Mexican chile
1   teaspoon annatto seeds (optional)
2   tablespoons extra-virgin olive oil
¼   pound silken tofu
2   cups unbleached flour
½   teaspoon salt

ANNATTO SEEDS, ALSO KNOWN AS *ACHIOTE*, ARE FROM THE PODS OF A TREE THAT GROWS IN THE YUCATÁN, IN MEXICO. WIDELY AVAILABLE IN MARKETS THAT CATER TO MEXICANS AND CARIBBEANS, THEY ARE PRIMARILY A COLORING AGENT, GIVING FOOD A BRIGHT ORANGE GLOW. THE HARD SEEDS LAST INDEFINITELY IN A CLOSED JAR.

• Remove the stems and seeds from the dried chiles and place in a bowl. Pour boiling water over the chiles and let sit for 10 to 15 minutes, or until they are softened.

• Meanwhile, if you are using the annatto seeds, heat them with the oil in a small saucepan just until the oil is warm and has turned orange. Strain the oil, discarding the seeds.

• Place the softened chiles and 2 tablespoons of the chile soaking liquid, the oil, and the tofu in the blender and blend until smooth.

• Sift the flour onto a work surface (a large wooden board is good) in a mound and make a hollow in the middle. Pour the chile-tofu mixture into the hollow and add the salt. With a fork, first mix the salt into the tofu mixture, and then gradually draw in the flour from the edge, incorporating it little by little until a paste begins to form. Then use both hands to gather the remaining flour together and work it into the dough.

• Work in as much of the flour as you can; there will be a few little straggly pieces of dough and a little flour that does not get worked in. Wash your hands to remove dough. Scrape up the excess dough pieces and flour sticking to the board with a pastry scraper or knife, and sift them through a strainer so that the flour falls back onto the board. Discard the pieces caught in the strainer. Knead, working in the last bit of flour, with vigorous rhythmic motions, for 5 to 10 minutes, or until the dough has a firm, slightly elastic consistency, is not sticky, and has become smooth and pliable. Cover with plastic wrap and let rest for about 1 hour at room temperature.

white bean and garlic sauce

As they are cooking, these garlicky beans send delightful scents wafting through the house. For the best results, use beans you soak yourself. Pressure cooking yields especially fine results, although canned beans make this sauce a snap. The fresh herbs are also really important here.

This is a textured sauce, but you can make it creamy smooth by puréeing it in a blender or food processor.

1½ cups navy beans or great
   northern beans, soaked, or
   2 15-ounce cans, drained and
   rinsed
   Salt
2 tablespoons extra-virgin olive oil
2 onions, finely chopped (2 cups)
8 garlic cloves, thinly sliced
5 sprigs of fresh sage
   Handful of fresh thyme sprigs
1 bay leaf
2 teaspoons lemon juice
   Freshly ground black pepper

• Drain the soaked beans. Cover with 6 cups of water and pressure cook about 8 minutes for the navy beans, or 10 minutes for the great northern beans. Season with salt to taste. Let the beans sit in the cooking liquid for a few minutes to absorb the salt. Drain the beans, reserving the cooking liquid.

Alternatively, on the stovetop, simmer the beans in 8 cups of water, partially covered, for about 1½ hours, or until the beans are soft. Season with salt to taste. Let the beans sit in the cooking liquid for a few minutes to absorb the salt. Drain the beans, reserving the cooking liquid.

• Warm the olive oil in a medium saucepan. Add the onions and cook over medium-low heat for about 7 minutes, or until the onions are softened and starting to brown. Add the garlic and cook for a few more minutes, until fragrant. Add the cooked beans and 2½ cups of the bean cooking liquid. (If you are using canned beans, add 2½ cups water.)

• Tie the herbs together with a cotton string and add to the pot, along with the bay leaf. Cover, bring to a boil over medium heat, reduce the heat, and simmer, partially covered, for 15 minutes to allow the flavors to marry. Add the lemon juice and salt and pepper to taste. Remove the bay leaf and tied herbs.

sautéed arugula

Sautéeing softens arugula's bite and it takes only a few moments. Count on one full bunch of arugula for every two people. The umeboshi vinegar adds a sour-salty pop to the greens.

SERVES 6

1 tablespoon extra-virgin olive oil
3 bunches of arugula, torn into
bite-size pieces
Splash of umeboshi vinegar
Freshly ground black pepper

• Heat the oil in a medium skillet over medium-high heat. Add the greens and cook, tossing with tongs, until heated through and slightly wilted, about 30 seconds. Add the umeboshi vinegar and pepper. Do not overcook or the greens will wilt down to nothing before you know it.

frizzled leeks

Typically, frizzled leeks are deep-fried, but roasting them makes for great flavor with a fraction of the fat. Choose leeks with a long white section, if possible, and avoid the very large leeks, as these can sometimes be tough.

You need to pay close attention to the leeks as they roast. They take a little while to get started, but once they start to cook, they cook fast. Keep an eye on them, removing any that brown faster than the rest.

3 medium leeks (about 1½ pounds)
1 tablespoon extra-virgin olive oil
Salt

• Preheat the oven to 375° F.

• Trim the leeks, leaving only about 1 inch of the green part. (Reserve the rest of the green part for stock.) Cut the leeks in half lengthwise, then cut into 2-inch pieces. Cut each 2-inch segment into very thin matchsticks. Immerse the matchsticks in a bowl of cold water and swish around with your fingers to loosen the dirt. Lift the leeks out of the water to let the dirt sink to the bottom of the bowl. Repeat with clean water if necessary. Dry the leeks well.

• Place the leeks in a medium bowl and toss with the olive oil and salt. Spread on a parchment-covered baking sheet and roast for about 30 minutes, stirring every 5 minutes, until most of the leeks are brown and crispy. Set them aside, and be careful not to snag too many before they go out on the plate, or you won't have enough!

Herbed Ravioli with Porcini Pesto and Tofu "Ricotta"

Basil-Walnut Pesto

Roasted Peppers

SERVES 6

This is an ideal meal for when you're craving extravagant Italian flavors. Put on some Puccini or Verdi to accompany you as you grind the pesto and roll the dough. Make the ravioli in a relaxed moment and freeze it to have on hand so you can entertain at a moment's notice.

The strong flavors in this meal marry beautifully. The mushroom and tofu filling is explosive on its own, but it combines harmoniously with the basil-walnut pesto along with the mellowing qualities of the pasta dough. The basil-walnut pesto is a good all-purpose sauce to have on hand for a quick meal over pasta or to enliven simple grains and vegetables.

cook's notes

If you want, you can make the raviolis well in advance and freeze them.

• Make the pasta dough first.

• While the dough rests, make the filling, then stuff the ravioli.

• Roast the red peppers.

• Put together the basil-walnut pesto.

• To serve, drizzle the basil-walnut pesto in a circle around the plate. Put a spot of pesto in the middle. Place raviolis around the plate. Put the peppers on the spot in the center. Sprinkle the plate with chopped walnuts.

herbed ravioli with porcini pesto and tofu "ricotta"

Not one but two layers of filling make these festive raviolis seem extra special. Although the tastes of the tofu cheese and porcini pesto on their own may seem strong—heavy on the salt and garlic—this is intentional. When encased in dough and cooked, then eaten with the other dishes on the menu, the filling fulfills its roll in the overall balance.

Since the ravioli dough is somewhat translucent, it looks better to have the tofu layer of the filling facing up. If you use a mold, that will mean putting the tofu in first. Just a dab of the porcini pesto is needed, as the dried mushrooms are intensely flavorful.

SERVES 6

tofu "ricotta"

½   pound tofu, pressed (see page 76)
3   tablespoons extra-virgin olive oil
2   tablespoons fresh lemon juice
½   teaspoon salt
2   garlic cloves, peeled
1   teaspoon mellow barley miso
1   tablespoon fresh rosemary, finely chopped
    Herbed Pasta Dough (page 186)

porcini pesto

1½   ounces dried porcinis (1½ cups)
3   medium garlic cloves, peeled
¼   cup pine nuts or walnuts
¼   cup extra-virgin olive oil
½   teaspoon salt, plus more to taste
    Freshly ground black pepper
¼   cup finely chopped chives

make the tofu "ricotta":

• In a food processor fitted with a metal blade, combine the tofu, oil, lemon juice, salt, garlic, and miso. Process, stopping a few times to scrape down the sides, until the tofu is smooth with a slightly granular texture. Add the chopped rosemary and pulse to combine. Remove from the processor and set aside. Wash out the bowl of the food processor.

make the porcini pesto:

• Place the mushrooms in a bowl, pour boiling water over them, and let soak for 20 minutes. Drain the mushrooms and clean them thoroughly to remove all the sand attached to the stems. Discard the soaking liquid.

• Combine the mushrooms, garlic, pine nuts, oil, salt, and pepper in the food processor and process until smooth. Add the chives and pulse to combine. Taste for seasoning.

• Roll out the dough and fill the raviolis according to the directions on page 185, spooning in ½ teaspoon of tofu "ricotta" first, then adding a heaping ½ teaspoon of porcini pesto on top. Cover with the second sheet of dough to encase the filling. The raviolis can be frozen at this point.

• Cook the raviolis in a large skillet filled with 2 inches of simmering water for 3 to 5 minutes, depending on the dryness of your pasta and whether or not they were frozen.

• Use a slotted spoon to gently lift the raviolis out of the water. Drain briefly, then serve immediately.

herbed pasta dough

2 tablespoons extra-virgin olive oil
¼ pound silken tofu (preferably firm Mori-Nu)
2 tablespoons water
½ teaspoon salt
2 cups unbleached white flour
⅓ cup minced fresh herbs (a combination of flat-leaf parsley, chives, and rosemary)

• Combine the oil, tofu, water, and salt in the blender and blend until smooth.

• Sift the flour onto a work surface (a large wooden board is good) in a mound and make a crater in the middle. Pour the tofu mixture into the hollow. Mix the minced herbs into the tofu mixture with a fork, then gradually draw in the flour from the edges of the crater.

• Continue to incorporate the flour little by little until a viscous paste begins to form. Then, with both hands, gather the remaining flour together and put it over the paste. Work the flour into the paste. If the paste does not absorb all the flour, and if the ingredients cannot be easily worked, add a little water and work it in with both thumbs. But be patient and work the dough thoroughly before you resort to this.

• Press the dough into a ball and work in as much of the flour as you can; there will be a few little straggly pieces of dough and a little flour that does not get worked in. Wash your hands to remove dough. Scrape up the excess dough pieces and flour sticking to the board with a pastry scraper or knife, and sift them through a strainer so that the flour falls back onto the board. Discard the pieces caught in the strainer. Knead, working in the last bit of flour, with vigorous rhythmic motions, for 5 to 10 minutes, or until the dough has a firm, slightly elastic consistency, is not sticky, and has become smooth and pliable. Cover with plastic wrap and let rest for about 1 hour at room temperature.

basil–walnut pesto

The addition of the miso intensifies the pesto and gives it a "cheese-like" quality, which is necessary since it will be diluted when served. I often serve it on top of polenta, bruschetta, or roasted potatoes.

Thin out the pesto with ½ cup boiling water right before serving (use the water in which you simmered the ravioli). If you are serving only a portion of the pasta, thin out enough pesto in the ratio of 2 parts pesto to 1 part water.

¾ cup walnut halves for the pesto, plus ½ cup for garnish

2 cups fresh basil leaves, firmly packed

1 garlic clove

2 tablespoons fresh lemon juice

⅓ cup extra-virgin olive oil

1 teaspoon mellow barley miso

½ teaspoon salt

¼ teaspoon freshly ground black pepper

PULL BASIL LEAVES FROM THEIR STEMS AND WASH AND DRY LIKE GREENS.

• Preheat oven to 350°F. Place all of the walnuts on a baking sheet and lightly toast for 10 minutes. Remove from the oven and place in a strainer. Rub the walnuts against the strainer (over the sink or wastebasket) to loosen some of the skins. Don't make yourself crazy doing this. Whatever readily comes off is enough.

• Remove the walnuts from the strainer and add ¾ cup to a food processor fitted with a metal blade. Then add all the other ingredients. Process until smooth. By hand—not in the food processor—chop the remaining ½ cup of walnuts into pieces. Reserve for garnish.

roasted peppers

These simple peppers—a great basic to have in your refrigerator—make a bright and tasty accompaniment to pasta; moreover, a little roasted pepper tossed into a vegetable sauté, a salad, or a sandwich adds color and flavor. Covered, the peppers keep well in the refrigerator for a week.

SERVES 6

3 medium red bell peppers
1 tablespoon extra-virgin olive oil
1 teaspoon balsamic vinegar
Salt and freshly ground black pepper

• Place 1 of the peppers directly on the grate over a gas burner. Turn the heat to high and leave the pepper to cook until one side is blistered and charred. Use tongs to turn the pepper and cook each side until the whole surface is blackened. This should take only a few minutes. Place the pepper in a plastic or paper bag or under an inverted bowl to steam the skin loose. Repeat with the remaining peppers. Leave for about 15 minutes, and the skin will steam itself loose. When the peppers are cool enough to handle, remove the charred skin, using a paring knife if necessary. Don't run the peppers under water to remove the skin, as that washes away a lot of flavor. (I like to have a small bowl of water nearby to dip my fingers in—this makes slipping off the skin much easier.) Discard the stem and seeds.

As an alternate method, halve the peppers and remove the stems, seeds, and white membranes. Place cut-side down on an oiled or parchment-covered baking sheet. Place in a very hot oven or under a broiler. Roast or broil until evenly charred. Remove from the oven or broiler and cover immediately, and proceed as above.

• Cut the peppers into 1-inch strips. Toss with the oil and vinegar and season to taste with salt and pepper.

Tofu-Leek Tart with Pine Nut Crust

French Lentil Sauce

Fennel and Asparagus Salad with Beets

SERVES 6

Quiche, a savory custard encased in pastry, originated in Lorraine, a territory to which both France and Germany have laid claim at various points in history. Originally, quiche had a breadlike crust; in fact, the French word *quiche* derives from *kuchen*, the German word for cake.

The tofu-leek tart in this recipe is quichelike; it comprises an egg-free "custard" made up of whipped, flavored tofu that is baked with leeks and sautéed mushrooms. The versatile and piquant French lentil sauce paired with it makes a perfect counterpart to the milder tart. It's a simple supper that would work well as a brunch or lunch dish, if you substituted a tossed green salad for the fennel and asparagus one.

cook's notes

- Press the tofu.
- Put the beets and lentils up to cook.
- Make the crust and prebake it for a few minutes. Prepare the topping, and then the filling.
- While the tart is baking, finish the sauce and the salad.
- To serve, put a puddle of sauce on one side of the plate with a wedge of tart on top. Place the salad on the side of the plate on a bed of wilted beet greens or other greens.

tofu-leek tart with pine nut crust

The tofu in this tart is ultra-creamy and slightly tangy. Sweated leeks and a thick crown of sautéed mushrooms give it substance and an elegant appearance, but feel free to change the vegetables. The puréed tofu serves as a good vegan base for endless possibilities of toppings.

A mixture of wild, or at least of wild and cultivated, mushrooms is most pleasing for the tart. I often choose oyster, shiitake, and crimini with very good results. The simple press-in crust is enriched with pine nuts; for a tasty variation, replace the pine nuts with sesame seeds.

SERVES 6

crust

½   cup pine nuts
1   cup whole wheat pastry flour
¼   teaspoon baking powder
2   tablespoons extra-virgin olive oil
¼   cup unflavored soy milk
    Salt

mushroom topping

1   tablespoon extra-virgin olive oil
6   cups thinly sliced mixed
    mushrooms (about 1 pound)
2   tablespoons shoyu

tofu-leek filling

4   tablespoons extra-virgin olive oil
3   cups chopped leeks, white part
    only (see page 191)
1   pound firm tofu, pressed (see
    page 76)
2   tablespoons rice vinegar
2   medium garlic cloves, peeled
2   teaspoons mellow barley miso
1   teaspoon salt
    Freshly ground black pepper
1   tablespoon arrowroot powder
2   teaspoons chopped fresh
    rosemary

make the crust:

- Preheat oven to 350°F.

- In a food processor fitted with a metal blade, grind the pine nuts with a few tablespoons of the flour until finely ground. The flour will keep the nuts from turning into paste. Transfer to a medium bowl, add the remaining flour and the baking powder, and whisk to combine thoroughly.

- In a small bowl, whisk the oil, soy milk, and a pinch of salt. Add to the flour mixture, stirring until the dry ingredients are completely moistened.

- Press the crust into an oiled 9-inch tart pan. (Placing a piece of plastic wrap between your fingers and the dough will facilitate pressing.) Press the last few times with your thumb around the sides where the bottom of the pan meets the side to make sure there is no excess crust there. Use a knife to cut off any excess along the top of the tart pan, then poke holes all over the crust with the tines of a fork. Bake the shell for 5 minutes, then remove from the oven and set aside. Do not turn off the oven.

make the mushroom topping:

- Heat the oil in a medium saucepan over medium-low heat. Add the mushrooms and sauté for several minutes, then add the shoyu and cook for 10 to 15 minutes, or until the mushrooms have released their juices and shrunk considerably. The pan should be almost dry. Set aside.

make the tofu-leek filling:

- Warm 1 tablespoon of the oil in a medium skillet. Add the leeks and sauté over medium-low heat for 10 to 12 minutes, or until the leeks have softened. They should be only lightly browned. Set aside in a medium mixing bowl.

- In a food processor, combine the tofu, the 3 remaining table-spoons of oil, the rice vinegar, garlic, miso, salt, and pepper to taste and process until completely smooth. It takes a good few minutes of running the food processor to change the texture from gritty to creamy. Stop the processor frequently to scrape down the sides. When the tofu is very smooth, add the arrowroot and rosemary and process for another 30 seconds to combine.

- Add the tofu mixture to the bowl with the sautéed leeks and gently combine. Spread the filling evenly over the prebaked crust. Evenly distribute the mushrooms across the top of the tart and press them gently into the tofu. Bake for approximately 40 minutes, or until the filling is firm and the crust has lightly browned.

- Remove the tart from the oven and let it sit for a couple of minutes before removing the rim of the pan. Serve warm.

The white part of the leeks is the usable part, so look for medium leeks with the largest amount of white stem. The greens, however, are great in stock. Cut the greens off about an inch above the white part, and slice off the roots. Halve the leaves lengthwise and cut up the leeks according to the recipe. The cut leeks should be washed by immersing them in a bowl of cold water. Swish the pieces around in a bowl for a minute or two until no traces of dirt or sand are left clinging to them. You may have to rub away some dirt. Allow the dirt to settle at the bottom of the bowl, then carefully scoop out the leeks with a skimmer or strainer. Don't pour the leeks into a strainer, or the dirt will come right out of the bowl with them and get trapped in the leeks.

french lentil sauce

Half the lentils are puréed, then sautéed in olive oil with red pepper flakes to add a flavorful bite to this smooth, rich gravy. My recipe tester loves this so much she makes it practically every other day! The sauce is great on pasta, especially on small shapes like orecchiette.

In a pinch, you can use regular brown lentils, but French lentils (lentilles du Puy) hold their shape better and are more elegant.

1   cup French lentils
5   cups water
1   bay leaf
2   sprigs of fresh rosemary, plus 1
    teaspoon minced fresh rosemary
4   sprigs of fresh thyme, plus
    1 teaspoon minced fresh thyme
3   fresh sage leaves, plus 1 teaspoon
    minced fresh sage
    Salt
3   tablespoons extra-virgin olive oil
¼   teaspoon hot red pepper flakes
    Freshly ground black pepper

YOU CAN TIE THE HERBS IN A CHEESECLOTH TO MAKE THEIR REMOVAL EASIER, OR YOU CAN PUT THEM RIGHT INTO THE PAN WITH THE LENTILS. THE HERBS THEMSELVES WILL SOFTEN, BUT YOU WILL NEED TO REMOVE THE ROSEMARY AND THYME STEMS AND THE BAY LEAF BEFORE PURÉEING.

FOR MINCED ROSEMARY AND THYME, STRIP THE LEAVES OFF THE BRANCHES OPPOSITE THE DIRECTION IN WHICH THEY GROW. FOR SAGE, SIMPLY PULL THE LEAVES OFF THE STEM.

• Sort through the lentils and wash them in cold water. Place the lentils in a saucepan with the water, bay leaf, sprigs of rosemary and thyme, and sage leaves. Bring to a boil over high heat, then lower the heat to a simmer and cook, partially covered, for 25 to 35 minutes, or until the lentils are tender. Add salt to taste and remove the herb sprigs, sage leaves, and bay leaf.

• Remove 1 cup of the lentils with a slotted spoon and place in a blender with ½ cup of the cooking liquid. Blend until smooth. Transfer the puréed lentils to a fine strainer and press through with a wooden spoon into a small saucepan. Some of the skins and pulp will get caught in the strainer and you will be left with a fine purée. Discard the pulp.

• Add the oil and red pepper flakes to the lentil purée in the saucepan and heat just until the mixture reaches a boil. Whisk as you heat the mixture to make sure the oil completely works its way into the lentils.

• Return the lentil purée to the pot with the whole lentils. Simmer together for 5 minutes to allow the flavors to marry. Add more salt if necessary, and add pepper to taste. Stir in the minced herbs.

fennel and asparagus salad with beets

Keep the beets separate from the fennel and asparagus until the last minute to prevent the beets from bleeding onto the other vegetables. Beet greens, often overlooked, are sweet and tasty and work well here right under the salad. If you can't buy beets with their greens, place the salad on a bed of arugula, watercress, frisée, or mesclun.

SERVES 6

3 medium beets with greens (1 pound)
5 tablespoons balsamic vinegar
2 garlic cloves, peeled
2 teaspoons capers, rinsed
6 tablespoons extra-virgin olive oil
1 cup fresh basil leaves, packed
  Salt and freshly ground black pepper
½ pound asparagus
½ medium head of fennel

YOU CAN PREPARE THE BEETS IN A PRESSURE COOKER: COVER WITH WATER AND COOK OVER HIGH PRESSURE FOR 10 MINUTES. ALLOW THE PRESSURE TO COME DOWN NATURALLY, OR USE THE QUICK-RELEASE METHOD BY RUNNING WATER OVER THE TOP OF THE COOKER TO BRING DOWN THE PRESSURE.

A MANDOLINE, IF YOU HAVE IT, IS A HANDY DEVICE FOR CUTTING THE FENNEL PAPER-THIN. PLASTIC MANDOLINES ARE READILY AVAILABLE AT ASIAN MARKETS AND COOKWARE STORES.

• Separate the beets from the greens. Place the beets in a medium saucepan and cover with water. Bring to a boil over high heat, lower the heat to a simmer, and simmer for about 45 minutes, or until the beets are tender.

• Meanwhile, make the dressing. Place the vinegar, garlic, capers, oil, and basil in a blender and blend until smooth. Season with salt and pepper to taste. Set aside.

• Remove the beets from the hot liquid and place in a bowl of cold water until cool enough to handle. Remove the skins; they should slip off quite easily. Cut the beets in half and slice each half into ½-inch wedges. Place the beets in a small bowl and toss with one third of the dressing.

• Bring a large pan of salted water to a boil. Trim off the hard stem ends of the asparagus (about 1 inch from the end). Slice the spears on the diagonal into 2-inch pieces. Blanch in the boiling water, uncovered, 3 to 5 minutes, or until they are cooked but still crisp. Drain the asparagus and place it in cold water to stop the cooking. Transfer to a medium bowl.

• With a paring knife, cut out the fennel's hard core. Slice the bulb lengthwise very thin and add to the asparagus. Pour the remainder of the dressing over and mix thoroughly.

• Cut off and discard any thick stems from the beet greens, and cut the greens into bite-size pieces. Wash thoroughly, then put the beet greens in a skillet and toss gently over medium heat. The water from the greens is enough liquid to cook them—you don't need to add more. Remove the greens when they are lightly wilted, after about 3 minutes.

• To serve the salad, arrange some beet greens on each plate. Place some of the asparagus–fennel mixture on top and finish with some of the beets.

Millet–Sunflower Croquettes with Smoky Black Bean Sauce

Roasted Asparagus

"Sour Cream" with Ginger and Chives

Jicama, Radish, and Watercress Salad with Avocado Dressing

SERVES 4

This is probably the easiest menu in the book to prepare, and you can even make the croquette mixture a day in advance. The delicate colors and refined flavors would lend themselves to a luncheon gathering. The millet–sunflower croquettes with their soft bodies and light crusts lie in a pool of smoky black bean sauce. With the gingery "sour cream," crunchy salad, and roasted asparagus, this meal is ideal for early spring.

cook's notes

You can make the tofu cream and salad dressing the night before. You can, in fact, make everything but the roasted asparagus in advance.

• Start the beans in one pot and the millet and grits in another. Meanwhile, toast the sunflower seeds.

• Make the tofu cream, then the salad dressing.

• Form the croquettes. Put the asparagus in to bake at the same time. Add the croquettes 5 minutes later. While they are baking, make the salad and finish the sauce.

• For a beautiful circular presentation, make three equidistant puddles of black bean sauce on each serving plate, and place a croquette on each. Top each croquette with a dollop of the tofu cream. Mound the salad in the middle, with a border of tortilla chips separating the salad from the beans. Arrange a couple of asparagus spears over each of the croquettes.

millet–sunflower croquettes

These tasty little croquettes have a little oil in the mixture, which makes them golden and crusty when baked. I inevitably end up eating some of the mixture before it gets formed into cakes, as it makes a tasty porridge. I love these as leftovers, for breakfast especially, and in a pinch they make a good snack on the run, right out of the refrigerator!

The millet is not toasted here and is cooked with an unusually high ratio of grain to liquid, which makes the croquettes hold together well. Quick-cooking corn grits, found in natural food stores, add flavor and textural contrast; they also help to solidify the croquette.

SERVES 4

½ cup sunflower seeds
4   cups water
½ teaspoon salt
3   tablespoons canola oil
¾ cup millet, washed
¼ cup corn grits
1   onion, finely diced (1 cup)
1   tablespoon fresh thyme leaves

• Preheat the oven to 350°F. Spread the sunflower seeds on a baking sheet and toast for about 10 to 12 minutes, or until they are golden brown. Do not turn off the oven.

• Meanwhile, in a medium pot or saucepan, bring the water to a boil. Add the salt and 2 tablespoons of the oil. Add the millet and corn grits, turn the heat down to a simmer, and cook, uncovered, for 20 to 25 minutes, stirring every so often to make sure the grains are not sticking. As it becomes thicker, you will have to stir more frequently.

• Meanwhile, in a medium skillet, warm the remaining 1 tablespoon of oil over medium-high heat. Add the onions and sauté until browned, about 8 minutes. Stir the onions into the millet pot as it cooks. When most of the liquid has been absorbed, and the millet is cooked, turn off the heat and let it sit for a few minutes. Stir the sunflower seeds and fresh thyme into the millet.

• Using a ¼-cup cookie scoop or measuring cup, make mini croquettes. To help keep the mixture from sticking to your scoop, either oil your scoop or dip it in cold water after every 2 scoops. Push the mixture firmly into the scoop to form croquettes. Place the croquettes on a parchment-covered baking sheet.

• Bake the croquettes for 20 minutes, or until they are crusty and golden. Serve hot.

smoky black bean sauce

These mild, saucy, flavorful beans get a hint of smoky spice from a chipotle chile, which cooks along with them but is discarded before puréeing. Use these beans as an accompaniment to polenta or spread them on corn tortillas with salsa and avocado.

The pressure cooker gives these beans the perfect saucy consistency and they do not need to be puréed. To achieve that same consistency if using beans cooked on the stovetop, and especially canned ones, purée half the beans.

1½ cups soaked black beans, or
    2 15-ounce cans, drained and
    rinsed
1   chipotle chile, or any hot smoked
    chile
4   cups water
1½ teaspoons salt
1   tablespoon extra-virgin olive oil
1   medium onion, cut into small dice
    (1 cup)
2   garlic cloves, minced
1   teaspoon ground coriander
    Freshly ground black pepper
1   teaspoon fresh lemon juice

• To a medium pot or saucepan, add the beans, chile, and the water. Bring the liquid to a boil, lower the heat, and simmer, partially covered, for about 1½ hours, or until the beans are soft. Add the salt to the beans, remove the chile, and discard. Take out 1 cup of beans, purée them in a blender, and return them to the pot. Or use an immersion blender to thicken the beans.

Alternatively, place the soaked beans, the chile, and 3 cups of water in a pressure cooker. Bring up to boil with the lid loosely covering, then lock it down and cook at high pressure for 12 to 16 minutes. Let the pressure release naturally. Add the salt to the beans, remove the chile, and discard.

If using canned beans, drain and rinse the beans and place in a saucepan. Add 1 cup of water and the chile and simmer for 20 minutes, partially covered, to allow the chile flavor to develop. Remove the chile and discard, and salt beans to taste (you won't need the full 1½ teaspoons). Take out 1 cup of the beans, purée them in a blender, then return them to the pot. Alternatively, use an immersion blender to thicken the beans.

• Warm the oil in a medium skillet and cook the onions and garlic over medium heat for 10 minutes, or until the onions are soft and beginning to brown. Add the coriander and cook a couple more minutes.

• Stir the onions into the beans and adjust the salt. Add black pepper to taste, then mix in the lemon juice.

roasted asparagus

Roasting is not the most obvious way to cook asparagus, but it's delicious, and the frizzled tips are especially tasty. It's a handy way to cook large quantities of asparagus for a crowd, too, as it doesn't require watching or split-second timing.

SERVES 6

1 pound medium asparagus, washed
Extra-virgin olive oil
Salt

• Preheat the oven to 375° F. Cut off the hard ends of the asparagus and discard. In a bowl, toss the asparagus with oil to coat lightly, then sprinkle with salt. Spread the asparagus on a parchment-covered baking sheet and roast for about 20 minutes—more or less, depending on size—until it is tender and beginning to brown. If baking the asparagus with the croquettes, they will need an extra 5 to 10 minutes at 350° F.

"sour cream" with ginger and chives

The creamy texture and sour, refreshing taste of this cream make it an appealing partner for burritos and baked potatoes as well as for the savory croquettes. It keeps well for up to four days refrigerated.

½ pound silken or soft tofu
3 tablespoons canola oil
2 tablespoons fresh lemon juice
2 teaspoons brown rice vinegar
¾ teaspoon salt
1 tablespoon peeled, chopped ginger, or 1 tablespoon ginger juice (see Note)
2 tablespoons minced fresh chives or thinly sliced scallions

• In a food processor fitted with a metal blade, combine the tofu, oil, lemon juice, brown rice vinegar, salt, and ginger. Process until very smooth. Add chives or scallions and pulse to combine.

TO MAKE 2 TABLESPOONS OF GINGER JUICE, GRATE A 2-INCH PIECE OF GINGER, SKIN INCLUDED. SQUEEZE THE JUICE OUT WITH YOUR HANDS OVER A SMALL BOWL, OR PLACE GINGER IN A CHEESECLOTH AND SQUEEZE THROUGH THE CHEESECLOTH. GRATE AN ADDITIONAL 1-INCH CHUNK OF GINGER FOR EVERY TABLESPOON MORE OF JUICE THAT YOU WANT.

jicama, radish, and watercress salad with avocado dressing

Despite the sharp flavors, this is a delicate, dainty salad. The creamy green avocado dressing balances, in texture as well as in taste, the three crunchy vegetables.

dressing

½ medium avocado (ripe, preferably Hass)
½ medium cucumber, peeled and seeded
¼ cup fresh lemon juice
2 garlic cloves, peeled
½ cup chopped fresh cilantro
½ teaspoon salt
¼ cup water

salad

Salt
4 medium carrots
5 radishes, washed and trimmed
1 medium jicama (¾ pound)
¼ cup chopped fresh cilantro
1 bunch of watercress, washed and dried

ORIGINALLY FROM CENTRAL AND SOUTH AMERICA, NOW CULTIVATED IN ASIA, JICAMA LOOKS LIKE A LARGE YAM-LIKE TUBER. ITS EXTERIOR MASKS A SWEET VEGETABLE WITH WATERY AND CRUNCHY FLESH THAT IS BEST EATEN RAW. IT IS GREAT FOR ADDING A SWEET CRUNCH TO SALADS AND IS A PERFECT VEGETABLE FOR DIPS. PEEL THE HARD BROWN SKIN WITH A WIDE VEGETABLE PEELER.

make the dressing:

• Combine the dressing ingredients in a food processor or blender. Blend until creamy.

make the salad:

• Bring a pot of salted water to a boil. Peel and cut the carrots in a thin diagonal cut. Blanch the carrots in the boiling water for 2 or 3 minutes, or until they are cooked but still crisp. Drain the carrots and refresh in cold water to stop the cooking. Drain again and place in a bowl.

• Slice the radishes thin. Peel the jicama and cut it into large matchsticks (page 13). Add the jicama, radishes, and cilantro to the bowl with the carrots and toss. Add the dressing, toss again, and serve on watercress.

Spring Vegetable Ragù

Red Bhutan Rice and Adzuki Beans

Hijiki "Caviar"

Asian Slaw

SERVES 4 OR 5

Here is a meal to herald the coming of spring. The ragù highlights artichokes, snow peas, and brilliant green fava beans, which start appearing in markets in late April and May. Some of these vegetables, such as fresh fava beans and artichokes, are ingredients that you might not use regularly. They're not difficult to master, but there is a little hand work involved in prepping them. I think of this meal as a whole experience in the craft of food making, starting with a satisfying process, and ending with rich reward. The flavors and colors of red adzuki beans, black hijiki "caviar," and green snow peas play off one another like dancers in a ballet. The meal is substantial but light, and is easy to digest. It feels like a refreshing spring tonic after the heavier fare of winter.

cook's notes

In advance: Soak the adzuki beans. Hijiki "caviar" and slaw can be made in advance.

• Put the beans up to cook. Press the slaw and soak the hijiki.

• Prep the ragù. (You need the most time for this.)

• Finish the slaw and make the hijiki "caviar." Put up the rice to cook while you cook the ragù.

• To serve, ladle the ragù into a wide bowl or pasta plate. Place a mound of rice and adzuki beans to one side of the bowl and top with a spoonful of hijiki "caviar." Serve the slaw on a side plate with a few fresh greens popping out from under the slaw.

spring vegetable ragù

A citrus-ginger undertone and the refreshing bright flavors of spring vegetables make this an exceptionally appealing dish. It is not difficult to cook, the only labor-intensive part being shelling the fava beans and trimming the artichokes. A pound and a half of pods yields about one cup of beans when peeled. Grab a chair, have a seat at your kitchen table, and listen to some good music while you shell the beans.

Put up the dashi to cook while you prepare the vegetables. Once they are done, the ragù comes together very quickly. Add the snow peas just before eating. If you are saving some to eat the next day, reserve some blanched snow peas to toss in at the last minute.

dashi

8   medium-size dried shiitakes
    3-inch piece of kombu
¼   cup fresh shiitake stems (see below)
8   cups water

KOMBU, A KELPLIKE SEA VEGETABLE, CAN BE FOUND IN NATURAL FOOD STORES. IT CONTAINS A NATURAL FORM OF MSG AND GIVES BODY TO FOOD COOKED WITH IT, IMPARTING A LOT OF FLAVOR. IT HAS A STRONG TASTE, HOWEVER, AND SHOULD BE REMOVED AFTER 5 MINUTES OF SIMMERING.

ragù

    Salt
¼   pound snow peas, strings removed
1½ pounds fresh fava beans, shelled
2   tablespoons extra-virgin olive oil
¼   cup minced shallots
½   pound shiitakes, stems removed (use for dashi), caps thinly sliced (3 cups)
3   medium to large artichokes or 14 baby artichokes, trimmed (see page 63)
½   cup white wine
1   tablespoon shoyu
4   cups dashi (recipe precedes)
2   tablespoons kudzu dissolved in ¼ cup water

make the dashi:

• Place the dried shiitakes, kombu, and fresh shiitake stems in a 4-quart pot. Cover with the water and bring to a boil over medium heat. Lower the heat and simmer, uncovered, for 5 minutes. Remove the kombu and simmer for 15 minutes more. Strain, discarding the mushrooms.

make the ragù:

• Bring a pot of salted water to a boil. Add the snow peas and blanch for about 1 minute, just until the snow peas are bright green and still crisp. Use a slotted spoon to transfer the peas to a bowl of cold water to stop the cooking. Drain, and set aside. Keep the water on the stove for the fava beans.

• Separate the fava beans that are smaller than a thumbnail from the larger ones, which need to have the peel removed. (The small ones are tender enough to go in the ragú unpeeled.) Blanch the larger beans for 1 minute in the boiling water, then drain, and cool them under cold water. Use your thumbnail and fingertips to break the skins, and peel them off to reveal the emerald-green bean inside. Set aside with the smaller fava beans.

• Warm the oil in a large, nonreactive pot over medium heat. Add the shallots, shiitakes, and trimmed artichokes, and sauté over medium heat for 8 to 10 minutes, or until the mushrooms have cooked down. Add the wine and shoyu, and reduce until the wine is almost evaporated.

• Add the 4 cups of dashi and bring to a boil. Reduce to a simmer and cook, uncovered, for about 10 minutes, or until the artichokes are almost tender. Add the fava beans and simmer, uncovered, just until tender, about 3 minutes.

(continued)

Freshly ground black pepper
2 tablespoons fresh lemon juice
3 tablespoons ginger juice (see page 197)
¼ cup chopped fresh flat-leaf parsley

• Add the dissolved kudzu and stir just until the liquid is thickened and returns to a simmer. Turn off the heat and add salt and pepper to taste, the lemon juice, and the ginger juice. Stir in the snow peas right before serving. Sprinkle with the parsley.

red bhutan rice and adzuki beans

The similar colors of the red Bhutan rice and the adzuki beans blend together handsomely. There is no need to soak adzuki beans if you are pressure cooking, since they take so little time to cook. Soaking, however, does cut down the time on beans cooked on the stovetop. Since the texture of adzuki beans rapidly passes from just cooked to overcooked, I prefer to cook them the minimum time in the pressure cooker, then finish simmering for a few minutes if necessary on the stovetop. The Bhutanese red rice has a pleasingly singular taste and appearance; if you can't find it, however, substitute another short-grain rice.

SERVES 4 OR 5

½ cup adzuki beans, soaked if
   cooking on the stovetop
   Salt
½ cup red Bhutan rice

RED RICE HAS BEEN GROWN IN BHUTAN FOR CENTURIES BUT HAS JUST RECENTLY BEEN IMPORTED INTO THE UNITED STATES. IT IS AVAILABLE IN MANY GOURMET AND NATURAL FOOD STORES. THE SHORT-GRAINED RICE HAS A NUTTY TASTE, A LIGHT, FLUFFY TEXTURE, AND A DARK ROSY-PINK COLOR. IT QUADRUPLES IN SIZE WHEN COOKED.

• In a large pot, cover the beans with 6 cups of water and cook, partially covered, for about 1 hour, or until tender. Salt to taste and let the beans sit in the cooking water for 10 minutes to absorb the salt. Drain.

Alternatively, add the beans to a pressure cooker with 4 cups of water and bring to a boil. Secure the lid and bring up to high pressure. Lower the heat just enough to maintain high pressure and cook for 3 minutes if soaked, or 6 minutes unsoaked. Allow the pressure to come down naturally and release the lid. Add salt to taste. Leave the beans in the liquid for 10 minutes to absorb the salt. Drain.

• While the beans cook, place the rice in a large bowl with cool water. Swish with your fingers, then let the rice settle to the bottom. Pour off the water, catching the last grains of rice in a strainer. Place the rice in a small pot and toast over medium heat until no liquid remains. Add 1½ cups of water and a pinch of salt, bring the liquid to a boil, then reduce the heat and simmer, uncovered, for about 15 minutes, or until most of the liquid is absorbed. Cover, lower heat to very low, and cook an additional 5 minutes. Remove from the heat and let stand, covered, for 5 minutes. Mix in the adzuki beans and fluff the rice. Add more salt if necessary.

Adzuki beans (also spelled Aduki or Azuki) are small, reddish-brown beans with a white stripe along one edge, and are popular in the cooking of Japan and China, where it is even used in desserts. It has a sweet, almost nutty flavor when cooked and is among the highest in protein and lowest in fat of all beans. It is also packed with minerals. According to traditional Chinese medicine, adzukis strengthen the kidneys. Since ancient Chinese folk wisdom says kidneys govern the emotion of fear, adzuki beans are considered a source of strength that helps people confront their challenges bravely. Thus, in China they are served on New Year's Eve to bring courage and good fortune.

hijiki "caviar"

This is a great way to eat hijiki. Chopped into caviar-sized pieces and sautéed with lots of garlic, a small bit on top of milder foods like rice really packs a powerful punch. It keeps very well in the refrigerator for at least a week.

Hijiki is a thin, black twiglike sea vegetable that doubles in size when soaked. It is already precooked (the process involves drying and cooking for hours under pressure, then drying again), so theoretically you need to cook it for only a few minutes. I find, however, that with a good 20-minute soak and a 25-minute braise, its briny flavor is mellowed considerably. The soaking liquid, loaded with minerals, is good for house plants.

½   cup dried hijiki (½ ounce)
2   tablespoons toasted sesame oil
3   garlic cloves, minced
1   tablespoon mirin (sweet Japanese sake)
1   tablespoon plus 1 teaspoon shoyu
    Salt (optional)
1   tablespoon fresh lemon juice

HIJIKI IS ONE OF THE MOST MINERAL-RICH SEA VEGETABLES, WITH APPRECIABLE AMOUNTS OF CALCIUM, IRON, PROTEIN, MAGNESIUM, VITAMIN A, AND VITAMIN C.

• Soak the hijiki for 20 minutes in 2 cups of cold water. Drain. Mince the hijiki so that it resembles caviar.

• Warm the sesame oil in a pan over medium heat. Add the minced hijiki and the garlic and sauté for about 3 minutes. Add the mirin and shoyu and scrape to loosen any bits sticking to the pan. Add water to cover (about 1 cup) and gently simmer for 25 to 30 minutes, or until the water has evaporated.

• Add more shoyu or a sprinkling of salt if necessary. Add lemon juice and stir to combine.

asian slaw

This slaw is a quick version of the spicy Korean cabbage pickle, kimchee, minus the fiery heat. It is light and bright, with pungent flavors and crispy texture. I prefer the mild flavor of napa cabbage here, but everyday cabbage (Dutch head) will work fine.

SERVES 4 OR 5

6 cups shredded napa cabbage
1 teaspoon salt
3 garlic cloves, minced
2 tablespoons minced peeled ginger
1 jalapeño, stem removed and seeded, minced (use red if you can find it)
½ cup chopped fresh cilantro
2 tablespoons apple cider vinegar

CUT OFF THE HEAVY PART OF CILANTRO STEMS. IF USING FOR A GARNISH, PULL OFF THE LEAVES. OTHERWISE, YOU CAN CHOP UP THE DELICATE PARTS OF THE STEM THAT ARE ATTACHED TO THE LEAVES.

• Place the cabbage in a large bowl. Sprinkle the salt over the cabbage and toss to mix. Place another bowl over the cabbage and a put a weight in the bowl. (Anything heavy will do.) Set aside for 30 minutes to let the cabbage wilt. It will shrink considerably. Drain off the liquid.

• Add the garlic, ginger, japapeño, and cilantro to the cabbage, and mix well to distribute the flavorings. Add the vinegar and mix again. Taste to see if more salt is necessary. Let sit at least 30 minutes to let flavors marry.

Napa cabbage, or Chinese cabbage, has yellow to dark green outer leaves with broad white ribs. The large mature heads make wonderfully tender cole slaw. Use the whole cabbage, white ribs and all. It has a mild flavor, is very digestible, and cooks quickly. There is no need to wash the cabbage. All you have to do is remove any wilted or bruised outer leaves.

864 0151

Indonesian Sambal

Rice Noodles with Thai Peanut Sauce

Stir-Fried Vegetables

Mango Slices

SERVES 4

The colors of this dish are as striking as its variety of tastes. The light, crisp vegetables play off against the noodle combination, which, though heavier than the vegetables, is actually quite light itself. The coconut-peanut sambal in this dish is the exotic condiment that unites the flavors of the stir-fried vegetables, noodles, and mango slices in an exotic Southeast Asian mélange with hints of Thailand as well as Indonesia.

Sambals, the Indonesian term for chutneys, are based on fresh fruit, ginger, coconut, herbs, spices, and chiles, among other ingredients, soured with tamarind or citrus. All the ingredients in sambals must be finely chopped. If you're in the mood for a culinary adventure on a hot summer night, this is a fun meal to make.

cook's notes

- Make the sambal. (This can be done up to two days in advance.)
- Make the peanut sauce.
- Prep the stir-fry, then soak the noodles. Meanwhile, cut the mangos into pieces.
- Heat the peanut sauce. Cook the stir-fry and toss the noodles with peanut sauce.
- To serve, place a mound of noodles in the middle of a plate or wide pasta bowl. Top with the stir-fried vegetables. Sprinkle the sambal around the edges of the plate, so that it encircles the vegetables but does not cover them. Lay four or five mango slices around the edges.

indonesian sambal

This sambal is really fun to sprinkle over the stir-fry and noodles, as well as other dishes. Mango slices dipped in the sambal also make an exotic snack. Although it appears to be little more than toasted coconut and chopped peanuts, the taste tells you there is more here than meets the eye. A medley of flavor comes from cumin, ginger, garlic, fried onions, and tamarind. Refrigerated, the sambal stays good for over a week.

Tamarind, the fibrous pod of the tamarind tree, is a brown sticky substance that is used in East Asian and Indian cooking as a souring agent. It is readily found in Indian groceries, and comes in a caked paste or a jar of concentrate.

SERVES 4

1   tablespoon finely chopped peeled ginger
1   garlic clove, minced
½   cup unsweetened coconut flakes
    Pinch of salt
    Pinch of cayenne pepper
½   teaspoon ground cumin
1   teaspoon tamarind concentrate
2   tablespoons peanut oil
¼   cup finely diced onion
¼   cup chopped roasted, unsalted peanuts

• In a medium bowl, mix together the ginger, garlic, coconut, salt, cayenne, and cumin. Work in the tamarind concentrate until it is evenly distributed.

• Warm the oil in a medium skillet. Add the onions and sauté over medium heat for about 5 minutes, or until they are just starting to brown. Add the coconut mixture and sauté over medium-low heat for about 5 minutes, stirring constantly, until the mixture is browned. Remove from the heat and add the chopped peanuts. Add more salt to taste.

I PREFER TAMARIND CONCENTRATE TO THE PASTE, SINCE IT IS EASIER TO USE, BUT THEY CAN BE USED INTERCHANGEABLY. TO RECONSTI-TUTE THE PASTE, COMBINE 3 TABLESPOONS HOT WATER TO 1 TEASPOON TAMARIND PASTE IN A SMALL BOWL AND WORK THEM TOGETHER WITH THE BACK OF A SPOON TO DISSOLVE AND BREAK UP THE PASTE AS MUCH AS YOU CAN. PASS THROUGH A STRAINER AND DISCARD THE TAMARIND PULP. THIS SHOULD YIELD 1 TABLE-SPOON OF STRAINED SYRUP.

rice noodles with thai peanut sauce

This peanut sauce evokes Thai cuisine in a single burst of flavor. In addition to partnering it with noodles, use this as a dipping sauce for spring rolls or baked tempeh, or drizzle it over simple rice. The amount of rice noodles in this recipe (5 ounces) yields a heavy noodle-peanut combination. If you like it lighter, use a few more noodles (7 ounces). Rice noodles often come in 3.5-ounce packages; the thicker recipe (below) calls for 1½ packages; the thinner, a full 2 packs.

SERVES 4

5 to 7 ounces rice noodles (see introduction)
1 cup coconut milk
2 lemongrass stalks, cut into 1-inch pieces
¾ cup crunchy peanut butter
2 teaspoons maple syrup
2 garlic cloves, minced
¼ cup shoyu
2 tablespoons fresh lime juice
1 teaspoon grated lime zest
1 jalapeño, stem and seeds removed, minced
½ teaspoon salt
   Cayenne pepper
2 scallions, thinly sliced on the diagonal

THE BEST PEANUT BUTTER IS MADE SOLELY FROM PEANUTS; IT HAS NO ADDED STABILIZERS, HYDROGENATED OIL, SUGAR, OR SALT. PEANUT BUTTER OFTEN HAS A NATURALLY OCCURRING LAYER OF OIL AT THE TOP BECAUSE NO STABILIZERS ARE ADDED. JUST STIR IT BACK INTO THE NUT BUTTER BEFORE USING.

RICE NOODLES ARE AVAILABLE AT NATURAL FOOD STORES, GOURMET MARKETS, AND ASIAN GROCERIES. THEY DO NOT NEED TO BE BOILED. A 10-MINUTE SOAK IN BOILING WATER IS ENOUGH TO SOFTEN THEM.

• Place the rice noodles in a bowl. Pour boiling water over the noodles and let sit for 10 minutes.

• Combine the coconut milk and lemongrass in a small saucepan and bring to a boil over medium heat. Turn off the heat and let the lemongrass steep in the hot liquid for 10 minutes. Strain out the lemongrass, then whisk in the peanut butter, maple syrup, garlic, shoyu, lime juice and zest, jalapeño, salt, cayenne to taste, and scallions.

• Drain the rice noodles and place in a serving bowl. Pour the sauce over the noodles and toss to mix well.

stir-fried vegetables

No need to use a wok for this quick stir-fry; a large skillet works perfectly well. Fresh soybeans (edamame) or other shell beans such as cranberry beans are a welcome addition if you are able to find them. Have everything ready before you start to stir-fry, as the cooking is done in a matter of minutes.

SERVES 4

6	tablespoons fresh orange juice
2	tablespoons fresh lime juice
2	tablespoons shoyu
2	tablespoons peanut oil
¾	pound asparagus, hard ends discarded, and spears cut diagonally into 2-inch pieces
1	large red bell pepper, stem, seeds, and membrane removed, flesh cut into 1-inch pieces
6	bok choy leaves, stems cut into ½-inch slices, leaves cut into bite-size pieces
½	pound fresh soybeans or cranberry beans, shelled (optional)
3	garlic cloves, minced
2	tablespoons finely chopped peeled ginger
2	scallions, finely chopped
1	cup basil chiffonade (see page 15)

• In a small bowl, mix together the orange juice, lime juice, and shoyu and set aside.

• Heat the peanut oil in a large skillet over high heat until almost smoking. Add the asparagus pieces, red pepper pieces, and bok choy stems and stir-fry for about 2 minutes. Add the bok choy leaves and shelled beans (if using) and stir for another 30 seconds or so until the leaves start to wilt. Push the vegetables to the side of the pan and add the garlic, ginger, and scallions in the middle; cook for about 30 seconds.

• Add the reserved juice mixture to the pan and toss to coat all the vegetables. Make sure the garlic, ginger, and scallions are well distributed. Cover with a lid and let the vegetables steam for about 1 minute. Remove the lid and stir in the basil. Serve immediately.

mango slices

The mangos are a very important part of this menu both for the cooling, sweet touch they lend and for the visual appeal. The mangos should be ripe but not so soft that it is impossible to cut them into slices.

2   mangos, ripe but not very soft

• Cut a slab off each side of the mango, cutting as close as possible to the pit. Cut the two thinner side pieces similarly. Score the flesh at 1/2-inch intervals. Carefully cut the flesh away from the skin with a paring knife. You should have 1/2-inch wide wedges. Repeat with the other pieces.

Potato Salad with Tarragon Vinaigrette

Chickpea Crepes with Grilled Spring Vegetables, Tofu "Cheese," and Spinach–Basil Sauce

SERVES 4 OR 5

This meal celebrates the fleeting moments of that shortest of seasons, spring. In late April and the first part of May, vegetables that make their way to market for the briefest time are stars. Baby artichokes, ramps, fiddlehead ferns, baby spinach, asparagus, and fresh herbs signal the end of winter and the start of a new season of growth.

To make the most of spring's riches, I like to fill a delicate chickpea crepe with grilled seasonal vegetables, a bright spinach–basil sauce, and a zesty herbed tofu "cheese." It is accompanied by a salad of new potatoes dressed with a lively tarragon vinaigrette.

These eggless crepes are very handy to have in your fridge or freezer. If you have made the crepes a day ahead or defrosted some you've made previously, this meal is simplicity itself. See page 79 for a discussion of crepes.

cook's notes

- Make the crepe batter first and let it sit for at least 20 minutes. (You can make it up to 1 day in advance.)

- Make the potato salad, followed by the spinach sauce and the tofu "cheese."

- Make the crepes.

- Grill the vegetables, then fill and serve the crepes.

- To serve, place two crepes on a plate. Spread with spinach–basil sauce. Fill the crepes with tofu "cheese" and grilled vegetables. Close up one crepe and top with spinach-basil sauce. Leave the other crepe open to display the colorful vegetables inside. Serve with a side of potato salad.

potato salad
with tarragon vinaigrette

This tasty potato salad is redolent of fresh herbs and is amazingly light. Use medium- to low-starch potatoes such as new potatoes, Yellow Finns, or Yukon golds. My favorites are small, low-starch red bliss or white creamers. They look best unpeeled and need only to be halved or quartered. Very small ones do not need to be cut at all. The one potato not to use is an Idaho, or russet, since this starchy tuber tends to break down in salads and is far too heavy tasting.

SERVES 4 OR 5

2 pounds potatoes (low-starch), cut into 1-inch cubes
4 teaspoons salt
7 tablespoons extra-virgin olive oil
1 onion, finely diced (1 cup)
1 celery stalk, cut into small dice (½ cup)
4 tablespoons fresh lemon juice
1 scallion, thinly sliced
1 tablespoon chopped fresh tarragon
4 tablespoons chopped fresh flat-leaf parsley
1 garlic clove, minced
20 scrapes of fresh nutmeg (¼ teaspoon ground)
Freshly ground black pepper

• Place the potatoes in a large pot with cold water to cover and 2 teaspoons of the salt. Bring to a boil, lower the heat to a simmer, and simmer, uncovered, for about 10 minutes, or just until the potatoes are tender when pierced with a fork. Drain the potatoes and carefully transfer to a large bowl.

• Warm 1 tablespoon of the olive oil in a medium skillet. Add the onions and sauté over medium-low heat for 8 to 10 minutes, or until the onions are soft and lightly browned. Add to the potatoes along with the celery.

• In another bowl, combine the lemon juice and the remaining 6 tablespoons of oil, adding the oil in a slow, steady stream and whisking vigorously until emulsified. Whisk in the scallions, tarragon, parsley, garlic, nutmeg, the remaining 2 teaspoons of salt, and pepper to taste.

• Pour the dressing over the potatoes while the potatoes are still warm and gently mix everything together. Let sit for at least 30 minutes to absorb flavors. Add more salt if necessary.

chickpea crepes with grilled spring vegetables

Spring is a marvelous time for grilling vegetables. Most of the young vegetables can go right on the grill, without preblanching. Choose the season's most ephemeral delicacies: baby artichokes, ramps, and fiddlehead ferns are all good examples. Then cook them the simplest way: with olive oil, salt, and pepper. Heaven.

The vegetables suggested below are for the height of spring. As summer approaches, add summer squash and pattypan squash, eggplant, and corn.

The chickpea crepes are the same that were filled with wild mushrooms, roasted cauliflower, and chickpeas for an autumn meal on page 80. Crepes work well in any season.

SERVES 4 OR 5

8   baby artichokes
½   lemon
1   pound asparagus (medium stalks if possible)
1   medium red bell pepper
1   medium zucchini
¼   pound ramps, or 4 scallions
2   ounces fiddlehead ferns (optional)
2   tablespoons extra-virgin olive oil
     Salt and freshly ground black pepper
12   Chickpea Crepes (page 80)

FIDDLEHEAD FERNS ARE THE GREEN SHOOTS OF THE OSTRICH FERN. THESE TIGHTLY SCROLLED VEGETABLES HAVE A DELICATE ASPARAGUS-LIKE FLAVOR AND ARE IN SEASON FOR ONLY A LIMITED TIME IN SPRING; ONCE THEY OPEN AND GROW INTO FERNS, THEY ARE NO LONGER EDIBLE. TO PREPARE THE FERNS, CUT OFF THE HARD STEM ENDS AND IMMERSE IN WATER, AND WASH LIKE GREENS.

• Trim the baby artichokes (see page 63), cut in half, and rub the cut surfaces with the lemon half. Cut off the hard ends of the asparagus and discard.

• Cut the pepper in half lengthwise. Remove the stem end, seeds, and membrane. Cut lengthwise into 1-inch pieces. Cut the zucchini lengthwise into ½-inch slabs.

• Trim and discard the root ends of the ramps or scallions. Trim the ends of the fiddlehead ferns, if you are using them. Place all the vegetables in a large bowl and toss with the oil so that each vegetable gets a light coating of oil. Season with salt and pepper.

• Heat the grill or grill pan. Working in batches if necessary, add the vegetables in a single layer (make sure each vegetable touches the grill) and grill without moving them until they are well seared. The zucchini will grill faster than the asparagus. The ramps will take very little time. Turn and grill on the other side.

RAMPS ARE IN THE LEEK AND SCALLION FAMILY. THEY LOOK LIKE SCALLIONS WITH BROADER, FLAT LEAVES AND A SMALL, WHITE BULB AT THE ROOT END. THEY SURFACE IN THE SPRING FOR ONLY A FEW WEEKS, BUT THEIR UNUSUAL ONION FLAVOR IS SO DELICIOUS (ESPECIALLY GRILLED) THAT THEY ARE WORTH SEEKING OUT.

• When all the vegetables are cooked, cut them into 1-inch pieces (leave the baby artichokes and fiddleheads whole). They are ready to be folded in the crepes, or place them in a baking dish to be heated for a few minutes before serving.

If you choose to roast the vegetables instead of grilling them, you need to add them in stages, with the slower-cooking ones added first. Toss each vegetable separately in a small bowl with a little oil, salt, and pepper. Preheat the oven to 400° F. Add the artichokes to a parchment-covered baking sheet and roast for 10 minutes. Remove from the oven, mix the artichokes around, and add the asparagus and peppers to the same tray with the artichokes. Roast everything for 10 minutes, and remove the sheet. Mix the vegetables around, and add the zucchini and ramps (or scallions) to the same tray. Roast for 10 minutes more, or until all the vegetables are cooked.

tofu "cheese"

Versatile tofu here appears in yet another guise, as an herby mass of cottage cheese–like curds. It can be eaten at room temperature or baked until golden. The tofu does not need to be pressed, since gentle simmering cooks it and firms up the texture. Barley miso gives it a richer taste. Mix it with chopped vegetables and use it for a sandwich spread or bake it into turnovers.

Salt
1 pound firm or extra-firm tofu, drained and cut into 1-inch cubes
3 tablespoons extra-virgin olive oil
2 tablespoons fresh lemon juice
1 garlic clove, minced
2 teaspoons mellow barley miso
   Freshly ground black pepper
1 tablespoon chopped fresh tarragon
1 tablespoon chopped fresh chives

• In a pot of simmering, lightly salted water, gently cook the tofu for 5 minutes. Remove the tofu from the water with a slotted spoon, drain on paper towels, and pat dry. Place in a medium bowl.

• In a small bowl, add the oil, lemon juice, garlic, miso, ½ teaspoon of salt, and pepper to taste, and whisk to combine. Pour over the tofu. Use a potato masher or fork to mash flavorings into the tofu until all the liquid has been absorbed and curds have formed. Stir in the fresh herbs.

• Preheat the oven to 350° F. Place the tofu in a baking dish and bake for about 20 minutes, or until the tofu starts to brown.

a word about grilling

Nothing is more inviting than the taste, look, and smell of grilled foods, and I pull out the charcoal as soon as the snow melts. When grilling outdoors, make sure the fire goes out before you begin to cook. When the coals are covered with ash and glowing within, it's time to begin grilling. Make sure you have everything ready—vegetables tossed or brushed in olive oil to keep them from sticking (then sprinkled with salt and pepper) and a pair of tongs. Be sure to leave the vegetables exactly where you put them on the grill until they are half cooked and ready to turn. You'll get the best-looking grill marks that way.

An indoor gas grill or even a grill pan can give very good results if you don't have an outdoor grill. You won't be able to infuse your vegetables with mesquite flavors (as you can with a charcoal grill), but you will get that special seared vegetable flavor and the requisite grill marks. Do make sure you have proper ventilation; even grill pans create a good deal of smoke.

As an alternative, you can toss the vegetables in oil, salt, and pepper and roast them in a 400° F. oven.

spinach–basil sauce

This bright-green sauce, akin to a spinach pesto, brightens the flavors of tofu or steamed vegetables. Two things to remember to keep the color bright green: add the lemon juice right before you are going to serve the sauce, and heat only what you are going to use. If you won't use all the sauce at one meal, add lemon only to what you will serve; this way, it can sit in the refrigerator for a couple of days and still maintain the bright green color. If you use the fresh oregano, which adds a lot of flavor, stir it in by hand to preserve the flavor of the oregano.

¾ pound fresh spinach
4 tablespoons extra-virgin olive oil
1 medium onion, finely chopped
   (1 cup)
3 garlic cloves, minced
1 cup fresh basil leaves
1 scallion, chopped into 1-inch
   pieces
1 teaspoon mellow barley miso
1 jalapeño, stem and seeds
   removed
½ cup water
2 tablespoons pine nuts
1 teaspoon sea salt
2 tablespoons chopped fresh
   oregano (optional)
2 tablespoons fresh lemon juice

• Prep the spinach by cutting off the bottom few inches of the stems and washing thoroughly. With just the water clinging to the leaves, cook the spinach in a large pot or skillet over medium heat. Stir frequently, or toss with tongs, to push the uncooked leaves to the bottom of the pot until they all have wilted and shrunk and are bright green. Transfer the spinach to a blender.

• Heat 2 tablespoons of the oil in a medium saucepan. Add the onions and garlic and sauté over medium-low heat until the onions are softened and beginning to brown, 8 to 10 minutes. Add to the blender with the spinach.

• Add the basil, scallions, miso, jalapeño, water, pine nuts, the remaining 2 tablespoons of oil, and the salt to the blender and blend until smooth. Remove from the blender and stir in the chopped oregano by hand, if using.

• Add the lemon juice no more than 1 hour before serving. Heat gently, just until warmed through. If necessary, add a little water to make the sauce the perfect consistency.

Paella

Roasted Tomato Sauce

Tofu–Roasted Garlic "Aïoli"

Sautéed Cherry Tomatoes

SERVES 4

Though almost all of them include saffron, there are endless varieties of paella, most of which are nonvegetarian. In my travels throughout Spain, I found the vegetarian paellas consistently disappointing. The imagination and flavor put into the more traditional varieties seemed to be lacking in the vegetarian versions. Taking this as a challenge, I devised a version that includes roasted chickpeas and tempeh cubes along with a cornucopia of vegetables, olives, and capers. The pungent tofu aïoli and roasted tomato sauce round out the dish, which is finished off by the melting, succulent jewels of sautéed cherry tomatoes.

The word *paella* originally referred only to the *paellera*, or wide shallow pan in which the food was cooked. Paella is usually made in large portions for a crowd, an approach that allows for a harmonious medley of ingredients. This dish is a meal unto itself, requiring nothing in the way of side dishes. The pungent garlic sauce serves as a traditional condiment.

cook's notes

- Put the ingredients for the tomato sauce in to roast. Put the garlic in to roast for the aïoli.

- Make the aïoli and the tomato sauce.

- Put in the chickpeas, cauliflower, and tempeh to roast for the paella.

- Make the rice and prep the vegetables.

- Sauté the vegetables and add the rice and roasted items.

- Sauté the cherry tomatoes at the last minute.

- To serve, ladle some tomato sauce onto each large dinner plate. Spoon a large mound of paella over the sauce. Serve the aïoli in a small ramekin. Garnish with the cherry tomatoes and some fresh greens such as mizuna or arugula.

paella

Few dishes make a more impressive party presentation than paella. You can easily double or even triple this recipe to feed a crowd; be sure to scale up the garlicky cream accompaniment, too! Small, even cuts of the vegetables are important for a beautiful appearance. Have everything ready before you begin to sauté, since at that point everything cooks very quickly.

The Moors reintroduced saffron to Europe in the eighth century, and the most sought-after saffron today still comes from Spain. Since its singular flavor is the hallmark of paella, the saffron should be of good quality, which means you're best off purchasing it in the thread form, not the powder. Although it is expensive, a little bit goes a long way.

SERVES 4

roasted chickpeas and cauliflower

1½ cups cooked chickpeas or
    1 15-ounce can chickpeas,
    drained and rinsed
½ medium cauliflower, cut into small
    florets (2 cups)
2   tablespoons extra-virgin olive oil
¾   teaspoon salt

roasted tempeh

1   8-ounce package tempeh
2   tablespoons extra-virgin olive oil
1   teaspoon toasted sesame oil
2   tablespoons shoyu
1   teaspoon paprika

saffron rice

2   tablespoons extra-virgin olive oil
1   onion, cut in half and thinly sliced
    (1 cup)
2   medium tomatoes, stems removed
    (½ pound)
1   cup brown basmati rice
2½ cups water
    Pinch of saffron
½   teaspoon salt

make the roasted chickpeas and cauliflower:

• Preheat the oven to 375° F.

• Toss the chickpeas and cauliflower in the olive oil and sprinkle with the salt. Spread on a parchment-covered baking sheet and roast for 30 to 40 minutes, stirring every 10 minutes or so, until the chickpeas are browned and nutty and the cauliflower is cooked and lightly browned. Set aside.

make the roasted tempeh:

• While the chickpeas and cauliflower roast, cut the tempeh into ¼-inch cubes. Steam over boiling water for 10 minutes. Combine the oils, shoyu, and paprika in a mixing bowl. Add the steamed tempeh and toss to coat. Spread on a parchment-covered baking sheet and roast for 30 minutes along with the chickpeas and cauliflower, until the tempeh is crisp, stirring after 15 minutes.

make the saffron rice:

• Warm the oil in a medium skillet. Add the onions and cook over medium heat for 5 to 7 minutes, or until the onions are soft and translucent. Transfer the cooked onions to a blender. Add the tomatoes and blend until smooth.

• Place the rice in a bowl and cover with water, stirring and swishing around the submerged grains with your hand, then letting the water settle for a moment. Pour off the water, catching the grains at the last moment with a strainer. Transfer the rice to a medium pot and stir over medium heat for a few minutes, until it is toasted and dry. Add the tomato–onion

vegetables

2   tablespoons extra-virgin olive oil
1   small carrot (¼ pound), peeled and cut into small dice
1   celery stalk, cut into small dice (½ cup)
½   medium red bell pepper, stem, seeds, and membrane removed, cut into small dice (½ cup)
½   teaspoon salt
     Freshly ground black pepper
1   small zucchini (¼ pound), cut into small dice (1 cup)
¾   cup fresh or frozen peas
¼   cup sliced black olives, such as kalamata
1   tablespoon capers, drained

purée, the water, saffron, and salt to the pot and stir once to dislodge any grains that have stuck to the bottom.

- Let the liquid come to a boil, uncovered. Lower the heat and simmer, uncovered, for about 30 minutes, or until most of the liquid is cooked out. Cover, reduce the heat to low, and cook for another 5 minutes.

make the vegetables:

- Warm the oil in a large pot over medium heat. Add the carrots, celery, red peppers, salt, and pepper to taste and cook, stirring often, for 5 minutes, or until the vegetables are softened.

- Add the zucchini and cook a few minutes more. Add the peas and cook 5 minutes more, or until the peas are tender. Add the tempeh, chickpeas and cauliflower, olives, and capers and cook, stirring, until everything is warmed through. Add the saffron rice and mix thoroughly. Adjust salt and pepper to taste.

roasted tomato sauce

Roasting tomatoes concentrates their flavor and makes the sauce a snap to prepare. It is especially delicious made from midsummer through autumn, when locally grown tomatoes are abundant.

3   pounds tomatoes
2   onions, halved and thinly sliced (2 cups)
1   jalapeño, stemmed, halved, and seeded
5   garlic cloves, unpeeled
¼   cup extra-virgin olive oil
1   teaspoon salt
     Freshly ground black pepper
8   sprigs of fresh thyme

- Preheat the oven to 375° F. Cut out the stem end of the tomatoes, then cut them in half. Arrange the onions, jalapeño, and garlic cloves in two 9 X 11-inch baking dishes. Arrange the tomatoes cut-sides up on top of the onions. Drizzle the oil over everything, then sprinkle with the salt and pepper to taste. Lay the thyme sprigs over the tomatoes.

- Roast, uncovered, for 40 to 50 minutes, or until the tomatoes are really cooked. Discard thyme. Squeeze the garlic from their skins, then place in a blender with the tomatoes and onions. Pass the sauce through a food mill or sieve. Adjust salt and pepper if necessary.

tofu–roasted garlic "aïoli"

It would be unthinkable to serve paella without aïoli, the garlicky mayonnaise that contains eggs. Tofu is the basis of this eggless cream, but it packs just as much garlic power. Granted, this aïoli by itself is strong. But a little bit served with the paella really enlivens it.

1 small head of garlic, unpeeled (or ½ medium head), plus 1 small garlic clove, peeled
2 tablespoons plus 1 teaspoon extra-virgin olive oil
   Salt
½ pound silken tofu
1½ teaspoons fresh lemon juice

• Preheat the oven to 375°F. Peel off the papery outer layers of the garlic head and cut off the top fifth. Lay the garlic on a piece of aluminum foil large enough to enfold the garlic. Drizzle 1 teaspoon of the oil and a sprinkle of salt over the cut top. Wrap in foil and roast for 30 to 40 minutes, or until the garlic is soft. You want the garlic to be soft enough that it squishes out of the skin when pressed.

• In a food processor, combine the tofu, the raw garlic clove, the remaining 2 tablespoons of oil, the lemon juice, and ½ teaspoon salt. Squeeze the garlic out of its skins into the food processor. Purée until creamy.

sautéed cherry tomatoes

Remember this fast and easy side dish for the cold months, when that fresh tomato taste is so welcome. You have to keep these babies in motion so that they cook evenly—you don't want to overcook any one side or break the skin. When they start to crack and are more or less evenly cooked all around, they are done.

SERVES 4

1 tablespoon extra-virgin olive oil
1 pint cherry tomatoes, stems removed, washed and dried

• Heat the oil in a medium skillet over medium-high heat. Add the cherry tomatoes and sauté until they are heated through and the skin begins to shrivel, about 2 to 3 minutes.

Summer Ratatouille Lasagna

Fresh Tomato Sauce

Mixed Lettuces with Reduced Balsamic Vinaigrette

SERVES 6

One of the most familiar creations from Provence in the south of France, ratatouille is a versatile dish that can be eaten hot or cold. In this menu, it is layered between noodles and olive-caper tofu "cheese." It is anything but an ordinary vegetarian lasagna. Topped with a layer of walnuts, the casserole showcases summer's succulent vegetables. The tomato sauce is not baked into the casserole, but ladled under it. Sourdough batons lend a light crunch to the mesclun salad, which is served with a vinaigrette of walnut oil and reduced balsamic vinegar. It's light fare for a summer night that will transport you to a Mediterranean hillside.

cook's notes

- Sweat the eggplant. Press the tofu.
- Make the ratatouille and set aside.
- Soak the lasagna noodles while you make the tofu "cheese."
- Toast the walnuts while you assemble the casserole. (At this point you can refrigerate the lasagna overnight or even freeze it.)
- Bake the lasagna.
- Make the tomato sauce, salad dressing, and batons while the lasagna bakes.
- To serve, ladle a small pool of tomato sauce onto the plate. Top with a wedge of lasagna. Include a side of salad.

ratatouille

Some ratatouilles are stewed until the vegetables meld into an indistinguishable but tasty heap. Here, the vegetables are sautéed separately, then finished with a short simmer together, so they keep their basic shape and character and don't break down too much. Don't overcook the vegetables, since they are going to bake for 30 minutes in the lasagna.

This is a classic summer side dish that goes with virtually any meal, so make a double batch of ratatouille while you're at it and serve some later in the week as a sandwich filling or a pasta topping.

SERVES 6

2   1-pound eggplants
6   to 8 tablespoons extra-virgin
    olive oil
2   onions, cut in half and thinly sliced
    (2 cups)
1   yellow bell pepper, seeds and
    membrane removed, cut into
    1-inch squares
1   red bell pepper, seeds and
    membrane removed, cut into
    1-inch squares
3   garlic cloves, minced
3   medium zucchini (about 1 pound),
    halved lengthwise and cut into
    1-inch pieces
1   pound tomatoes (3 medium),
    seeds removed, cut into large dice
    Salt and freshly ground black
    pepper
½   cup basil chiffonade (see
    page 15)

• Use a peeler to remove strips of the eggplant skin; it will appear striped. Cut the eggplants into 1-inch cubes. Salt the eggplant cubes, and place them in a colander over a bowl for 30 minutes to sweat. Quickly rinse the eggplant cubes and blot them dry.

• Warm 2 tablespoons of the oil in a large pot. Add the onions, peppers, and garlic and cook over medium-low heat for about 15 minutes, or until the onions and peppers are softened. Remove from the pot and set aside.

• Wipe out or wash the pot and warm 2 more tablespoons of oil. Sauté the zucchini over medium heat for 2 to 3 minutes on each side, or until just browned on all sides. Rather than stirring the zucchini, allow the pieces to sit in place until browned on one side, then turn to brown another side. Set aside.

• Warm 2 more tablespoons of the oil in the large pot and cover with a single layer—no more—of eggplant cubes. Cook over medium heat, turning to brown all sides, just until the eggplant is softened and browned, about 4 minutes. If necessary, wipe out the pot, add 2 more tablespoons of oil, and cook the remaining eggplant cubes. Be careful not to mash the eggplant.

• Return all of the cooked vegetables to the large pot with the eggplant. Add the chopped tomatoes and cook, uncovered, over medium-high heat for 15 minutes, stirring every so often, to allow the flavors to meld. Do not let the vegetables get too mushy or overcooked. Season with salt and pepper. Remove the ratatouille from the heat and stir in the basil chiffonade.

summer lasagna

Capers and olives give the "cheese" an unexpected zing. This lasagna fits perfectly into a deep 7 × 9-inch glass baking dish, my favorite for casseroles. Use your favorite type of lasagna noodle. I prefer a good-quality semolina here; whole-wheat noodles seem too heavy for this dish.

    The noodles are not preboiled but are soaked for 20 to 25 minutes just until they are pliable, not soggy and limp. They bake into the casserole beautifully, and you do not have to worry about piecing together a lot of broken noodles, which inevitably occurs when you cook them first.

SERVES 6

12 lasagna noodles
1 pound firm tofu, pressed (see page 76)
2 garlic cloves, peeled
2 tablespoons fresh lemon juice
3 tablespoons extra-virgin olive oil
½ teaspoon salt
  Freshly ground black pepper
½ cup black olives (preferably imported ones), chopped
1 tablespoon capers (drained if in brine, rinsed if salted)
½ cup walnut halves
1 recipe Ratatouille (page 222)

- Place the lasagna noodles in a shallow baking dish large enough to hold them without breaking. Cover them with hot water and let them sit for 20 to 25 minutes, or until the noodles are softened. Drain in a colander.

- In a food processor, combine the tofu, garlic, lemon juice, oil, salt, and pepper to taste. Process until smooth, scraping down the sides once or twice. Stir in the olives and capers.

- Preheat the oven to 350° F.

- Meanwhile, place the walnuts on a baking sheet and lightly toast just until fragrant, about 10 minutes—don't let them burn. Remove from the oven and place in a strainer. Rub the walnuts against the strainer (over the sink) to loosen the skins. Remove the walnuts from the strainer and hand-chop into small pieces.

- Arrange a layer of lasagna noodles in the bottom of the baking dish. Cut to fit if necessary. Spread one third of the ratatouille mixture over the noodles, then use a spatula to spread half of the tofu cheese evenly over the vegetables.

- Top with another layer of noodles, then another third of the vegetables. Place a third layer of noodles over the vegetables, and finish with the remainder of the vegetables. Top with the rest of the tofu cheese, spreading it evenly. Sprinkle the chopped walnuts over the top.

- Bake the lasagna for about 30 minutes, or until the vegetable juices bubble around the sides of the dish. Remove from the oven and let sit for a few minutes before cutting.

fresh tomato sauce

This simple sauce adds a familiar touch of tomato succulence to many dishes, including the ratatouille lasagna. It's the perfect use for a backyard bumper crop, to serve over polenta, steamed tempeh cubes, or any pasta, and it freezes well, too. The amount here allows for a small pool of sauce spooned under each piece. If you like a lot of sauce—remember, though, the lasagna is very juicy—double the recipe.

2   pounds fresh tomatoes, peeled and seeded, or 1 2-pound can whole tomatoes, drained
3   tablespoons extra-virgin olive oil
2   garlic cloves, minced
1   teaspoon dried basil
    Salt and freshly ground black pepper

• Chop the tomatoes into 1/2-inch dice. In a medium saucepan combine the oil, garlic, basil, and tomatoes. Cook over medium heat for 25 to 35 minutes, or until the tomatoes have released their juices and the water has cooked out. Add salt and black pepper to taste. You can purée the sauce in a blender, or serve it as is.

peeling and seeding tomatoes

Bring a pot of water to a boil. Cut out the core of the tomato by inserting the tip of a paring knife about 1 inch into the tomato at an angle just outside of the core. With a paring knife, cut around the stem, with blade angled inward, until you've made a cone around the stem. Lift it out and discard. Drop the tomatoes in boiling water and leave them 15 to 30 seconds, depending on ripeness. Ripe tomatoes will need less time. Remove the tomatoes with a slotted spoon and let them cool a minute. Skins should peel right off. To seed, cut in half and squeeze the seeds out of the tomatoes. Scoop out the remaining seeds with your fingers or a spoon.

mixed lettuces with reduced balsamic vinaigrette

Reducing balsamic vinegar sweetens it and concentrates its flavor. Hazelnut oil works very well in this recipe also. Make sure to keep nut oils refrigerated to keep them from becoming rancid.

SERVES 6

½ sourdough baguette
½ teaspoon dried basil
1 teaspoon extra-virgin olive oil
½ cup balsamic vinegar
½ cup walnut oil
 Salt and freshly ground black pepper
6 to 12 cups mixed lettuces or mesclun

• Preheat the oven to 350° F. Cut the baguette into ¼-inch slices on an extreme diagonal. Cut each slice into ¼-inch strips or batons. You should have 2 cups of batons. Place them in a bowl, sprinkle with the dried basil, and drizzle with the olive oil. Toss the batons to evenly distribute the oil. Spread on a baking sheet and bake for about 10 minutes, or until the batons are crispy.

• Place the balsamic vinegar in a small saucepan. Bring to a boil and cook for about 5 minutes, or until reduced by half. Measure to be sure you have ¼ cup. Pour it into a small bowl.

• Drizzle in the walnut oil, whisking with one hand while pouring with the other until the oil and vinegar are emusified. Sprinkle with salt and pepper to taste. Toss with the mesclun and sprinkle with the batons.

Pasta with Fresh Shiitakes, Tomatoes, and Basil

Mediterranean Salad

Mushroom "Nuggets"

SERVES 4

It doesn't get much easier than this: pasta, salad, and flavorful mushroom patties. This is a good-looking, light-and-easy spread, portions of which can be prepared in advance. It goes without saying that the tomatoes should be ripe and bursting with flavor. Try to choose a few different varieties and colors to make the presentation even more vibrant. The meal can be made wheat-free if you choose a wheat-free pasta.

cook's notes

- Make the salad first and allow it to marinate while you make the rest. Or make the salad a day ahead.
- Make the mushroom "nuggets" and roast the shiitakes for the pasta.
- Cook the pasta. Have the ingredients ready for the pasta sauce so you can make it at the last minute.
- Stir the lettuce into the salad right before serving.
- To serve, in a wide bowl or pasta plate, accompany pasta with six or seven mushroom "nuggets" around the edges. Top with a sprinkle of shiitake mushrooms. Serve the salad in a separate small dish or bowl.

pasta with fresh shiitakes, tomatoes, and basil

This is a simple and flavorful pasta that celebrates the fresh, ripe tomato. Fresh tomatoes are warmed through and mixed with cooked pasta and basil. I like to use short pasta such as fusilli. Sometimes I mix spinach pasta with whole wheat for a subtle variety of color and flavor.

The shiitake mushrooms transform amazingly when you cook them until they shrivel. They become chewy and crispy and are a great complement to the pasta.

This is a pasta that can easily be made for company. Cook the pasta in advance and toss it in a bit of olive oil, so that the pasta pieces will not stick together. Have all the other ingredients ready to go, including the basil chiffonade. The sauce only takes five minutes to cook, so heat it through at the last minute, right before eating.

SERVES 4

½ pound fresh shiitake mushrooms
2 tablespoons plus ½ cup extra-virgin olive oil
2 tablespoons shoyu
Salt
8 ounces pasta such as penne or fusilli
6 garlic cloves, minced
4 medium tomatoes, seeded and cut into ½-inch dice (4 cups)
1 cup basil chiffonade (see page 15)

• Preheat the oven to 375° F. Remove the stems from the shiitake mushrooms and discard them or save them for stock. Thinly slice the caps. In a medium bowl, toss the mushrooms with 2 tablespoons of the oil and the shoyu. Spread on a parchment-covered baking sheet and roast for 20 to 30 minutes, stirring every 10 minutes, until the mushrooms have shrunk and become crispy. Set aside for garnish.

• In a large pot of boiling, salted water, cook the pasta until it is barely al dente. Drain. If you are holding the pasta for a while before serving, toss it at this point with a little olive oil to prevent it from sticking together or drying out.

• Warm the ½ cup of oil in a large pot or skillet. Add the garlic and cook for 3 minutes, or until the oil is shimmering and the garlic just barely starts to color. Add the diced tomatoes and stir until they are hot. Add the drained pasta and basil, and stir over medium heat for 2 to 3 minutes, or until the pasta is warmed through. Season with salt (make sure you taste here to determine how much you need) and pepper. Serve immediately.

mediterranean salad

This sunny, crisp salad is ideal for a midsummer day. It has very little oil, yet lots of flavor. It is important to cut the peppers small so the flavors can meld into a whole greater than the sum of the individual parts. Jicama can be replaced by celery hearts, but the fresh, crunchy, distinctive taste of jicama lends something special. This is the ideal salad to make ahead. In fact, it improves if left to marinate for a few hours or even up to two days. Remember to stir in the lettuce at the last minute so it does not wilt.

SERVES 4

Salt

1 medium red onion, cut in half and thinly sliced (1 cup)

1 medium cucumber

1 small jicama

1 small red bell pepper

1 small yellow bell pepper

½ cup olives, such as kalamata, Gaeta, or Niçoise

1 cup cherry tomatoes, red or yellow

¼ cup chopped fresh flat-leaf parsley

1 tablespoon chopped fresh marjoram (substitute oregano or tarragon, if preferred)

2 teaspoons capers, drained

2 tablespoons red wine vinegar

3 tablespoons extra-virgin olive oil
  Freshly ground black pepper

4 cups lettuce, preferably bibb or butter lettuce, torn into bite-size pieces

THE TINY "SUN-GOLD" TOMATOES ARE PERFECT FOR THIS SALAD; THEY USUALLY ARE SUPER-SWEET.

• Bring a pot of salted water to a boil. Add the red onions and blanch for about 1 minute, or just until they lose their raw bite. Drain the onions and place in a medium bowl.

• Peel the cucumber, cut it in half lengthwise, and scoop out the seeds with a spoon. Cut the cucumber halves into ¼-inch half-moon pieces and add to the onions.

• Peel the jicama and cut it into ¼-inch slabs. Cut each slab into 2-inch-long matchsticks. You should have 1 cup. Add to the bowl.

• Cut the peppers in half and remove the stems, seeds, and membranes. Cut the peppers into ¼-inch dice and add to the other vegetables.

• Pit and chop the olives into ¼-inch pieces. If the cherry tomatoes are small, leave them whole. Otherwise, cut them in half. Add the olives, tomatoes, parsley, marjoram, capers, vinegar, oil, and salt and pepper to taste to the bowl and combine well.

• Let the vegetables sit for at least a few minutes to allow the flavors to marry. At this point, you can refrigerate the vegetables for up to 2 days. Stir in the lettuce just before serving.

mushroom "nuggets"

Serve six or seven of these taste little morsels per plate of pasta. You'll have some extra—but they have a way of disappearing! I suggest cremini and portobello mushrooms, but you can use a blend of whichever mushrooms you prefer. As an alternative to serving with pasta, you can make larger patties and pan-fry or bake them and serve between two pieces of bread. The mixture can also be baked into lasagna, or stuffed into mushroom caps and baked.

The tofu paste binds the "nuggets" and imparts a lot of flavor. Make that first and set it aside while you are cooking the mushrooms. Soft tofu, which is softer than firm tofu but firmer than silken, is the tofu of choice here. The "nuggets" look best when they are small.

tofu paste

½ pound soft tofu
2 garlic cloves
1 teaspoon light miso
1 teaspoon umeboshi paste
2 tablespoons extra-virgin olive oil

mushrooms

½ pound cremini or cultivated mushrooms
1 8-ounce portobello mushroom
2 tablespoons extra-virgin olive oil, plus more for brushing
1 onion, minced (1 cup)
2 garlic cloves, minced
2 teaspoons ground cumin
1 teaspoon dried thyme
½ teaspoon dried sage
½ teaspoon dried oregano
¼ teaspoon cayenne pepper
1 tablespoon shoyu
½ cup fresh breadcrumbs
¼ cup finely chopped fresh flat-leaf parsley
Salt and freshly ground black pepper

make the tofu paste:

• In a food processor, blend the tofu with the garlic, miso, umeboshi paste, and oil. Run the processor for a few minutes to get the mixture as creamy as possible, scraping down the sides of the bowl as needed. Remove the tofu paste and set aside while you sauté the mushrooms.

make the mushrooms:

• Trim the stems of the cremini mushrooms and wipe the caps with a damp paper towel. Discard the stem of the portobello and cut the cap into chunks. Combine the mushrooms in a food processor and pulse until finely chopped, scraping down the sides of the bowl as necessary. Do not overprocess the mushrooms, or they'll turn to paste.

• Warm the oil in a medium skillet. Add the onions and sauté over medium heat for 5 minutes, or until translucent. Add the garlic, mushrooms, cumin, thyme, sage, oregano, cayenne, and shoyu, and cook over medium-low heat, stirring constantly, for about 10 minutes, or until the mushrooms have released their juices and the mixture is moist but the pan is almost dry. Do not cook the mixture so long that it starts to stick to the pan.

• Remove from the heat and stir in the breadcrumbs, tofu paste, and parsley. Add salt and pepper to taste and set aside to cool slightly.

• Preheat the oven to 350° F. Use a measuring spoon to form balls from 1 heaping teaspoon. Or, even better, use a very small cookie scoop. Place the balls on a parchment-covered baking sheet. With a brush, lightly dab each with olive oil. Bake for 20 minutes, or until the "nuggets" are heated through.

Pickled Red Onions

Masa Harina Tamales with Black Beans and Tomatillo-Cilantro Sauce

Chayote, Red Pepper, and Corn Salad

SERVES 4 OR 5

Tamale making has a long and venerable history in Mexico. Records from the Conquistadores indicate that tamales were offered to the gods at special times of the year, and they remain a celebratory food. For this fun, south-of-the-border menu, tamales are served with a simple tomatillo sauce, complemented by a zesty chayote, red pepper, and corn salad and a garnish of pickled red onions. Each of the dishes in this vibrantly colored meal is easily assembled in advance, and they all make wonderful leftovers.

cook's notes

- Make the onions the day before, if possible—or make them first. Soak the beans.

- Cook the beans and make the salad. (These two steps can be done the day before.)

- Make the *masa,* and set it aside while you soak the corn husks and refry the beans.

- Make the sauce while you steam the tamales.

- To serve, start with two tamales per person. Open the tamales so they are sitting in the corn husks. (If you do not have a very large plate, serve two on one corn husk.) Pour some of the sauce onto each tamale so that it flows onto the plate. Surround the tamales with a small mound of pickled red onions and some of the chayote, red pepper, and corn salad.

pickled red onions

These onions, with their appealing magenta color, are quick to make. Jalapeño, garlic, and herbs give the onions extra flavor and heat. While these onions are good right after they're made, they taste even better a few days later. It's a great condiment to have on hand, and they keep for up to a month in the refrigerator, so make a double batch.

2 cups red onions, cut in half and thinly sliced

½ teaspoon coriander seeds

½ jalapeño, cut in half, stemmed, seeded, and thinly sliced

2 garlic cloves, thinly sliced

½ teaspoon dried oregano, preferably Mexican or Greek

2 tablespoons umeboshi vinegar

¼ cup brown rice vinegar

½ cup water

½ teaspoon salt

• Bring a pot of water to a boil. Add the onions and blanch for 1 minute. Drain.

• In a mortar and pestle or a spice grinder, coarsely grind the coriander seeds. Place in a nonreactive bowl and add the onions, jalapeño, garlic, and oregano. Mix thoroughly.

• In a small pot or saucepan, bring the vinegars and the water to a boil. Stir in the salt and pour over the onions. Let stand for several hours if possible before serving or place in a tightly covered jar and refrigerate for up to 1 month.

masa harina tamales
with black beans

In Mexico, I learned a traditional way of making tamales, and a similar method is used in Quezaltenango, Guatemala, which leads me to believe that this technique is very old indeed. This version utilizes *masa harina*, dried field corn that is boiled briefly with slaked lime, then dried and ground into a fine powder. In Guatemala, these tamales are called *Talluyos de San Juan*, presumably named after the town in which they originated. The *masa harina* is rolled out very thin, spread with a layer of black bean paste (refried beans), then rolled together into a large pinwheel. This is in turn cut into pieces, each of which is wrapped in a soaked corn husk. The tied bundles are then steamed for 30 minutes.

SERVES 4 OR 5

4   ounces corn husks
2   cups *masa harina*
½   teaspoon salt
2   tablespoons canola oil
1   cup plus 2 tablespoons water
    Refried Black Beans (page 234)

• Place the corn husks in a large bowl and cover with warm water. Put a bowl or weight on top to keep them submerged. As the husks soften, separate them to allow water to penetrate all the layers. They should be soaked for at least 20 minutes, or until you are ready to use them.

• Place the *masa harina* in a medium bowl. Whisk in the salt, drizzle in the oil, and mix them through the *masa* until you have a coarse overall texture. Add the water, then lightly knead the dough for a minute or two until it is smooth. Cover with plastic wrap until ready to use.

• Separate the dough into thirds and place one third on a piece of parchment paper cut into a 12 × 8-inch rectangle. Cover the unused dough with plastic wrap. Place a second sheet of parchment paper or plastic wrap over the dough you're working with and roll out to the size of the paper. Trim the edges, rolling trimmed pieces back in, to get a thin, even rectangle.

• Spread refried beans over the *masa*, completely covering it. Use the plastic or parchment to help you roll the dough into a log. Cut the log into pinwheel pieces 3 to 4 inches thick. Repeat with the remaining dough and refried beans.

• Wrap each pinwheel in a corn husk, folding the sides of the corn husk around it so the two sides overlap. If the corn husks are not large enough, you can overlap two to make one large one. Tear ¼-inch strips off scrap pieces of corn husk to use as ties. Tie the tapered end tight, doubling the knot. Fold the bottom back under (see page 233).

step 1

step 2

step 3

step 4

step 5

step 6

step 7

step 8

step 9

- Fill a large pot with 1½ inches of water. Place a steamer insert over the water and stack the tamales in the pot. Cover and steam for 30 minutes, making sure the water does not boil away. Add more water if necessary.

refried black beans

Refried beans are so versatile and easy to make (especially with a pressure cooker) that they're a must for your cooking repertoire. Don't use canned beans here, since the canned ones are too firm; besides, you need some cooking liquid for mashing the beans. The beans make a great addition to other Mexican-style dishes besides these tamales; use them as a filling for burritos, enchiladas, and tostadas. Serve them as a bean dip with chips or spread them on tortillas with a few wedges of lime-splashed avocados. For a quick meal of leftovers, I like to stir them into quick-cooking corn grits and top them with sautéed greens.

Anasazi and pinto beans are interchangeable with the black beans.

SERVES 4 OR 5

1½ cups black beans, soaked and drained
1 dried chipotle or other smoked chile
1 mild dried chile, such as pasilla, ancho, or mulato
5 cups water
 Salt
3 tablespoons canola oil
2 onions, cut into small dice (2 cups)
3 garlic cloves, minced

• In a medium pot, combine the beans with the chiles and water. Bring to a boil over high heat, then reduce the heat and simmer for 1 to 1½ hours, or until soft. Add 1½ teaspoons salt. Let the beans sit in the liquid for 10 minutes to absorb the salt. Drain the beans, reserving 1 cup of the cooking liquid; discard the chiles.

As an alternate method, pressure-cook the beans with the chiles and 4 cups of water for 6 minutes, or until soft. Let the pressure come down naturally. Add 1½ teaspoons salt and let sit in the liquid for 10 minutes before draining. Reserve 1 cup of the cooking liquid. Discard the chiles.

• Warm the oil in a medium skillet, then add the onions and garlic and sauté over medium-high heat for 8 minutes, or until the onions are browned. Add one third of the cooked beans and ⅓ cup of the reserved cooking liquid to the onions in the skillet. With a potato masher, the back of a spoon, or a wooden spatula, mash the beans into the liquid. Continue cooking until the liquid evaporates. Add one third more of the beans and ⅓ cup of the liquid, and mash and cook again, stirring. Repeat one more time, mashing and cooking and stirring, until all of the liquid is absorbed and the beans hold together in the pan without sticking to it. They shouldn't be very soupy, but they shouldn't be too solid, either.

The combination of chiles has a broad range of flavors. The chipotle, a smoked jalapeño, has a smoky, sweet flavor. Pasilla, a dried chilaca, also known as chile negro, is a dark, elongated, tapered chile 5 to 6 inches long. Ancho, meaning "wide," is a dried poblano, a broad chile tapering to a round end, and is the sweetest of the dried chiles, with a mild fruity flavor. Mulato, like ancho, is a type of dried poblano, with a slightly smokier flavor. It tapers to a point 5 to 6 inches long and is rounded at the top. Pasilla, ancho, and mulato chiles are very important in the making of moles. They are medium hot, and they taste wonderful here in combination with the fiery chipotle.

tomatillo-cilantro sauce

This mild green sauce is thickened with a little bread. Once you get all the ingredients for this sauce ready, all you have to do is blend them. To keep the color vibrant green, heat only the portion that you're going to serve.

¼ pound tomatillos

½ small green bell pepper, stem, seeds, and white membrane removed, cut into 1-inch pieces

¼ cup chopped fresh flat-leaf parsley

¼ cup chopped fresh cilantro

½ jalapeño pepper, stemmed and seeded

1 scallion, chopped (¼ cup)

4 slices soft white bread, crust removed, torn into pieces

1 cup water

½ teaspoon salt

THE TOMATILLO IS A SMALL, PLUM-SIZE, TART-TASTING GREEN FRUIT SIMILAR IN APPEARANCE TO THE TOMATO—BUT IN FACT UNRELATED TO IT. TOMATILLOS HAVE LEAF-LIKE HUSKS THAT MUST BE REMOVED AND ARE THE FOUNDATION FOR MANY COMMON MEXICAN SAUCES.

TOMATILLOS LAST SEVERAL WEEKS STORED IN THE REFRIGERATOR. ALTHOUGH THEY CAN BE USED RAW IN A SALSA, THEY ARE USUALLY SIM-MERED OR DRY-ROASTED.

• Preheat the broiler. Remove the stems and husks from the tomatillos and rinse them. Place the tomatillos on a broiler pan and broil until the skins blister, crack, and begin to blacken. Remove from the broiler and cut off any black spots.

• Put the tomatillos and the remaining ingredients in a blender and blend until smooth. Just before serving, heat just the amount you'll be serving.

chayote, red pepper, and corn salad

Roasting corn gives it smokiness that enhances the vegetable's natural flavor. Chayote's mild sweetness and firm, slightly starchy texture lend a distinctive presence to the salad. This salad is just as good the next day, so it is a great dish to make ahead of time.

SERVES 4 OR 5

Salt
1   chayote
⅔   cup roasted red bell pepper
     (1 medium) (see page 188)
3   cups corn kernels (fresh from
     3 medium ears of corn, or frozen)
½   teaspoon cumin seeds
1   teaspoon dried oregano
1   garlic clove, minced
2   tablespoons extra-virgin olive oil
½   cup minced onion
⅛   teaspoon hot red pepper flakes
3   tablespoons apple cider vinegar

CHAYOTES ARE PEAR-SHAPED PALE-GREEN, STARCHY FRUITS WITH SMOOTH SKIN. THEY KEEP FOR A MONTH REFRIGERATED. CHAYOTES ARE INCREASINGLY EASIER TO FIND IN SUPERMARKETS AND SPECIALTY STORES. IN A PINCH, YOU COULD SUBSTITUTE ZUCCHINI.

• Bring a pot of salted water to a boil. Cut the chayote in half and cut out the central pit. Quarter, cut the quarters in half lengthwise, then slice crosswise into ⅜-inch pieces. Blanch the chayote until it is cooked through but still firm, about 3 minutes. Refresh in cold water, drain the water, then put the chayote in a medium bowl.

• Peel and seed the roasted pepper. Cut into ¼-inch strips, and cut those into 1-inch pieces. Add to the bowl.

• Heat a medium cast-iron skillet until very hot. (If you don't have a cast-iron skillet, be especially careful doing this in a regular skillet.) Add the corn and dry-roast the kernels, placing no more than 2 layers of the corn kernels in the pan at a time. Cook, stirring continuously, for 4 to 5 minutes, or until the corn is browned in places and cooked through. Add to the chayote and red pepper.

• In the same skillet, lightly toast the cumin and oregano, stirring frequently, until fragrant, about 1 minute. Place the toasted spices in a mortar and pestle or a spice grinder and grind. Add to the vegetables along with the garlic.

• Warm the oil in a medium skillet. Add the onions and red pepper flakes, and sauté over medium-low heat for 10 minutes, or until the onions are softened and have begun to brown. Pour the onions over the salad in the bowl and mix. Add the vinegar and ½ teaspoon of salt and stir to combine.

desserts

A much-admired pastry teacher once taught me that when you make dessert for a person, you make him or her your love slave. That may be overstating the case, but it is true that you will bring joy and pleasure to the lucky recipient. Desserts also take you back to that childlike state of innocence when a little sweet something was sheer unfettered bliss. A typical good-looking dessert, however, can raise your hopes with false promises; it looks so enticing, but after eating it you probably don't feel so great. A sugary dessert can send you on a blood-sugar roller-coaster ride.

Vegan desserts, however, are another story. You can feast on the desserts in this book and feel fantastic afterward. They use sweeteners that won't send your blood sugar racing like a bloodhound, and they are naturally low in fat. These are pleasures that have some real food value. They also provide just the right sweet sensation to round out a luscious meal. The taste of pure, high-quality ingredients comes shining through. Most important, these desserts are not the glumpy, heavy confections so often associated with vegan cooking. One taste of the chocolate coconut cake and you'll see what I mean.

Another upside to vegan desserts is that they are generally easier to make than their conventional counterparts. No temperamental butter creams or endless beating of egg whites. Once you master a few ingredients such as agar and arrowroot, the rest is easy.

Before proceeding with the recipes that follow, take the time to familiarize yourself with some basic ingredients and tools.

dry ingredients

No need to get a fancy sifter to aerate your dry ingredients. A metal strainer works fine. Put the dry ingredients in the strainer, hold it with one hand, and tap it with the other to sift the ingredients into a bowl.

For cakes and pastry dough, I use a combination of **whole-wheat pastry flour** and **unbleached white flour**. Make sure to purchase whole-wheat pastry flour, not bread flour, since the high gluten content in bread flour is what gives structure to bread—something not desirable in a cake.

Since eggs are not used in vegan cooking, **baking powder** and **baking soda** are critical leaveners. Get an aluminum-free double-acting baking powder, the kind sold in natural food and gourmet stores. Baking powder starts to react as soon as it is mixed with any wet ingredients and then again when it comes in contact with the heat of the oven, so once you mix your batter, don't delay in putting it in the oven! Baking soda requires the presence of something acidic, which is why my cake recipes usually have a small amount of vinegar in them.

Agar-agar is a vegetarian form of gelatin; it's the binding agent in the fruit kantens and the mousse toppings. **Kudzu** and **arrowroot** are natural thickeners. They are used to thicken liquids much in the way cornstarch does, and, in conjunction with agar-agar, they give mousses and other gelled desserts a fine custardy texture. Kudzu, moreover, has medicinal qualities; a little kudzu stirred into hot liquid soothes the stomach (page 240).

sweeteners

All sugars are powerful substances, and should be regarded with due respect, although some are more unwholesome than others. Not only is white sugar a highly refined product that contains no nutrients, it actually requires vitamins and minerals to absorb it. Furthermore, it sends the blood glucose level into an immediate tailspin, often causing letdown, fatigue, and irritability. Luckily, there are some luscious natural alternatives to white sugar that, although processed to some degree, still have some relation to their whole-food origins and have a more gradual effect on the body's blood sugar level. The way your body reacts to various sweeteners will likely determine which ones you prefer to use. Of all the dry sugars, **maple sugar**, which is crystallized maple syrup, is the mildest tasting and usually the most finely granulated. Of course, it is also the hardest to find. The other dry sugars will substitute in all cases, the difference being that they are a little grainier than the maple, and they are a little stronger-tasting.

There are some luscious alternatives to refined white sugar.

Date sugar is made from ground, dehydrated dates, so it has the same nutritional value as dried dates. It is coarsely granulated, so it works best when it's dissolved in liquid.

Pure maple syrup is a good all-purpose sweetener. It is worth getting a good-quality maple syrup, because cheaper brands might contain chemical antifoamers, mold inhibitors, and residue from formaldehyde pellets used to keep the tap-holes in the tree from healing. (Stay away from anything labeled "pancake syrup." This is a cheap product made from corn syrup or sugar syrup with artificial flavoring.) Maple syrup comes in various grades. Avoid grade C, which is thicker and darker than the other grades and can darken the desserts it's baked into. (Unfortunately, I learned this the hard way in front of a class when a dessert I was making turned a notably unvoluptuous shade of gray.)

Sucanat, a name coined from the first letters of the words "sugar cane natural," is a natural sweetener made from dried granulated cane juice. Only the water and fiber are removed, so the mineral salts and vitamins naturally present are retained. It is moist, and it has a slight taste of molasses and a coarse granular texture. **Rapidura** is another brand name for the same product. Use both as you would maple sugar. Furthermore, Sucanat is organic, which is important because pesticides are concentrated during the processing of sugar.

Barley malt syrup is made from sprouted barley; add hops and yeast and you've got beer. Barley malt is a fairly mild sweetener with a strong, distinctive flavor and the consistency and color of molasses. I usually use it in combination with other sweeteners.

Brown rice syrup is a very mild sweetener with a subtle butterscotch flavor, making it a great choice for savory foods as well as desserts. It is a good sweetener for those who barely want a sweetener at all. Brown rice syrup, as well as barley malt, still have complex carbohydrates left in them, and they pack a very mild sugar punch. Buy them as well as Sucanat in natural food stores.

Molasses is a by-product of the sugar-refining process. Thick, dark, and sweet, it retains vitamins and mineral loss in the process. Always use unsulphured molasses, since the sulfured tastes of residues of sulfur dioxide. Because molasses has a strong taste, I use small quantities as an accent in desserts such as pumpkin pie or glazed bananas.

chocolate

While not necessarily something to indulge in every day, chocolate is a heavenly ingredient. Why is it that a little chocolate sends people into a state of rapture? Chocolate is rich in phenylethylamine, which is what the brain manufactures when stimulated by the emotion of love.

Chocolate derives from the pods of the cacao tree. The pods are roasted, and the shells are removed. The seeds inside are ground into an oily paste called chocolate liquor. **Cocoa powder** is pure chocolate liquor with most of the cocoa butter pressed out of it. The remaining dry cake, which is then pulverized, becomes cocoa powder. If your cocoa powder is labeled "Dutched," it means the powder was treated with a mild alkali to mellow the flavor and make it more soluble. I usually use Dutched cocoa powder. When sugar, vanilla, extra cocoa butter, and lecithin are added to the chocolate liquor, it becomes chocolate in bar form. Several types of semisweet chocolates on the market are naturally sweetened with grain syrup, Rapidura, or Sucanat. My favorite chocolate is Tropical Source espresso chocolate chips. These chocolate chips feel velvety-smooth in the mouth and have the most chocolatey flavor. The chips melt readily, eliminating the need to chop up chunks.

Some other ingredients to have in your voluptuous pantry include a supply of nuts (if you have space, store them in the freezer to keep them fresh), apple cider vinegar, canola oil, cocoa, grain coffee or instant espresso, vanilla and almond extract, and, of course, sea salt. If you have these ingredients, you need only purchase some fresh fruit or specialty items when you set about making a scrumptious dessert.

Dessert making is infinitely more pleasurable if you have the right tools (see list at left). Fortunately, most of these are inexpensive and readily available.

Fun equipment to make your creations especially beautiful includes: plastic squeeze bottles for saucing plates and decorating desserts, and individual tart pans and cake molds (I favor small cheesecake molds, so that you can easily pop out the cakes, and so that you can make all the mousse cakes in miniature).

An ice-cream maker is a great piece of equipment to have. There are so many on the market now ranging in price from $45 to $500. The prepared vegan ice creams on the market are not that good. Making homemade ice cream, especially vegan, is easy. Be forewarned, though; it can become a passionate obsession.

So live it up! Pamper yourself with a luscious sweet. Sometimes it's best to let go of constricting attitudes about what you can and cannot have. Think abundantly. Abundance doesn't mean gluttony—you don't need to eat the whole cake yourself. Make yourself something delectable, and then consume just enough to make you feel good. After all, there's always more where that came from, especially if you can make it yourself. Make a dessert and bring someone (yourself included) some simple, unadulterated bliss.

a word about agar-agar, kudzu, and arrowroot

Agar-agar is a vegetarian form of gelatin, made from a red seaweed that is processed into flakes, bars, or powder. The bars are also known as kanten bars.

One kanten bar is equivalent to about ¼ cup of flakes. Either one bar or ¼ cup of flakes is the correct amount to gel 1 quart of liquid. This amount can vary depending on what else is in the recipe. The powder is five times as strong as the flakes, so 1 tablespoon of powder is equivalent to 5 tablespoons of flakes. Use the powder only when you are also using a sweetener such as maple syrup, never when you want to gel only juice. This is because the powder has a bit of a sea-taste that the flakes and bars do not have. The strong flavor of a sweetener will overcome this, whereas juice alone cannot. Because of its concentrated form, a little powder goes a long way and does not need much liquid to dissolve in. Also, powder is the only type of agar-agar you can bake with. It is a bit more difficult to find than the flakes or bars, which are readily available in most health food stores. You can order it by mail. It is expensive, but a little goes a long way and it lasts indefinitely.

Preparation methods are similar for all three forms of agar-agar. Agar flakes or powder are put in a pot with cold liquid and heated on the stove. Agar bars first have to be soaked in water for a few minutes until softened, and then squeezed to remove excess liquid. They should be ripped apart a bit before adding to the pot of cold liquid, to make dissolving easier. The liquid must be brought to a boil slowly, stirring every once in a while to make sure nothing has stuck to the pot. Once the liquid reaches a boil, immediately lower the heat and allow the liquid to simmer softly until all of the agar has definitely, thoroughly dissolved. The powder needs to simmer for only a few minutes to completely dissolve, but the flakes and bars need to simmer about 10 minutes. Be sure to pay close attention during this process—it is repugnant to find bits of undissolved agar in an otherwise carefully made dish. You are then ready to proceed with the next step, or to remove the pot from the heat.

Kudzu and arrowroot are pretty much interchangeable. Both are healthful substitutes for cornstarch. Agar thickens once the liquid has chilled. Kudzu and arrowroot thicken when the liquid is hot.

Agar gelatinizes; kudzu and arrowroot thicken. Together they give a custard-like texture. Arrowroot or kudzu can be used by themselves to thicken a sauce, but agar-agar is best used in conjunction with one of the two thickeners. This greatly improves the texture by softening and smoothing it. Never add arrowroot or kudzu directly to the pot. You'd end up with a lumpy mess. You need to dissolve the starch in a small amount of cool liquid—and that means really dissolve—before adding it to a pot of hot liquid. If you pour it in with visible lumps—well, you will get a lumpy, glumpy end product.

That is why I often favor arrowroot over kudzu. Kudzu comes in big white chunks and takes a bit of work to make sure it is properly dissolved. Kudzu is the root of the kudzu plant. Although it is a groundcover that grows wild all over the South to the chagrin of many farmers, the type we get that is ready to use is imported from Japan and is quite expensive. It is, however, a wonderful stomach soother, so if your purposes are medicinal, by all means take the extra trouble and expense and use it. Also, kudzu's smooth consistency makes it better for sauces served cold or at room temperature. On the other hand, if you're making Chocolate Mousse Cake (page 258), use arrowroot. In addition, you can also use arrowroot to thicken a pie.

After you add your dissolved arrowroot mixture (in the recipes it is called a slurry) to the pot with hot simmering liquid, stir, stir, stir. Do not leave to answer the telephone, do not leave for any other reason, but stay there, stirring continuously, stopping for a moment now and then to see what's happening, then continuing to stir, until the mixture has gone from cloudy to clear. When you see a few bubbles, this means your liquid is about to boil, and it's ready to remove from the stove. It would be a big mistake to let the liquid boil away after you've added the arrowroot. The arrowroot would break and lose its strength. Kudzu is a lot stronger in this regard. You can reheat anything thickened with kudzu without harming its integrity.

It's a good idea to do a test, just to make sure you won't end up with any ugly surprises when it comes to sampling your finished product. Simply put a little of the hot liquid in the freezer for a few minutes. It will gel quickly and you'll have a good idea whether or not you have the texture you want. If it's too firm, you could add more liquid. If it's too runny, dissolve more agar in a pot with a little liquid, and add it to your principal pot.

cranberry–orange tart

This bright red dessert is lovely to look at, and it makes a great finale to a holiday feast. Toasting the flour for the crust gives it a taste like graham crackers. Cranberries are readily available in November and December, but I like to buy several extra packages and freeze them, since it feels appropriate to eat cranberries in the dead of winter but they're sometimes difficult to find.

SERVES 8

crust

1¾ cups whole-wheat pastry flour
1   teaspoon baking powder
⅓   cup canola oil
⅓   cup pure maple syrup
     Pinch of salt

filling

1   cup walnut halves
3   cups cranberries, fresh or frozen
¼   cup apple juice or apple cider
¾   cup pure maple syrup
1   teaspoon ground cinnamon
1   tablespoon orange zest, finely minced
1   tablespoon agar flakes
1   tablespoon arrowroot powder
⅓   cup fresh orange juice
¼   cup almond butter (optional)

make the crust:

• Preheat the oven to 350° F. Oil a 9-inch tart pan. Spread the flour evenly on a parchment-covered baking sheet. Place in the oven and toast the flour for 20 minutes, or until it is fragrant. Remove from the oven and use the parchment paper to transfer the flour to a medium mixing bowl. Let cool a few minutes.

• Add the baking powder and whisk to mix. In another small bowl combine the oil, maple syrup, and salt, and whisk until thoroughly combined and emulsified.

• Add the wet ingredients to the dry, stirring just enough to incorporate the dry ingredients. The dough should hold together easily when squeezed with your hands. If it feels a little dry, work in a couple of tablespoons of apple juice or water until the dough is wet enough to press easily.

• Press the dough into the tart pan. Be careful not to make it too thick at the juncture where the bottom of the tart pan meets the side; press against the sides with your thumb to lift out the excess that tends to accumulate here. Trim off any excess at the top of the tart pan with a knife.

• Bake the crust for about 15 minutes, or until it is browned. (Don't turn off the oven.) Remove the crust from the oven and let it cool while you prepare the filling.

The crust should be smooth, moist but not too wet, and easy to press. You can use a piece of plastic wrap between your hands and the dough to keep your hands dry and make sure the crust presses in smoothly. The baking powder in the crust will make it puff a bit, so it is important that the crust be even.

make the filling:

- Spread the walnuts on a baking sheet. Lightly toast for about 10 minutes, or until fragrant. Place the walnuts in a strainer while they are still warm and rub them against the sides to loosen the skins. (It's neatest to do this over the sink or a garbage can.) Chop the walnuts into small pieces. Set aside.

- Go through the cranberries and discard any that are soft or rotten. Place in a small saucepan with apple juice, maple syrup, cinnamon, orange zest, and agar flakes. Cook, uncovered, over medium heat until the agar flakes have dissolved, the cranberries have started to pop, and the liquid reaches a boil, about 8 to 10 minutes.

- Meanwhile, in a small bowl dissolve the arrowroot in the orange juice to make a slurry. When the cranberries start to bubble, add the slurry, stirring constantly until liquid changes from cloudy to clear and the cranberries begin to bubble once again. Remove from the heat.

- Spread a thin layer of almond butter over the bottom of the crust. (Although the tart tastes good without it, the almond butter adds a delicate richness.) Sprinkle a layer of chopped walnuts evenly on the bottom of the crust. Pour in the cranberry mixture, spreading it evenly, and refrigerate for about 45 minutes to set.

Remember to stir the cranberry mixture continuously after the arrowroot has been added. Do not remove the mixture from the heat until you see a few bubbles appear on the surface and you feel it thicken.

raspberry-cornmeal tart with raspberry sauce

Whole raspberries, toasted almonds, and swirls of raspberry purée baked into a golden cornmeal batter—the result is a delectably elegant dessert that is quite simple to make in three easy stages. For the best flavor, be sure to make the accompanying raspberry sauce (recipe follows) while the cake is cooling (or it can be made ahead).

Before you mix the batter for the cake, have your raspberies and toasted almond ready for the garnish, because you need to assemble the tart quickly once the batter is mixed.

SERVES 8 TO 10

raspberry purée

½ cup raspberries, fresh or frozen
2   teaspoons pure maple syrup

almond crust

¾ cup blanched sliced almonds
¾ cup whole-wheat pastry flour
3   tablespoons canola oil
3   tablespoons pure maple syrup
½ teaspoon almond extract
    Pinch of salt

ORDINARILY, I'D RECOMMEND USING WHOLE ALMONDS AND BLANCHING THEM FOR THE CRUST. SINCE YOU ALREADY HAVE THE SLICED ONES THAT YOU'RE USING FOR THE TOP, HOWEVER, YOU CAN SAVE YOURSELF SOME WORK BY USING SLICED, BLANCHED ALMONDS FOR THE CRUST AS WELL. THEY TOAST MORE QUICKLY THAN THE WHOLE ALMONDS, SO CHECK THEM AFTER 5 MINUTES.

make the purée:

• Blend the raspberries. Push the raspberries through a strainer into a bowl with a rubber spatula, scraping the bottom of the strainer as you go. (The strained raspberry purée tends to stick to the bottom of the strainer—this is the stuff you want.) You should have about ¼ cup of strained purée. Mix the maple syrup into the purée. Set aside.

make the crust:

• Preheat the oven to 350° F. Oil a 9-inch tart pan. Spread the almonds on a baking sheet and bake for 5 to 6 minutes or or until lightly toasted. Reserve ¼ cup for garnish.

• In a food processor fitted with a metal blade, grind the ½ cup of toasted, blanched almonds with the pastry flour and process until the nuts are finely ground into the flour. Transfer to a medium bowl.

• In another small bowl, whisk the oil, maple syrup, and almond extract together with the salt. Pour into the flour–nut mixture and mix with a wooden spoon or rubber spatula until the dry ingredients are thoroughly moistened.

• Press the crust mixture evenly into the bottom of the oiled tart pan. You may wish to use a piece of plastic wrap between your fingers and the nut mixture to help press it in smoothly and easily. Do not press the crust mixture up the sides of the pan. Bake for 10 to 15 minutes, or until the crust is lightly browned. Remove from the oven and leave the oven on.

cornmeal cake

¼ cup whole-wheat pastry flour
¼ cup unbleached white flour
½ cup cornmeal
¾ teaspoon baking powder
½ teaspoon baking soda
3 tablespoons canola oil
6 tablespoons pure maple syrup
6 tablespoons water
1 teaspoon vanilla extract
1 teaspoon almond extract
¾ teaspoon apple cider vinegar
¼ teaspoon salt

½ cup whole raspberries, fresh or frozen, for garnish

Raspberry Sauce (recipe follows)

make the cake:

- Into a medium bowl sift the flours, cornmeal, baking powder, and baking soda. Whisk to combine.

- Add to another medium bowl the canola oil, maple syrup, water, vanilla, almond extract, vinegar, and salt. Whisk until thoroughly combined. (You could do this in a blender.)

- Pour the wet ingredients into the dry, and whisk for a few moments to blend the two just until the dry ingredients are thoroughly moistened.

- Pour the batter evenly over the crust in the tart pan. Drizzle the raspberry purée in decorative swirls or spoon it over the batter. Arrange the fresh whole raspberries in clusters on the top and strew the remaining ¼ cup of blanched almonds over the surface.

- Bake for 20 to 30 minutes, until a toothpick inserted in the center comes out clean. Let the tart cool for a few minutes before popping it out of the pan.

raspberry sauce

1 pint raspberries, fresh or frozen
2 tablespoons pure maple syrup
½ teaspoon vanilla
2 tablespoons water

- Purée the raspberries with the maple syrup in a food processor or blender. Push through a strainer to remove the seeds. Stir in the vanilla and water.

chocolate pudding tart

This is a chocolate lover's delight—the brownie layered with a creamy filling satisfies those who love their pudding and want cake too. Make this sensuous dessert for your sweetheart on Valentine's Day.

The recipe calls for a small amount of tofu. I generally do not like tofu in desserts, but I make an exception when the results are excellent. I get superior results by using the boxed firm silken tofu for desserts such as this one. It has virtually no taste of soy and a very light, creamy, but firm texture.

SERVES 8 TO 10

brownie layer

¼ cup whole-wheat pastry flour
¼ cup unbleached white flour
¼ teaspoon baking powder
¼ cup Sucanat
3 tablespoons cocoa powder
¼ cup canola oil
¼ cup pure maple syrup
2 tablespoons original flavored soy milk
1 teaspoon vanilla extract
¼ teaspoon salt

pudding layer

¾ pound firm silken tofu (boxed Mori-Nu)
2 tablespoon canola oil
½ cup pure maple syrup
¼ teaspoon salt
2 teaspoons vanilla
1 cup water
1 tablespoon agar flakes
2 tablespoons cocoa powder
1 teaspoon arrowroot powder
¼ cup soy milk
¼ cup whole chocolate chips plus ¼ cup chocolate chips, chopped into small pieces, for garnish

make the brownie layer:

• Preheat the oven to 350° F. Oil a 9-inch tart pan.

• In a medium bowl, combine the flours, baking powder, Sucanat, and cocoa powder.

• In a small bowl, thoroughly whisk the oil, maple syrup, soy milk, vanilla, and salt to combine. Pour the wet ingredients into the dry, whisking just until the dry ingredients are thoroughly moistened. Pour the batter into the prepared tart pan and spread evenly with a metal spatula to cover the bottom of the pan. It will be a thin layer. Bake for about 10 minutes, or until a toothpick inserted in the cake comes out clean.

make the pudding layer:

• In a food processor fitted with a metal blade, add the tofu, oil, maple syrup, salt, and vanilla and process until smooth.

• In a small saucepan, combine the water with the agar flakes and cocoa powder. Heat until the liquid reaches a boil, then lower the heat and gently simmer for 10 to 15 minutes, or until the agar is completely dissolved. In a small bowl, mix the arrowroot with the soy milk to make a slurry. Stir the slurry into the hot liquid and cook, stirring constantly, until the liquid just starts to bubble. Turn off the heat and add the whole chocolate chips. Let sit for a few minutes in the hot liquid, then whisk thoroughly to blend.

• Pour the chocolate mixture into the food processor and process until everything is thoroughly combined. Pour the mixture into the tart pan to cover the brownie crust. The chocolate mixture should completely fill the pan.

• Let the filling set for a few minutes, then sprinkle the chopped chocolate chips around the edges to line the pan. Place in the refrigerator for 45 minutes, or until completely set and cool. Unmold and serve.

a word about tarts and tart pans

Using a piece of plastic wrap over your hands to press in a tart crust makes the job really easy. Besides leaving you with clean, unsticky hands, it allows you to work much faster and with very smooth results. Press along the sides to get rid of any thick parts, making sure you have the same even thickness where the side crust meets the bottom crust. It is easy to deposit extra dough there accidentally. Another pitfall to avoid is making the crust too thin. If you can see a bit of the tart pan peeking through the crust, it's too thin.

Tart pans with fluted sides also make it easy to get rid of excess dough you've just pushed up the sides. Just run a knife along the top edge.

Tarts should be removed from the tart pans before serving. If the crust appears to have stuck to the sides, don't panic. Look under the tart pan and you can see the little lip where the two pieces of metal overlap. Run a dull knife between them, and even the most stubborn crusts will release with relative ease.

Fresh fruit on a tart benefits from a glaze, often a jam that has been strained and heated. The glaze should be a nice liquidy consistency to coat the fruit. There should be enough glaze on the brush so that it can be dabbed on the fruit in a light caress. If the glaze cools before you have finished, by all means heat it up again. If it gets too thick, add a bit of water to thin it out.

Finally, tarts are really best eaten the day they are made. They won't be terrible the next day—indeed, some people might not know the difference—but the crispy texture of the crust will suffer the longer it sits with filling in it. You can, however, have as much preparation as possible done beforehand, so that the actual making of the tart is minimal work. You can, for example, have dry ingredients blended in one container, wet in another. You can have filling ingredients measured out. You can have a jam glaze strained. You can even make most crusts the day before. With all that done it won't take long to put together the tart, and you'll probably be thankful you did it that way so it can be served at its maximum freshness. You can eat the leftovers with a slightly soggy crust and nobody will complain.

apple spice streusel cake

This cozy country dessert consists of a velvety cake with a moist apple filling and a crunchy streusel topping—an autumn classic that fills the kitchen with the aroma of spices and apples.

Measure the ingredients for each section as you go along. Once you mix the batter, you have to make the cake immediately—you don't want the batter to sit around. Also, cut your apples right before sautéing. For best results, use a springform pan, since it's not a good idea to invert a cake with a streusel topping.

In the autumn, use any type of apple that is crisp and good for baking: Rome, Mutsu, Northern Spy, Cortland, Ida Red, and Jonagold, to name a few. In the winter, I fall back on Golden Delicious.

The cake will stay fresh for three or four days in the refrigerator and it tastes delicious served with ice cream.

SERVES 10 TO 12

filling

1   cup pecan halves
1   tablespoon canola oil
2   medium apples, peeled and cut into ⅜-inch dice (about 2 cups)
1   teaspoon ground cinnamon

streusel

1   cup whole-wheat pastry flour
½   cup maple sugar or natural cane sugar
1   teaspoon ground cinnamon
½   teaspoon baking powder
    Pinch of salt
6   tablespoons canola oil

WHEN A BATTER IS AS WET AS THIS, I USE A WHISK TO MIX THE WET AND DRY INGREDIENTS TOGETHER.

make the filling:

• Preheat the oven to 350° F. Spread the pecans on a parchment-covered baking sheet and toast for about 12 minutes, or until they are fragrant. Transfer to a cutting board and coarsely chop.

• Heat the oil in sauté pan. Add the apple pieces. Stir continuously over medium-high heat for about 3 minutes, or until the apples start to soften. Remove from the heat. Place the apples in a bowl and stir in the chopped pecans and the cinnamon until the apples are thoroughly coated. Set aside.

make the streusel:

• In a medium bowl, combine the pastry flour, maple sugar, cinnamon, baking powder, and salt. Stir to blend thoroughly. Slowly drizzle in the oil, tossing with your fingers until the mixture is moistened. The mixture should be like wet sand, with pebbles of various sizes, ranging from crumbs to large pebbles. Add a few drops of water if necessary to get there.

make the cake:

• Preheat the oven to 350° F. Oil a 9-inch springform pan and set aside.

• Into a medium bowl, sift the flours, baking powder, baking soda, and spices. Stir to blend.

• In a second bowl, whisk the oil, maple syrup, water, vinegar, vanilla, and salt until thoroughly blended and emulsified. (This can be done in a blender.)

cake

1 cup whole-wheat pastry flour
1 cup unbleached white flour
2 teaspoons baking powder
2 teaspoons baking soda
1 teaspoon ground cinnamon
1 teaspoon ground ginger
1 teaspoon dry mustard
½ teaspoon ground cloves
⅓ cup canola oil
¾ cup pure maple syrup
¾ cup water
1 tablespoon apple cider vinegar
2 tablespoons vanilla extract
½ teaspoon salt

• Pour the liquid ingredients into the flour mixture and whisk until the liquid ingredients are completely absorbed. Scrape down the sides of the bowl with a rubber spatula to make sure all of the dry is mixed in. Don't worry if there are a few small lumps, as they will bake out.

assemble the cake:

• Cover the bottom of the springform pan with batter (about 2 cups). Evenly distribute the filling on top, then pour on the remaining batter to cover the filling completely. Sprinkle the streusel evenly on top. Bake on the center rack of the oven until a toothpick or cake tester inserted in the center comes out dry, 50 to 60 minutes. Remove from the oven and set on a cake rack to cool for 30 minutes. Remove the cake from the pan and let it cool completely.

things to watch out for

Check the cake after 40 minutes to see how it's cooking. Make sure you don't open the door too soon, but rather wait until the cake has developed some structure—at least 20 minutes. On the other hand, if you have a temperamental oven, and it tends to jump temperature, you need to check up on it (which is why it is so important to have an oven thermometer in the oven in plain sight when you open the door). If the top looks like it's getting dark, but the inside is still unbaked, cover loosely with aluminum foil and lower the temperature to 300° F. to dry out the filling.

date-pecan coffee cake

Even if you're not a date aficionado, you'll love this date-pecan streusel cake, inspired by my friend and colleague Lynnie Martinez. Pure comfort food, this is my favorite dessert to have in the late afternoon with a cup of tea. It tastes great with the Cashew-Cinnamon Ice Cream (page 285).

Remember not to mix the cake until you're ready to bake it.

SERVES 10 TO 12

filling

1   cup pecan halves
2   tablespoons pure maple syrup
2   tablespoons maple sugar, Sucanat, or dry sugar of your choice
½   cup dates, about 5 or 6 large
1   cup apple cider or apple juice
1   teaspoon cinnamon powder

SUGARED PECANS ARE SO TASTY THAT YOU MIGHT WANT TO DOUBLE THE RECIPE TO HAVE SOME ON HAND TO SPRINKLE OVER FROZEN DESSERTS OR PUMPKIN PIE, OR TO JUST PLAIN SNACK ON.

streusel

¾   cup whole-wheat pastry flour
½   cup pecan halves
⅓   cup maple sugar, Sucanat, or dry sugar of your choice
1   teaspoon cinnamon powder
½   teaspoon baking powder
    Pinch of salt
6   tablespoons canola oil

make the filling:

• Preheat the oven to 350° F. In a small bowl, toss the pecans with the maple syrup and sugar. Spread on a parchment-covered baking sheet. Bake for 15 minutes, tossing the nuts every 5 minutes to keep from sticking and to distribute the sugar. Remove from the oven and cool. Chop the pecans by hand into small pieces.

• Cut the dates into ¼-inch pieces, making sure to remove any pits. In a small pot or saucepan, heat the dates in the apple cider until the liquid reaches a boil. Immediately remove the pot from the heat and strain the liquid, reserving it for the cake batter. You should have about ¾ cup of liquid left. (If not, make up for the measurement with water. If you have extra, take some away to get ¾ cup.)

• Mix the dates with the chopped pecans. Stir in the cinnamon. Set aside.

make the streusel:

• In a food processor fitted with a metal blade, pulse the pastry flour, pecans, and sugar until you have a coarse meal. Remove the contents to a bowl and add the cinnamon, baking powder, and salt and mix well. Slowly drizzle in the oil, tossing with your fingers until the mixture is moistened. The mixture should be like that of wet sand, with pebbles ranging in size from crumbs to larger pebbles. Add a few drops of water if necessary to get the right texture. Set aside.

cake

1 cup whole-wheat pastry flour
1 cup unbleached white flour
2 teaspoons baking powder
2 teaspoons baking soda
⅓ cup canola oil, plus oil for
  greasing the pan
¾ cup pure maple syrup
¾ cup date soaking liquid
1 tablespoon apple cider vinegar
2 tablespoons vanilla extract
½ teaspoon salt

make the cake:

• Preheat the oven to 350° F. Oil a 9-inch springform pan and set aside.

• Into a medium bowl, sift the flours, baking powder, and baking soda. Stir to blend. In a second bowl whisk the oil, maple syrup, date soaking liquid, vinegar, vanilla, and salt until thoroughly blended and emulsified. (This may be done in a blender.)

• Pour the wet ingredients into the flour mixture. Whisk until the liquids are completely absorbed into the flour mixture. Scrape down the sides of your bowl with a rubber spatula to make sure all of the dry is mixed in. Don't worry if there are a few small lumps—they will bake out.

assemble the cake:

• Cover the bottom of the pan with batter (about 2 cups). Evenly distribute the filling on top, then pour on the remaining batter to completely cover the filling. Sprinkle the streusel on top to cover the cake. Bake on the center rack of the oven until a toothpick or cake tester inserted in the center comes out dry, 50 to 60 minutes. Remove the cake from the oven and set on a cake rack to cool for 30 minutes. Remove the cake from the pan and let it cool completely.

chocolate coconut cake
with chocolate fudge frosting

The marriage of chocolate and coconut in this rich-tasting cake (perfect for a birthday) is truly a match made in heaven. They'll never believe it's vegan! For a really tall cake, I bake it in two 8-inch cake pans instead of the 9-inch ones.

SERVES 10 TO 12

1 cup whole-wheat pastry flour
1 cup unbleached white flour
1¾ teaspoons baking powder
1 teaspoon baking soda
½ cup cocoa powder
1 cup coconut milk
6 tablespoons coconut oil (start with 8 solid and melt) or 6 tablespoons canola oil
1½ cups pure maple syrup
1½ teaspoons apple cider vinegar
2½ teaspoons coconut flavor
½ teaspoon vanilla extract
½ teaspoon salt
Chocolate Fudge Frosting (recipe follows)
1 cup unsweetened dried coconut, for garnish

• Preheat the oven to 350° F.

• Oil two 9-inch cake pans (or two 8-inch pans), line the bottoms with parchment circles, and oil again.

• Into a medium bowl, sift the pastry flour, unbleached white flour, baking powder, and baking soda.

• In a small saucepan over medium heat, dissolve the cocoa powder in coconut milk, stirring continuously. When the cocoa begins to bubble, remove it from the heat and pour it into an empty bowl. Add the remaining liquid ingredients and the salt to the cocoa and whisk until they are well combined.

• Pour the liquid ingredients into the dry, and whisk until the liquid is completely absorbed. Pour the batter into the pans and bake for 20 to 25 minutes, or until the cake starts to pull away from the sides of the pan and a toothpick comes out clean.

• Let the cakes cool in the pans on racks for 10 minutes. Loosen the sides with a spatula or knife and invert onto oiled wire racks. Remove the parchment circle. To prevent splitting, invert the cakes so that the tops face up. Cool completely before frosting with the Chocolate Fudge Frosting or wrapping overnight to store. Press the coconut into the sides of the cake for decoration.

chocolate fudge frosting

This smooth and delicious frosting seems as if has a lot of maple syrup, but it does not taste overly sweet. The recipe calls for agar powder, which is the easiest form of agar to use here since you need only 1 tablespoon, and it dissolves very easily. Agar powder is sometimes difficult to find, so you can substitute 4 tablespoons of agar flakes in this recipe. Dissolve the flakes the same way, only stir to make sure they don't stick to the side of the pan. Make sure to simmer for a good 10 minutes or more, stirring frequently, until all the flakes dissolve.

This fun decorative medium keeps well in the refrigerator for weeks.

1¼ cups water
1   tablespoon agar powder or
    4 tablespoons agar flakes
½   cup cocoa powder
1½ cups pure maple syrup
    Pinch of salt
2   tablespoons arrowroot powder
¼   cup soy milk
1   teaspoon vanilla extract
1   cup chocolate chips

- In a small saucepan combine the water and agar powder or agar flakes. Cook over medium heat, uncovered, stirring occasionally, until the water starts to boil. Reduce the heat and simmer for 3 minutes if using agar powder and about 10 minutes if using agar flakes. Stir the flakes frequently to make sure nothing sticks to the pot.

- Add the cocoa powder, maple syrup, and salt, stirring occasionally to dissolve the cocoa powder.

- In a small bowl, dissolve the arrowroot in the soy milk to make a slurry. When the cocoa liquid starts to boil, add the arrowroot slurry, stirring constantly (stopping every so often only long enough to see if it's bubbling), until you see bubbles starting to form. The mixture will thicken and lose its cloudy look when the liquid starts to bubble.

- Turn off the heat. (If you used agar flakes, pour the mixture through a fine-meshed strainer to catch any bits of undissolved agar.) Add the vanilla and chocolate chips. Let the chocolate chips sit in the liquid for a couple of minutes to heat. Then, whisk until smooth. Pour into a shallow pan and refrigerate for about 45 minutes, or until hardened. Scoop the frosting into the food processor and whip until smooth. Return the frosting to the refrigerator for about 10 minutes to let the frosting firm up a bit.

gingerbread with blood-orange sauce

This is gingerbread! Dark and moist, it scents the house with sweet-smelling spices. Great for packing in a lunch box or on a picnic, the cake is really enhanced and dressed up when paired with the gingery orange sauce. Although you can use a 9-inch springform or cake pan, it's irresistible baked in individual baby cake molds (3-inch cheesecake molds are great for their easy release). If you do use individual molds, do not fill the pan more than halfway, since the wet batter rises quite a bit while baking.

SERVES 10

1 cup plus 2 teaspoons whole-wheat pastry flour
1 cup unbleached white flour
2 teaspoons baking powder
1 teaspoons baking soda
½ teaspoon salt
1 tablespoon ground ginger
½ teaspoon ground cloves
¼ teaspoon ground cinnamon
½ cup canola oil
1 cup pure maple syrup
½ cup molasses
1 cup original flavored soy milk
1 tablespoon apple cider vinegar
2 tablespoons vanilla extract
Blood-Orange Sauce (recipe follows)
Chopped orange segments, for garnish

• Preheat the oven to 350° F. Oil a 9-inch springform pan or a cake pan. Line it with a parchment circle. Alternatively, oil and line with parchment paper ten 3-inch individual cake molds.

• In a medium bowl, sift together the flours, baking powder, baking soda, salt, and spices. Whisk to combine. In another medium bowl, combine the canola oil, maple syrup, molasses, soy milk, vinegar, and vanilla. Whisk vigorously until the ingredients are emulsified (you can do this in a blender).

• Pour the liquid ingredients into the dry, whisking together just until all the liquid ingredients are absorbed. The batter will be quite wet.

• Pour the batter into the oiled pan or pans and place on a middle rack in the oven. Bake for about 55 minutes, or until the cake is springy to the touch and a toothpick inserted comes out clean. If you are using individual cake molds, put them on a baking sheet for easy removal. The baby cakes take a little less time to cook, so start checking after 35 minutes.

• Serve the cakes warm or cool atop a pool of the blood-orange sauce. Sprinkle chopped orange pieces around the plate.

blood-orange sauce

Blood oranges have orange- to crimson-colored skins. The juice is a beautiful blood-red color, and they are more intensely flavored than juice oranges. Blood oranges are mostly available from January through March.

1½ cups plus 2 tablespoons orange juice, preferably from blood oranges

1   2-inch piece of fresh ginger, unpeeled and cut into 3 slices

2   tablespoons maple sugar, date sugar, or Sucanat

1   heaping tablespoon arrowroot, or 1 tablespoon kudzu

1   teaspoon orange zest

2   tablespoons ginger juice (see page 197)

• In a small saucepan, heat 1½ cups of the orange juice to a boil with the sliced ginger and sugar.

• In a small bowl, dissolve the arrowroot in the remaining 2 tablespoons of orange juice to make a slurry.

• When the orange juice reaches a boil, stir in the slurry. (Give the slurry a stir at the last minute right before adding, to dislodge any arrowroot that might have settled at the bottom of the bowl.) Stir continuously, lifting your spoon to look every so often for the first few bubbles to appear. The liquid will have lightly thickened.

• Immediately turn off the heat when the first bubbles appear and stir in the orange zest and ginger juice. Remove the ginger slices. Serve with the gingerbread cake.

carrot cake with coconut–cardamom sauce

There's nothing ordinary about this carrot cake. It's a twist on the classic, with dates and cardamom instead of the more traditional ingredients. The creamy coconut-cardamom sauce and toasted coconut-cardamom garnish accentuate the cake's flavors.

SERVES 9

1 cup walnut halves (10 to 12 walnuts)
1 cup whole-wheat pastry flour
1 cup unbleached white flour
2 teaspoons baking powder
2 teaspoons baking soda
2 teaspoons ground cinnamon
3 teaspoons ground cardamom
½ cup canola oil
⅔ cup pure maple syrup
⅔ cup soy milk
½ teaspoon salt
2 cups grated carrots
½ cup chopped dates
3 tablespoons dried coconut
Coconut-Cardamom Sauce (recipe follows)

• Preheat the oven to 350° F. Place the walnuts on a baking sheet and lightly toast for 10 minutes, or until fragrant. Remove from the oven and place in a strainer. Rub the walnuts against the strainer (over the sink or wastebasket) to loosen the skins. Remove the walnuts from the strainer and chop by hand into small (¼-inch) pieces. Set aside.

• Oil a 9-inch cake pan or springform pan, and line the bottom with a parchment circle and oil again. Alternatively, oil nine 3-inch baby cake molds and line the bottoms with parchment circles.

• Sift the flours, baking powder, baking soda, cinnamon, and 2 teaspoons of the cardamom into a medium bowl.

• In another medium bowl, whisk the oil, maple syrup, soy milk, and salt until the ingredients are emulsified. Pour the liquid ingredients into the dry and whisk together just until the dry ingredients are completely moistened. Stir in the chopped walnuts, grated carrots, and dates with a rubber spatula. The batter will be thick.

• Pour the batter into the oiled pan or pans and bake for 25 to 30 minutes, or until the top has formed a good crust. Test with a toothpick or cake tester to see if cake is baked. If the toothpick or cake tester comes out wet, cover the cake loosely with a piece of foil and bake for another 5 to 10 minutes, until the tester comes out clean. Remove from oven and let cool.

• While the cake bakes, in a small bowl, mix together the coconut and the remaining tablespoon of ground cardamom. Dry-toast the coconut in a heavy-bottomed or cast-iron skillet just until the coconut starts to brown. Set aside.

• Serve the cake beside a pool of Coconut–Cardamom Sauce and sprinkle with spiced, toasted coconut. Or pour the sauce over the cake and sprinkle the coconut on top.

coconut–cardamom sauce

The carrot juice gives the sauce a light salmon color that looks delectable under the carrot cake. Tamarind concentrate, which lends a singular sour note to the sauce, is readily available in Indian groceries. If you cannot find the tamarind, substitute a teaspoon of lemon juice.

1   14-ounce can light coconut milk
¼   cup fresh carrot juice
15 cardamom pods
¼   cup pure maple syrup
½   teaspoon tamarind concentrate
1   heaping tablespoon arrowroot powder
1   teaspoon vanilla extract

• Reserve 2 tablespoons of the coconut milk to mix with the arrowroot. Put the remainder in a small pot with the carrot juice, cardamom pods, maple syrup, and tamarind. Slowly bring the liquid to a boil. Turn off the heat and let sit for a few minutes to infuse the liquid with cardamom. Strain the liquid to remove the cardamom pods. Return the liquid to the pot and place it over the heat.

• In a small bowl, mix the arrowroot with the reserved coconut milk to make a slurry. When the coconut-milk mixture reaches a boil, stir in the slurry, stirring continuously until the liquid just starts to bubble. The liquid will have thickened. Remove it from the heat and stir in the vanilla. Refrigerate to cool the sauce.

chocolate mousse cake

This is an all-around winner for chocolate lovers—a rich, moist cake with a thick layer of hazelnut mousse. It keeps well for three to four days in the refrigerator; you can make the cake in two sessions if you like; it's elegant enough for special occasions; and it tastes delicious with the Raspberry Sauce (page 245). For a double-layer cake, double the cake part of the recipe, bake it in two 9-inch pans, and make the Chocolate Fudge Frosting (page 253).

The mousse topping calls for blanched hazelnuts, which are getting increasingly easy to find even in local supermarkets. If you cannot find blanched hazelnuts, you can remove the skins yourself by spreading nuts on a cookie sheet and baking for 12 minutes. While they are still warm, rub the nuts in a towel to remove the skins. As a substitution, raw cashews are delicious.

To get the best texture for the mousse, it is better to use a blender to mix the almond milk and hazelnuts. A food processor will work, but the texture will be much grainier.

SERVES 12

cake

1   cup whole-wheat pastry flour
1   cup unbleached white flour
2   teaspoons baking powder
1   teaspoon baking soda
½   cup cocoa powder
1   teaspoon ground cinnamon
1   cup water
½   cup canola oil
1½   cups pure maple syrup
1   teaspoon apple cider vinegar
2   teaspoons vanilla extract
½   teaspoon salt

YOU NEED TO USE A SPRINGFORM PAN FOR THIS CAKE TO ALLOW YOU TO REMOVE IT EASILY.

FOR MOCHA FLAVOR, I SOMETIMES USE INSTANT ESPRESSO, OR FOR A CAFFEINE-FREE ALTERNATIVE, A ROASTED GRAIN COFFEE. GRAIN COFFEE IS A CEREAL BEVERAGE MADE FROM VARYING INGREDIENTS SUCH AS BARLEY, RYE, MALTED BARLEY, CHICORY, AND ACORNS. NATURAL FOOD STORES USUALLY HAVE A GOOD SELECTION.

make the cake:

• Preheat the oven to 350° F.

• Oil a 9-inch springform pan.

• Sift the flours, baking powder, and baking soda into a medium bowl.

• In a small saucepan over medium heat, dissolve the cocoa powder and cinnamon in the water, stirring continuously. When the cocoa begins to bubble, remove from the heat and pour into another medium bowl. Add the remaining liquid ingredients and salt to the cocoa, and whisk until they are well combined.

• Pour the liquid ingredients into the dry, and whisk until the batter is smooth. Pour the batter into the pan and bake for 20 to 25 minutes, or until the cake starts to pull away from the sides of the pan and a toothpick comes out clean.

make the mousse topping:

• In a blender, blend the blanched almonds with the water. Line a strainer with cheesecloth and pour the blended almonds through it. Squeeze the cheesecloth to extract all the liquid from the pulp. You should have 3 cups of almond milk. If you are a little shy of 3 cups, make up the difference with water. Discard the pulp.

mousse topping

1 cup blanched almonds
3 cups water
1 cup store-bought blanched hazelnuts (cashews can be substituted)
3 tablespoons agar flakes
¼ cup cocoa powder
2 tablespoons grain coffee or instant coffee
1 cup pure maple syrup
½ teaspoon salt
2 tablespoons arrowroot powder
¼ cup original flavored soy milk
1 tablespoon vanilla extract

½ cup store-bought blanched hazelnuts, chopped, for garnish

Raspberry Sauce (page 245)

BUY BLANCHED ALMONDS (ALMONDS WITH THE SKINS REMOVED) OR BLANCH YOUR OWN. TO BLANCH: BRING A SMALL POT OF WATER TO A BOIL. DROP WHOLE ALMONDS IN FOR ABOUT 1 MINUTE, THEN DRAIN. THE SKINS WILL BE SUFFICIENTLY LOOSENED TO SLIP OFF EASILY.

• Finely pulse the hazelnuts in a food processor. Do not let the machine run more than a few seconds continuously, so as not to turn the nuts into nut butter. Add the ground nuts and the almond milk to the blender and blend until the mix is very creamy.

• To a small saucepan, add the almond–hazelnut milk, agar flakes, cocoa powder, grain coffee, maple syrup, and salt. Warm over a medium-high heat. Keep an eye on the mixture as it starts to boil, so that you make sure it does not boil over. In a small bowl, dissolve the arrowroot in soy milk to make a slurry.

• When the liquid begins to boil, lower the heat and gently simmer 5 to 10 minutes, to dissolve the agar fully. Add the arrowroot slurry and stir until the liquid just starts to bubble again. The liquid will have lightly thickened.

• Remove the mousse from the heat and stir in the vanilla. Pour the mousse over the cake in the pan and place it in the refrigerator for about 45 minutes to cool and set. You can line the border of the cake with toasted, chopped hazelnuts if desired.

• To unmold, run a knife around the inside edge of the cake pan to loosen the mousse and cake. Release the springform rim and carefully lift it away.

• Serve the cake as is or on a pool of raspberry sauce.

When the mixture is dark, it is difficult to see if the agar is fully dissolved. I usually take a spoonful of liquid from the pot and pour it onto a plate. If I can see little undissolved flakes, I simmer the mixture for a few more minutes and retest it.

peanut butter mousse cake

When I was a little girl, peanut butter was about the only food I would touch. Luckily, my tastes have widened considerably; however, I would still never turn my back on a good peanutty dessert.

The peanut taste here is delicate in the smooth-as-silk mousse that sits atop a rich-tasting blondie. Decorative peanut butter and chocolate sauce lines drawn into the topping provide a professional finish that makes it suitable for birthdays and other special occasions. Be sure to use a good-quality peanut butter, one whose sole ingredient is peanuts.

SERVES 10 TO 12

blondie layer

½ cup whole-wheat pastry flour
½ cup plus two tablespoons unbleached white flour
½ teaspoon baking powder
¼ cup Sucanat
¼ cup grain coffee such as Yannoh, or Inka
½ cup canola oil
½ cup pure maple syrup
¼ cup original flavored soy milk
2 teaspoons vanilla extract
2 tablespoons tahini
1 tablespoon creamy peanut butter
½ teaspoon salt

peanut butter–chocolate sauce

½ cup pure maple syrup
2 tablespoons cocoa powder or carob powder
2 teaspoons arrowroot powder
½ cup original flavored soy milk
¼ teaspoon vanilla extract
2 tablespoons creamy peanut butter

make the blondie layer:

• Preheat the oven to 350° F. Oil a 9-inch springform pan and set aside. In a medium bowl whisk the flours, baking powder, Sucanat, and grain coffee to combine.

• Add to a medium bowl the canola oil, maple syrup, soy milk, vanilla, tahini, peanut butter, and salt. Whisk together until the ingredients are well combined. Pour the liquid ingredients into the bowl with the dry ingredients, whisking all the ingredients together, just until the dry ingredients are completely moistened.

• Pour the batter into the oiled pan, spreading it evenly across the bottom. Place on the center rack in the oven and bake for 20 minutes, or until the cake has begun to pull away from the sides and a toothpick inserted in the center comes out clean.

make the peanut butter–chocolate sauce:

• Add the maple syrup and cocoa to a small saucepan, stirring until the cocoa is dissolved. In a small bowl, dissolve the arrowroot in the soymilk to make a slurry. When the maple mixture begins to bubble, add the slurry, stirring continuously, until bubbles appear on the surface and the liquid has thickened. Remove from the heat and stir in the vanilla and peanut butter. Cool the sauce for about 15 minutes and pour into a squeeze bottle if you have one. This makes putting decorative stripes on the top graceful and easy.

peanut butter mousse filling

1½ pounds firm silken tofu (the boxed kind, like Mori -Nu)
¼ cup canola oil
1   cup pure maple syrup
¼ teaspoon salt
½ teaspoon fresh lemon juice
1   tablespoon vanilla extract
6   tablespoons creamy peanut butter
1   cup water
2   tablespoons agar flakes
4   teaspoons arrowroot powder
½ cup original flavored soy milk

make the mousse filling:

• To a food processor fitted with a metal blade, add the tofu, oil, maple syrup, salt, lemon juice, vanilla, and peanut butter, and process until smooth.

• Add the water with the agar flakes to a small saucepan. Heat until the liquid comes to a boil, then lower the heat and gently simmer for 10 to 15 minutes, or until the agar is completely dissolved. In a small bowl, mix the arrowroot with the soy milk to make a slurry. Stir the slurry into the hot liquid and cook, stirring constantly, until the liquid just starts to bubble.

• Pour the agar mixture into the food processor and process until everything is thoroughly combined. Pour into the cake pan over the blondie layer.

• Let the filling set for a few minutes, then paint or pipe the peanut butter–chocolate sauce onto the top in stripes about ½ inch apart. Run a knife or toothpick through the stripes, pulling the design down. Pull the knife back and forth over the lines so that you get a feathered effect.

• Place the cake in the refrigerator for about 45 minutes to completely set and cool. Run a knife around the edge of the cake pan. Release the cake from the springform rim and serve.

lemon pudding cake with blueberry glaze

My testers dubbed this the "lazy man's way to make a fancy cake"—it looks elaborate but is actually quite easy to put together. The important thing to remember is to pour the blueberry glaze on top of the lemon pudding when the pudding is partially set, which will make the blueberry adhere perfectly to the lemon.

The lemon pudding alone makes an excellent tart filling. Pair it with the crust recipe from the Cranberry-Orange Tart (page 242) and top it with fresh raspberries.

SERVES 10 TO 12

cake

1   cup whole-wheat pastry flour
1   cup unbleached white flour
1½ teaspoons baking powder
¾   teaspoon baking soda
⅓   cup canola oil
¾   cup pure maple syrup
⅔   cup water
1   tablespoon vanilla extract
1   tablespoon lemon extract
2   tablespoons fresh lemon juice
½   teaspoon sea salt
1   tablespoon lemon zest

lemon topping

2   cups apple cider or apple juice
5   tablespoons agar flakes
⅛   teaspoon turmeric
    Pinch of sea salt
1   cup rice syrup
¼   cup pure maple syrup
¾   cup strained fresh lemon juice
½   cup soy milk
¼   cup arrowroot powder
1   tablespoon plus 1 teaspoon lemon zest, finely minced
2   teaspoons vanilla extract

make the cake:

• Preheat the oven to 350° F. Oil a 9-inch springform pan.

• Into a medium bowl, sift the flours, baking powder, and baking soda. Stir to blend. To another bowl (or in a blender) add the oil, maple syrup, water, vanilla, lemon extract, lemon juice, and salt and whisk together until thoroughly emulsified.

• Pour the liquid ingredients into the flour mixture. Whisk until the flour mixture is completely moistened. Stir in the lemon zest. Scrape down the sides of the bowl with a rubber spatula to incorporate all of the ingredients.

• Pour the batter into the prepared pan. Even it out with a spatula. Place on a middle rack in the oven and bake for 30 to 35 minutes, or until the cake starts to pull away from the sides of the pan and a toothpick inserted in the center comes out clean. Set aside to cool as you prepare the topping. Don't trim or worry if the top of the cake is not perfectly flat; the topping will cover any flaws.

make the lemon topping:

• To a 4-quart saucepan add the apple cider, agar flakes, turmeric, and salt. Cook over medium heat. Stir now and again to make sure the agar flakes are not sticking to the sides of the pot. When the mixture comes to a boil, lower the heat and gently simmer for 5 to 10 minutes to make sure the agar flakes have dissolved. Add the rice syrup, maple syrup, and lemon juice and raise the heat to medium.

• Meanwhile, in a small bowl, mix the soy milk and the arrowroot to make a slurry. (Make sure to give it another good mix right before you add it to the pot, to stir any arrowroot that has settled to the bottom.) When the mixture on the stove reaches a boil, add the slurry, stirring continuously. Keep stirring, raising your spoon every now and again to check if bubbles have formed. Cook until the liquid changes from cloudy to clear, thickens, and just starts to bubble.

- Remove the topping from the heat and stir in the lemon zest and vanilla. Let the topping sit in the pot to thicken for about 15 minutes. Then pour it onto the cake and let it set for about 10 minutes while you make the blueberry topping. Do not refrigerate at this time to speed the setting, since it is important that the lemon topping not be completely set before you add the blueberry glaze.

blueberry glaze

¾ cup plus 2 tablespoons apple cider
2 teaspoons agar flakes
1 tablespoon pure maple syrup
1 cup fresh blueberries
Pinch of salt
1 tablespoon arrowroot
1 teaspoon vanilla extract

2 kiwis
6 to 8 medium strawberries
½ cup fresh raspberries

make the blueberry glaze:

- To a medium pan, add ¾ cup of the apple cider, the agar flakes, maple syrup, blueberries, and salt. Cook over medium heat until the blueberries have imparted their blue color to the juice, some have burst, and the liquid begins to boil.

- In a small bowl mix the arrowroot with the remaining 2 tablespoons of apple cider to make a slurry. Stir the slurry into the blueberry mixture, stirring continuously until the liquid goes from cloudy to clear and just starts to bubble. Remove from the heat and stir in the vanilla.

- Carefully spoon the blueberry glaze over the lemon topping. The lemon pudding should be thickened enough that the glaze sits on top of the pudding without sinking into it. Cover the entire cake with a layer of the glaze and let it sit for a few minutes. Carefully move the cake to the refrigerator to set. Let it set for 20 minutes before garnishing.

- Peel the kiwis and slice them lengthwise in half. Slice each half into quarters. Wash the strawberries, cut off the stems, and cut each strawberry in half. Place each strawberry half flat on the cutting board. Cut thin slices down from the tip, without cutting through the tip, so that they are all connected at the tip. Fan out the sliced pieces of the strawberry half.

- Remove the cake from the refrigerator and arrange the strawberry fans and the kiwi slices alternately around the edge of the cake. Line the inner edge of the fruit with a ring of raspberries. Return to the refrigerator for about 30 minutes to finish setting. To unmold, run a knife around the edge of the cake. Carefully release the springform rim and lift it off.

poached pear and pecan strudel

Once you discover filo, I'm sure you'll be as enthusiastic as I am about it. For dinner parties, filo pastries such as this strudel can't be beat—I always make mine a few days ahead to eliminate last-minute hassle. When my guests are eating their main course, I pop it in the oven and let it bake. The strudel scents the kitchen deliciously, and the dessert is hot and fresh.

Fresh rosemary is suitable not only for savory food: it gives wonderful flavor to the poaching pears. Here, the infused pears are rolled in layers of flaky filo and baked to a golden crispness.

You can substitute one quart of apple-raspberry juice for the apple cider and the raspberry juice.

SERVES 6

3	pears (Bosc or Anjou)
2	cups apple cider
2	cups raspberry juice
2	sprigs of fresh rosemary
1	cinnamon stick
½	cup toasted chopped pecans
½	teaspoon ground cinnamon
1	tablespoon pure maple syrup
½	pound filo dough, defrosted
	Canola oil for brushing the filo
½	cup dry breadcrumbs

• Peel the pears, cut them in half, and remove the cores. Add the pears to a medium-large pot (large enough to hold the pears in a single layer) along with the cider, juice, rosemary, and cinnamon stick. Top the liquid with a parchment circle (with a steam vent cut in the middle) to keep the pears submerged (see Box.) Bring the liquid to a boil, reduce to a simmer, and cook until the pears are tender-firm. Remove the pears from the liquid and cool them separately from the liquid (so as not to cook the pears further). Strain the poaching liquid. Pour the cooled poaching liquid over the cooled pears to store. At this point they can be stored for several weeks.

• Remove the pears from the poaching liquid and drain well. Reserve the poaching liquid. Slice the pears into ½-inch pieces and place in a bowl. Toss with the toasted pecans, ground cinnamon, and maple syrup.

• Take the filo from its wrapping. Lay it out on a clean, dry surface and cover it with plastic wrap or a towel so it doesn't dry out.

• Take 1 sheet of filo and lay it on your work surface. Lightly brush the entire surface with oil. Take the second sheet of filo and lay it on top of the first, again oiling lightly. Add five more layers, brushing with oil in between each layer, to make a 7-layered strudel. Sprinkle the breadcrumbs over the last layer before adding the pears.

• Place the pears over half of the filo, starting 1 inch from the bottom edge and a few inches from the sides. Fold the sides in and then start rolling the filo until the whole piece is rolled into a log shape. Brush with oil to cover, and seal. At this point you can freeze the strudel until ready to cook.

parchment circle

When pears are added to liquid, they insist on bobbing around, refusing to stay submerged. They can be poached evenly, however, if you make a parchment circle to place right on top of the liquid. To make a parchment circle, fold your piece of parchment into a square that is bigger than the pot. (1 and 2) Fold it in half twice—see diagram—and then (3, 4, and 5) continue folding diagonally like a paper airplane. (6) Place the point at the center of the pot creating a radius and cut the side where it hits the edge. (7) Then cut ½ inch off at the tip to allow for a steam vent. (8) Open up your parchment, and you should have a circle about the size of your pot with a hole in the center.

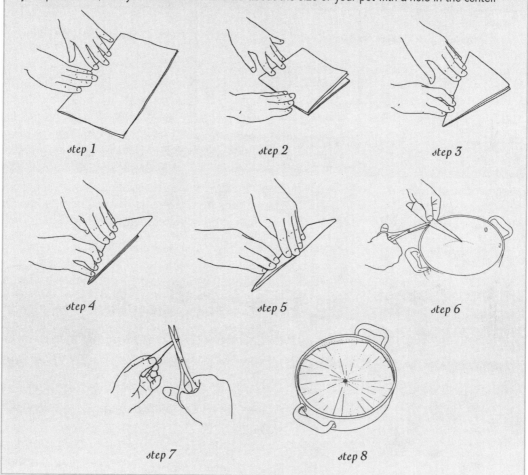

step 1   *step 2*   *step 3*

step 4   *step 5*   *step 6*

step 7   *step 8*

- Preheat the oven to 375° F.

- Make a glaze by placing the reserved poaching liquid in a pot and boiling for 45 minutes, or until it is reduced to ½ cup.

- Meanwhile, place the strudel on a parchment-covered sheet and bake until the filo is golden brown, about 30 minutes. Remove the strudel from the oven and serve drizzled with the glaze.

filo bundles with apples, pear, and quince

The pomegranate seeds surrounding these petal-leafed fruit dumplings look so delightfully festive that Persephone herself certainly would have been tempted to eat more than six. Served with caramel sauce, this is a great dessert for the finale to an autumn soirée, since it highlights those exciting but sometimes difficult-to-use fruits, quince and pomegranate. Like the Poached, Pear and Pecan Strudel, make this dessert in advance, freeze it, and bake it while you're serving the main course.

The filo for this dessert must be pliable, or it will be difficult to handle. You will need white cotton kitchen string to tie the bundles.

MAKES 7 TO 8

¾ cup walnut halves
1   medium apple
1   Anjou pear
1   medium quince
1   teaspoon ground cinnamon
2   tablespoons pure maple syrup
1   teaspoon strained fresh lemon juice
    Pinch of salt
½   cup red wine
1½ pounds filo dough, defrosted
    Canola oil or coconut oil for brushing the filo
    Caramel Sauce (page 268)
    Pomegranate seeds, for garnish

THE QUINCE, AVAILABLE THROUGH AUTUMN INTO EARLY WINTER, RESEMBLES A CROSS BETWEEN AN APPLE AND A PEAR, BUT IT HAS A DISTINCTIVE, FRAGRANT SCENT AND TASTE. IT BLENDS BEAUTIFULLY WITH THE APPLE AND PEAR. IF YOU CAN'T FIND ONE, YOU CAN SUBSTITUTE AN ASIAN PEAR FOR THE QUINCE OR DOUBLE UP ON THE APPLE OR PEAR.

• Preheat the oven to 350° F. Spread the walnuts on a baking sheet and toast them for 10 minutes, or until they are fragrant. Remove the walnuts from the oven and place in a strainer. Rub the walnuts, while warm, against the side of the strainer (over the sink or wastebasket) to loosen the skin. Remove the walnuts from the strainer and chop by hand into small pieces. Raise the oven temperature to 375° F.

• Peel and core the fruit and cut into small dice. In a medium bowl, combine the fruit, walnuts, cinnamon, maple syrup, lemon juice, salt, and wine. Toss well. Let the mixture sit for 15 minutes to allow the fruit to absorb the flavors, tossing every so often.

• Unroll the filo. Cut one edge to make the filo manageable. Cut other edges to make a 9-inch square. You can only get one 9-inch square out of the filo stack. Wrap up the cut strips of filo for another use. Remember to keep the filo covered at all times with a damp towel or paper towel when you are not working with it.

• Brush one sheet of filo with oil, lay another on top, oil that, then add another, and repeat until you have 4 sheets. Place ½ cup of filling in the center. Bring up the two opposite corners of the pastry over the filling, then fold up the other two to meet at the top. Press gently about 1½ inches down from the top. Tie string loosely around the pastry to hold it together. Pull the leaves down to form petals. Oil the outer surface of the pastry. Repeat with the remaining filo and fruit filling.

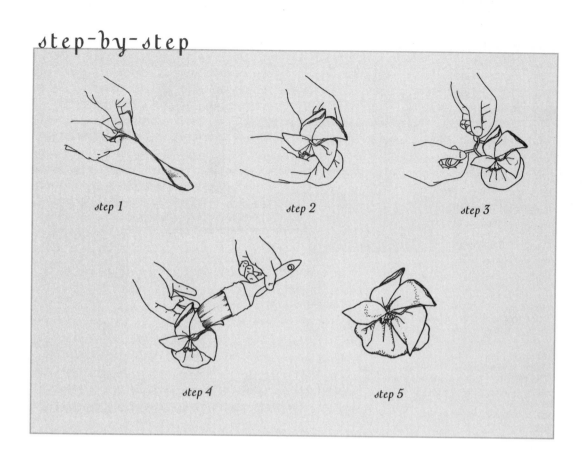

step 1

step 2

step 3

step 4

step 5

- Place the bundles on a parchment-covered baking sheet. Bake until they are golden, about 20 to 25 minutes. Or, freeze the bundles until ready to cook. (If frozen, do not defrost to bake. Take out of the freezer, place on a parchment-covered baking sheet, and bake until golden.)

- Remove from the oven, carefully cut the string, and discard it. Place each filo bundle on a plate and drizzle caramel sauce around it. Sprinkle with pomegranate seeds.

caramel sauce

This caramel sauce is golden, rich, and creamy. The syrups are cooked to a soft-ball stage—that is, when a spoonful of syrup is placed in a glass of ice water, it is soft and malleable. This is the correct point at which to add the other ingredients.

This sauce tastes scrumptious with other desserts as well; I like to eat it with the Cashew-Cinnamon Ice Cream (see page 285) and Chocolate Sorbet (see page 284). Kept refrigerated, it will last for several weeks.

1   teaspoon tahini
½   teaspoon creamy peanut butter
1   teaspoon vanilla extract
1   cup original flavored soy milk
½   cup pure maple syrup
½   cup rice syrup
1   teaspoon fresh lemon juice

WHEN HEATED, SUGAR GOES FROM A SOFT, PLI-ABLE STAGE TO A HARD, BRITTLE STAGE. FOR THE SAUCE TO BEHAVE PROPERLY, IT IS IMPOR-TANT THAT YOU NOT COOK IT PAST THE SOFT-BALL STAGE.

I LIKE TO HAVE A GLASS OF ICE WATER READY SO THAT I CAN TEST THE SUGAR SYRUP'S CONSISTENCY AS IT'S COOKING. I DO THIS BY DROPPING A LITTLE IN THE WATER TO COOL IT AND SEE WHAT STAGE THE SUGAR HAS REACHED.

• In a small bowl, mix the tahini, peanut butter, and vanilla with a rubber spatula. Slowly add the soy milk, whisking until it is incorporated.

• Have a glass of ice water on hand.

• In a small saucepan, bring the maple syrup and rice syrup to a boil over high heat. Reduce the heat slightly and let the sugars bubble and reduce until they thicken and go to the soft-ball stage. Start testing the syrup after 4 minutes to see how it's developing. If it's thread-like, loose, and stringy when placed in the ice water, it's not ready yet. Keep reducing and testing every minute. It is in the soft-ball stage when you put a spoonful into a glass of ice water and it has a soft, pliable consistency—a soft wax-like piece that holds together when you press it. This whole process takes 6 to 8 minutes.

• Slowly add soy-milk mixture, whisking until the mixture is completely incorporated. Whisk in the lemon juice and remove the pan from the heat. The sauce will thicken further when cool. Pour the sauce into a bowl or container and refrigerate.

For the sauce, I like to fill a squeeze bottle, the kind that is readily available at drugstores, art stores, and cooking supply stores. It makes drawing on the plate fast, easy, and fun!

a word about filo dough

Filo dough (or phyllo) is a paper-thin wheat dough most often associated with Greek or Middle Eastern specialties. Filo dough looks a lot more intimidating than it actually is. For all its delicateness, it is actually quite forgiving, and only a bit of practice yields impressive, professional results.

The main thing to remember is to keep the sheets you're not working on covered with a piece of plastic wrap, parchment, or a damp towel, to keep them from drying out. Uncover and lift each piece as needed, then cover again. Make sure you are working on a clean, dry surface.

Lightly—and that means lightly; no heavy hands here—brush a layer of oil between each layer, both to keep the filo from drying out and, more important, so the end product is light and flaky. The oil pushes the filo up and apart during baking. Without it, you'd have a glumpy, doughy mass, instead of the light, crispy layers we associate with baklava, strudel, and the like.

If your sheet of filo rips, don't worry. Once you layer and oil and layer again, you won't be able to tell. In this way filo is forgiving. As long as it hasn't dried out or become soggy, you shouldn't have any problems.

The best filo is made fresh in the area where you live. Even if you freeze this dough, it bears no resemblance to the stiff, cardboardy stuff you find in the freezer section in many gourmet-type shops. Once you use the fresh dough, you are destined to become a filo epicure, scoffing at the sight of a box in the freezer section.

Nonetheless, you have to use what you can get and you will get more than decent results with the boxed stuff. To defrost it, leave it in the refrigerator overnight, or on a counter for a few hours, and it is ready to use. Unused portions can be refrozen if they haven't been exposed to air.

oil crust

Creating a flaky, tender oil crust always poses a challenge for the baker. The smalll amount of baking powder in this crust lightens it; the small amount of sugar enhances its flavor; and the vinegar adds to the tenderness.

To ensure the flakiest crusts, all the ingredients must be very cold to start. Place canola oil in the coldest part of the freezer at least ½ hour (preferably more) before using. Canola oil is full of monounsaturates, which solidify somewhat when cold. Thus, the consistency of the canola oil changes quite a bit—it becomes thick and viscous and makes the flour pebbly, much the way butter does. The flour also works best if it is quite cold, so either store your flour in the freezer or place it in the freezer ½ hour before using. For the coldest water, simply place an ice cube in it to chill thoroughly.

As soon as the dough is made, it should be rolled and baked; this is not a good dough to make in advance and refrigerate.

MAKES ONE OR TWO 9-INCH PIE CRUSTS

single ccrust

¾   cup unbleached white flour, chilled
½   cup whole-wheat pastry flour, chilled
½   teaspoon baking powder
2   tablespoons unrefined cane sugar, Sucanat, or maple sugar
¼   teaspoon salt
¼   cup very cold canola oil
1   teaspoon apple cider vinegar
¼   cup to 6 tablespoons ice water

double crust

1½ cups unbleached white flour, chilled
1   cup whole-wheat pastry flour, chilled
1   teaspoon baking powder
4   tablespoons unrefined cane sugar, Sucanat, or maple sugar
½   teaspoon salt
½   cup very cold canola oil
1   teaspoon apple cider vinegar
½   cup ice water

• Toss the flours, baking powder, sugar, and salt together in a bowl. Drizzle in the oil a little at a time, tossing lightly with your fingers or a wooden spoon. The flour should lump in different-size pebbles, from very small to ½-inch lumps.

• Add the cider vinegar to the ice water. Drizzle this mixture a little at a time into the dough, tossing in the same way as with the oil. There is enough water when the dough starts to hold together when pinched. Do not add too much water, but just enough to hold the dough together when you squeeze it. You may not need all the water.

• Separate the dough into one or two balls (if you are making the double dough recipe). For the single crust, roll the one ball immediately. For the double crust, wrap the ball for the top crust in plastic, while rolling out the bottom crust, to prevent the dough from drying out.

coconut oil crust

More and more information has been coming to light in support of the notion that coconut oil is a very healthy product. Make sure to use organic unrefined oil (see Resources and Mail-Order).

Coconut oil produces a very tender, flaky, flavorful crust. This is my favorite completely vegan crust. Although coconut oil is solid at room temperature, the warmth of a kitchen melts it quite quickly. Therefore—for crusts especially—keep the oil in the refrigerator to harden it into a white, semisolid block. Measure the oil in dry measuring cups. Make sure to measure it in its solidified form.

A coconut oil crust is no more difficult to make than any other crust. You have to work the pieces of fat into the dough until it is pebbly, very closely resembling a butter crust. This recipe has a bit of baking powder to give it a lift, a bit of sugar for extra sweetness, and vinegar to make the crust especially tender.

MAKES ONE OR TWO 9-INCH PIE CRUSTS

single crust

¾ cup unbleached white flour, chilled
½ cup whole-wheat pastry flour, chilled
½ teaspoon baking powder
2 tablespoons maple sugar, Sucanat, or cane sugar
¼ teaspoon salt
6 tablespoons (¼ cup plus 2 tablespoons) coconut oil
1 teaspoon apple cider vinegar
3 to 5 tablespoons ice water

double crust

1½ cups unbleached white flour, chilled
1 cup whole-wheat pastry flour, chilled
1 teaspoon baking powder
4 tablespoons maple sugar, Sucanat, or cane sugar
½ teaspoon salt
¾ cup coconut oil
2 teaspoons apple cider vinegar
8 to 10 tablespoons ice water

• Toss the flours, baking powder, sugar, and salt together in a medium bowl.

• Measure the coconut oil. You have to scrape it out of the container with a spoon, since it hardens in the refrigerator. Toss the coconut oil with the dry ingredients, coating the hardened pieces with flour, which makes the pieces easier to break up and work in. Work the oil into the flour with your fingers. The coconut oil should be distributed into different-size pebbles, all of them small. Break up any large clumps or pebbles into smaller pebbles. Make sure there are no pebbles larger than a pea.

• Add the cider vinegar to the ice water. Drizzle the water into the dough a spoonful at a time, mixing in each as you go. You have enough water in the dough when the dough holds together when squeezed. Do not add any more water than is absolutely necessary.

• Gather the dough into a ball and flatten it into a disk. If you are making a double crust, divide the dough into two equal-size balls and flatten into disks. Wrap each disk in plastic wrap. Refrigerate for 45 minutes before rolling. The dough keeps for 2 days in the refrigerator, or for 2 weeks in the freezer.

peach–blueberry crumb pie

Every year I rush to make peach-blueberry pie in July, when succulent peaches come out in full force. This version with a sweet-crumb topping is one of my absolute favorites.

My preferred sweetener for the crumb topping is maple sugar, available in gourmet and specialty stores and some natural food stores. Sucanat, Rapidura, and unrefined cane sugar make satisfactory substitutes. They vary in their taste and graininess. Experiment until you find the one that suits you best.

Important: Let the pie sit for at least four hours before cutting into it so that the juices can thicken.

SERVES 8 TO 10

crumb topping

½ cup pecan halves
¾ cup whole-wheat pastry flour
½ cup maple sugar
½ teaspoon baking powder
1 teaspoon ground cinnamon
½ teaspoon salt
4 to 5 tablespoons canola oil or melted coconut oil

filling

4 cups peaches (2 pounds)
2 cups blueberries
¾ cup maple sugar, Sucanat, or date sugar
¼ teaspoon salt
2 teaspoons fresh lemon juice
1 teaspoon lemon zest
4 tablespoons arrowroot or tapioca flour, or 3 tablespoons instant tapioca

1 single-crust recipe Coconut Oil Crust (page 271) or Oil Crust (page 270)

make the crumb topping:

• Preheat the oven to 350° F. Lightly toast the pecans for 5 minutes. Chop the pecans into small pieces. Keep the oven on.

• In a medium bowl, toss together the flour, pecans, sugar, baking powder, cinnamon, and salt. Slowly drizzle in the oil, 1 tablespoon at a time, tossing with your fingers until the mixture is moistened. The mixture should be the consistency of damp sand, with pebbles of various sizes, ranging from crumbs to large pebbles. Use the last tablespoon of oil only if the topping seems dry.

make the filling:

• Peel the peaches, cut them in half, and remove the pits. Thinly slice each half.

• Add the peaches, blueberries, sugar, salt, lemon juice, and lemon zest to a medium bowl and toss to combine. Add the thickener of your choice and toss together to coat thoroughly.

assemble the pie:

• Have a 9-inch pie plate ready. Roll out the dough on a lightly floured board, or between 2 pieces of parchment paper. Start from the center and move outward, rolling the dough until it is as thin as possible (about ¹⁄₁₆ inch). Transfer the dough to the pie plate. Lightly push in the crust to meet the contours of the plate. Trim the overhang to extend ½ inch past the rim. Fold the overhang under and tuck it in so that it's flush with the plate. Make a decorative edge by pressing a piece of the dough between the forefinger of one hand and the thumb and forefinger of the other hand. Repeat this motion to make a handsome decorative border around the edge of the entire pie.

- Pour the filling into the crust and smooth it down evenly. Sprinkle the crumb topping over the fruit, covering all of it. Loosely cover the pie with foil. Place on a middle rack in the oven and bake for 30 minutes. Uncover and bake for another 20 to 30 minutes, or until the crust is cooked and the pie juices start to bubble.

- Remove the pie from the oven and let it cool to room temperature before slicing.

a word about pie thickeners

Fruit pies need added thickeners to sop up and contain their juices. Thickeners include flour, cornstarch, arrowroot, and tapioca. Cornstarch is an unhealthful ingredient, one that I do not consider an option. For the most part, I prefer the root starches over flour, since flour makes a weak thickener and too much flour makes for a pasty consistency. (I use flour to thicken the apple pie, however, since it doesn't dull the taste of the apples and very little flour is needed.)

I use 4 tablespoons of arrowroot or tapioca (cassava) flour to thicken the cherry and peach—blueberry pies. Tapioca comes from the root of the cassava plant. Tapioca flour, also known as cassava powder, has not undergone the beading process, which is what gives pearl tapioca a notably pebbly texture. You can find tapioca flour in Asian markets or the King Arthur catalogue (see Resources and Mail-Order Sources, page 293). Tapioca more commonly comes in quick-cooking (Minute) or pearl forms.

Three tablespoons of Minute tapioca work beautifully to firm up the fruit pies in this book. They hold together and retain their juices. If you can't find instant tapioca, you can grind the pearl variety in your spice grinder to make your own "quick-cooking." Minute (or ground pearl) tapioca is not great for open or lattice pies because the surface pellets bake into dry, hard bits. For that reason, I use arrowroot powder or tapioca flour when I make a lattice-top crust or an open-faced cobbler. The Minute tapioca, however, works beautifully in the apricot-plum cobbler when the crust is baked on top or in pies that have a double crust or a crumb topping.

apple pie

For me, apple pie is the the bread and butter of all desserts. One of the best things about autumn is the great variety of excellent apples available for pies—Ida Red, Winesap, Cortland, Mutsu, Rome, Northern Spy, and Jonagold are my autumn favorites; in the winter I use a combination of Golden Delicious and Granny Smith.

Half the apples are cut into chunks and precooked in a skillet; the other half are thinly sliced and added to the cooked ones before baking, creating a wonderful textural contrast.

This pie lasts a good four days in the refrigerator.

SERVES 8 TO 10

3   pounds apples (6 medium apples)
¼   cup apple juice or apple cider
     Pinch of salt
1½ teaspoons ground cinnamon
½   teaspoon allspice
¾   cup maple sugar, Sucanat, or date sugar
1   teaspoon lemon zest
1   tablespoon fresh lemon juice
2   tablespoons unbleached white flour
1   double-crust recipe of Coconut Oil Crust (page 271) or Oil Crust (page 270)
1   tablespoon barley malt or rice syrup mixed with 1 tablespoon water, for the glaze

• Peel, core, and quarter half of the apples. Cut each quarter into 4 slices lengthwise, and then in half (they should be no larger than ½ inch). In a medium skillet add the apple juice, salt, chunked apples, cinnamon, and allspice, stir to combine the spices, and cook over low to medium heat until the apples are barely tender, 3 to 5 minutes. Remove from the heat.

• Peel, core, and quarter the remaining apples. Cut each quarter into thin slices, no thicker than ¼ inch. Toss with the cooked apples and add the sugar, lemon zest, and lemon juice. Sprinkle the flour over the top, and stir to combine. Set the mixture aside while rolling the dough.

• Preheat the oven to 350° F. Start with one disk of dough. On a lightly floured board, or between 2 pieces of parchment paper, roll out the dough. Start from the center and move outward in all directions, rolling the dough until it is as thin as possible (about 1⁄16 inch). Transfer to a 9-inch pie plate. Lightly push in the crust to meet the contours of the plate, but leave the overhang.

• Add the filling to the crust, neatly mounding it in. Roll out the second crust in the same way as the first, and center it over the pie. Trim the two crusts together around the edge of the pie plate using a small knife or kitchen scissors. Pinch the two crusts together. Make a decorative edge by pressing a piece of the dough in between the forefinger of one hand and the thumb and forefinger of the other hand. Repeat this motion to create a zigzag pattern around the rim of the pie.

• Make 5 or 6 slashes in the top crust to vent steam.

• Bake for 50 minutes, or until the crust begins to brown. Paint the glaze all over the crust and bake 10 minutes, or until golden brown. Remove the pie from the oven and let it cool to room temperature before cutting.

cherry pie

In the middle of summer, when cherries are ripe and succulent, there's nothing like a pie to bring out the cherry's finer qualities. Make the crust, sit down, pull up a chair, and relax while you pit the fruit.

Use arrowroot powder or tapioca (cassava) flour for this lattice-topped pie. Instant tapioca, while a good thickener for pies that have a top crust, will not work here, as the tapioca hardens in the exposed parts.

SERVES 8 TO 10

2½ pounds cherries, pitted and quartered (6 cups)

¾ cup maple sugar or Sucanat

2 teaspoons fresh lemon juice

1 teaspoon lemon zest

½ teaspoon almond extract

1 teaspoon ground cinnamon
Pinch of salt

4 tablespoons tapioca flour or arrowroot powder

1 double-crust recipe of Coconut Oil Crust (page 271) or Oil Crust (page 270)

1 tablespoon barley malt or rice syrup, for the glaze

1 tablespoon water, for the glaze

TO PIT CHERRIES, USE A PITTER OR HALVE THE CHERRY FROM STEM TO BOTTOM ALL THE WAY AROUND. REPEAT THE CUT FROM STEM TO BOTTOM TO MAKE EQUAL QUARTERS. PIECES SHOULD COME OFF THE PIT EASILY.

- To a medium bowl add the cherries, sugar, lemon juice, lemon zest, almond extract, cinnamon, salt, and thickener. Stir to combine.

- Preheat the oven to 350° F. Have a 9-inch pie plate ready. On a lightly floured board, or between 2 pieces of parchment paper, roll out one disk of dough. Start from the center and move outward, rolling the dough until it is as thin as possible (about ¹⁄₁₆ inch). Transfer the dough to the pie plate. Lightly push in the crust to meet the contours of the plate. Leave the overhang for now. Add the filling to the pie.

- Roll the second disk of dough out on a floured surface or parchment paper until it is thin. Cut the dough into ¾-inch-wide strips. A fluted pastry cutter makes a very nice edge. Or, you could use a knife instead. Lay 6 parallel strips across the filled pie. Fold back every other strip on itself. (See diagram.)

- Lay 1 strip across the pie perpendicular to the other strips.

- Unfold the folded strip over the top of the perpendicular piece. Fold back every other piece. Lay another strip across the pie. Unfold the folded strips and fold back the ones that had been lying flat. Continue the process on each side of the center piece until the lattice is woven across the pie.

- Use a knife or scissors to trim the lattice strips and bottom crust to ½-inch overhang. Fold the overhang over the strips and pinch them together. Make a decorative edge.

- Place on the middle rack of the oven and bake for 45 minutes, or until the crust starts to turn golden.

- In a small bowl, mix together the barley malt and water. Use a pastry brush to paint the lattice and all exposed crust with the glaze. Return to the oven for another 10 minutes, until the crust is golden brown. Remove the pie from the oven and let it sit until it cools to room temperature.

step 1

step 2

step 3

step 4

step 5

step 6

step 7

step 8

step 9

To make a collar for the crust, take a piece of foil larger than the pie plate. Fold the piece into quarters. Cut out a quarter circle the size of a quarter of the pie plate. Open up the foil. You should have a circle of foil with a cut circle in the center. Trim off excess foil at the corners to form a ring. Shape the ring so it will curve over the rim of the pie crust, leaving the filling exposed.

pumpkin pie with glazed pecans

If you're a pumpkin pie lover, you're sure to enjoy this version with a caramelized pecan topping. Butternut squash is available for a longer period than any other squash, and it makes a reliable filling. In the autumn, however, try some of the other good pie squash, such as blue hubbard, red kuri, sugar pumpkins, or my favorite, milk (or cheese) pumpkins. These appear at local greenmarkets and specialty stores; they all taste best after the first frost, usually sometime in October.

SERVES 8 TO 10

pecan topping

1½ cups pecan halves
1   tablespoon molasses
¼   cup pure maple syrup
1   teaspoon arrowroot powder

pumpkin filling

3   cups cooked pumpkin or butternut squash
½   cup pure maple syrup
½   cup original flavored soy milk
4   teaspoons canola oil
¾   teaspoon ground cinnamon
¾   teaspoon ground ginger
¼   teaspoon freshly grated nutmeg
½   teaspoon salt
2   tablespoons arrowrooot powder
1   teaspoon agar powder
1   single-crust recipe of Coconut Oil Crust (page 271) or Oil Crust (page 270)

TO GET 2½ CUPS OF SQUASH PURÉE, START WITH 2½ TO 3 POUNDS OF SQUASH. CUT A SQUASH IN HALF AND PLACE IT FACE DOWN ON A BAKING SHEET. BAKE FOR 45 MINUTES, OR UNTIL THE FLESH IS TENDER WHEN PIERCED WITH A FORK. REMOVE THE SQUASH FROM THE OVEN AND LET IT SIT FOR A FEW MINUTES TO COOL. REMOVE AND DISCARD THE SEEDS. SCOOP OUT 3 CUPS OF FLESH. WHEN PROCESSED, THIS WILL MAKE 2½ CUPS PURÉED.

AGAR POWDER IS A VERY IMPORTANT INGREDIENT IN THIS PIE. IT IS WHAT MAKES THE PIE HOLD TOGETHER WHEN IT COOLS DOWN. UNFORTUNATELY, AGAR FLAKES WILL NOT SUBSTITUTE. A LITTLE GOES A LONG WAY, AND AGAR POWDER KEEPS INDEFINITELY.

make the pecan topping:

• Chop the pecans coarsely. Toss in a bowl with the molasses, maple syrup, and arrowroot. Set aside.

make the pumpkin filling:

• To a food processor fitted with a metal blade, add the pumpkin flesh, maple syrup, soy milk, canola oil, cinnamon, ginger, nutmeg, and salt. Process until smooth. Taste and adjust the sweetness by adding a touch more sweetener if necessary, since not all winter squashes are equally sweet. Add the arrowroot and agar powder and process to mix them in completely. Set aside while you roll the dough.

• Preheat the oven to 350° F. Have a 9-inch pie plate ready. On a lightly floured board, or between 2 pieces of parchment paper, roll out the dough. Start from the center and move outward, rolling the dough until it is as thin as possible (about ¹⁄₁₆ inch). Transfer the dough to the pie plate. Lightly push in the crust to meet the contours of the plate. Trim the overhang to extend ½ inch beyond the rim of the plate. Fold the overhang under and tuck it in so that it is flush with the plate. Make a decorative edge by pressing a piece of the dough between the forefinger of one hand and the thumb and forefinger of the other hand. Repeat this motion continuously around the edge of the entire pie.

• Pour the filling into the pie shell. Cover the crust with an aluminum foil collar. Bake for 50 minutes. The filling should look firm at this point.

• Remove the pie from the oven and remove the foil collar. Evenly distribute the reserved pecans over the top of the pie. Bake, uncovered, for another 20 minutes. Remove the pie from the oven and let it cool for a couple of hours before cutting.

apple-walnut crisp

This dessert is the quintessential comfort dessert with a crusty oat-nut topping; toasting the walnuts first makes all the difference. I use any apple suitable for an apple pie, including Ida Red, Jonagold, Northern Spy, and Rome. In winter, when the pickings are scarcer, I use a mix of Granny Smith and Golden Delicious. Dried cherries add a special touch, but you can substitute other favorite dried fruits or eliminate them altogether.

SERVES 6 TO 8

oat-nut topping

1   cup walnut halves
¾   cup rolled oats
⅔   cup unbleached white flour
½   cup maple sugar
¼   teaspoon salt
6   tablespoons canola oil
2   tablespoons water
1   teaspoon cinnamon, for dusting the top
1   teaspoon maple sugar, for dusting the top

apple filling

3   pounds medium apples
½   cup dried cherries, cut in half
1   teaspoon ground cinnamon
½   teaspoon ground allspice
2   tablespoons pure maple syrup
2   tablespoons maple sugar or cane sugar
1   teaspoon fresh lemon juice
½   teaspoon lemon zest
      Pinch of sea salt
¼   cup apple cider or apple juice

TO CORE APPLES, FIRST QUARTER THEM. THEN LAY THE QUARTERS DOWN ON A BOARD. CUT THROUGH THE CORE IN EACH WITH A DIAGONAL STROKE.

make the oat-nut topping:

• Preheat the oven to 350° F. Place the walnuts on a baking sheet and toast for 10 minutes, or until fragrant. Remove from the oven and place in a strainer. Increase the oven to 400° F. Rub the walnuts against the strainer (over the sink or wastebasket) to loosen the skins. Remove the walnuts from the strainer and chop into small (¼-inch) pieces.

• In a medium bowl, toss together the rolled oats, flour, sugar, walnuts, and salt. Drizzle in the oil, stirring lightly with a wooden spoon. Drizzle in the water and toss. The topping should be crumbly, like wet sand. Set aside.

• Mix the cinnamon and sugar in a small bowl. Set aside.

make the filling:

• Peel and core the apples. Slice the apples into ¼-inch slices. Cut each slice into thirds. In a large bowl, toss all the filling ingredients together. Pour into an 8 × 8-inch glass baking dish, preferably Pyrex.

assemble the crisp:

• Sprinkle the reserved oat-nut topping over the apples evenly, to completely cover the apples; sprinkle the cinnamon-sugar over the top.

• Bake for 15 minutes at 400°F., then reduce the heat to 350° F. and bake an additional 15 to 20 minutes, or until the topping is cooked and a toothpick inserted into the apples indicates they're cooked. If your crisp topping is browned before the apples are completely tender, cover with a piece of aluminum foil to finish baking.

• Remove the crisp from the oven and let it cool.

☞ THE APPLES BECOME JUICY, BUT THERE IS NO NEED TO THICKEN THE JUICE. FOR JUICIER FRUITS SUCH AS PEACHES AND BERRIES, YOU NEED TO ADD 2 TABLESPOONS OF ARROWROOT TO THE FRUIT TO THICKEN THE LIQUID.

apricot-plum cobbler

Apricots and plums with a layer of biscuit get a new lift by being baked upside down. Made this way, the cobbler has to be eaten the day it's baked; by the second day, the exposed fruit fades in color. You can put the fruit in first with the dough on top, and the cobbler will last for days. You need to use different thickeners for each version. Arrowroot or tapioca flour work best to thicken the exposed fruit, while instant tapioca works best the second way. Make sure to serve the cobbler warm, preferably with a frozen dessert or creamy whip.

SERVES 6 TO 8

apricot-plum filling

4 cups apricots, cut in half, pitted and sliced ½ inch thick (about 10 apricots, or 1½ pounds)
2 cups plums, cut in half, pitted and sliced ½ inch thick (about 4 plums, or 1 pound)
⅓ cup apricot fruit spread
4 tablespoons maple sugar or Sucanat
½ teaspoon vanilla extract
3 tablespoons arrowroot (for dough layered under the fruit), or 2 tablespoons instant tapioca (for dough layered on top)

biscuit layer

½ teaspoon fresh lemon juice
6 tablespoons soy milk
¾ cup whole-wheat pastry flour
¾ cup unbleached white flour
1 teaspoon baking powder
¼ teaspoon baking soda
¼ cup maple sugar or Sucanat
¼ teaspoon salt
½ teaspoon ground cinnamon
¼ teaspoon ground ginger
4 tablespoons very cold canola oil

¼ teaspoon ground cinnamon
¼ teaspoon maple sugar

make the filling:

• In a bowl, mix together the apricots, plums, fruit spread, sugar, vanilla, and thickener. Set aside.

make the biscuit:

• Preheat the oven to 350° F. In a small bowl, combine the lemon juice with the soy milk and let it sit for a few minutes until the soy milk curdles.

• Meanwhile, mix the flours, baking powder, baking soda, sugar, salt, and spices in a medium bowl. Whisk to combine. A tablespoon at a time, drizzle the very cold oil with one hand as you toss with a wooden spoon in the other hand. Do this until the topping is pebbly—no longer.

• Add the soy milk mixture to the topping and stir to combine. Gather the dough into a ball. Place the ball on a piece of parchment or wax paper. Cover with another piece. Roll the dough until it's a few inches larger than the baking dish. Peel off the top sheet of paper and use the bottom one to help you lift the dough. Lay the dough in the dish first, then pour the fruit in the center. Fold the irregular pieces over the fruit, leaving the fruit exposed in the center.

As an alternate method, place the fruit in the baking dish. Roll the dough out to a piece about the size of the pan. Place the dough on top of the fruit, tucking in any excess dough.

• Mix the cinnamon and sugar and sprinkle over the crust folds (or entire top crust). Bake for 25 minutes, or until the dough is golden and cooked through and the fruit juices are bubbling. Cool for 20 minutes and serve warm with Cashew-Cinnamon Ice Cream (page 285) or tofu whip.

trio of kantens

Though it is essentially made of gelled juice and fruit, kanten is somehow so much more than the ingredients. With no added sugar, kanten still satisfies a nagging sweet tooth. I love sweets, but when I've been indulging a little too much, I find myself returning again and again to simple kanten. It's a dessert you can eat free of guilt absolutely every day.

This recipe is as simple as it gets; each kanten takes only about 15 minutes of labor from start to finish. The fruit melts into the juice, producing a custardy jelled dessert. The agar and arrowroot (or kudzu) is what makes the texture custardy—neither too loose nor too firm.

Layered in a parfait glass with the peach cream, the jewel hues of the following three flavors make a striking presentation. Make up extra while you're at the stove; kanten keeps refrigerated for a good week.

EACH RECIPE SERVES 4

blueberry kanten

1 tablespoon kudzu or arrowroot
  powder
2½ cups apple cider or apple juice
2 tablespoons agar flakes
2 cups blueberries

- In a small bowl, dissolve the kudzu in ½ cup of the apple cider to make a slurry, and set aside.

- Put in a medium pot the remaining 2 cups of cider, the agar flakes, and 1 cup of the blueberries. Bring the liquid to a boil. Lower the heat and simmer for 5 to 10 minutes, or until the agar flakes are thoroughly dissolved.

- Add the slurry to the liquid, stirring constantly, until the mixture just starts bubbling again—no longer. Turn off the heat and stir in the second cup of blueberries. Pour into a shallow pan and refrigerate for about 30 minutes, or until cool and set. Pour into a container and serve.

apricot kanten

1 tablespoon kudzu or arrowroot powder
2½ cups apple-apricot juice
2 tablespoons agar flakes
2-inch piece of ginger, unpeeled and cut into 3 slices
2 cups thinly sliced apricots

- In a small bowl, dissolve the kudzu in ½ cup of the apple-apricot juice to make a slurry, and set aside.

- Put in a medium pot the remaining 2 cups of juice, the agar flakes, the ginger, and 1 cup of the apricots. Bring the liquid to a boil. Lower the heat and simmer for 5 to 10 minutes, or until the agar flakes are thoroughly dissolved.

- Add the slurry to the liquid, stirring constantly until the mixture just starts bubbling again—no longer. Turn off the heat and stir in the second cup of apricots. Remove the ginger slices and pour the liquid into a shallow pan and refrigerate for about 30 minutes, or until cool and set. Pour into a container and serve.

cherry kanten

1 tablespoon kudzu or arrowroot powder
2 tablespoons agar flakes
2½ cups apple-cherry juice
2 cups cherries, pitted and quartered
½ teaspoon almond extract

- In a small bowl, dissolve the kudzu in ½ cup of the apple-cherry juice to make a slurry, and set aside.

- Put in a medium pot the remaining 2 cups of juice, the agar flakes, the almond extract, and 1 cup of the cherries. Bring the liquid to a boil. Lower the heat and simmer for 5 to 10 minutes, or until the agar flakes are thoroughly dissolved.

- Add the slurry to the liquid, stirring constantly until the mixture just starts bubbling again—no longer. Turn off the heat and stir in the second cup of cherries. Pour into a shallow pan and refrigerate for 30 minutes, or until cool and set. Pour into a container and serve.

peach nut cream

This pale cream layers beautifully between the fruity kantens.

1   cup blanched almonds
¼   cup rice syrup
2   medium peaches, peeled, and pit removed
     Pinch of salt
¼   teaspoon almond extract
½   teaspoon vanilla extract
1   teaspoon orange zest

• Place all of the ingredients in a food processor fitted with a metal blade and process until creamy. Run the processor a few minutes, stopping now and again to scrape down the sides. The longer you process it, the smoother it gets.

a word about frozen desserts

You need an ice-cream maker to make the following frozen desserts. There are a wide variety on the market, ranging in price from $45 to $500 or more. The less expensive ones work well if your freezer is cold enough. They have removable canisters that need to be kept in a very cold freezer for at least twelve hours before being used and between batches. The pricier models have self-contained refrigeration units so that you can make batch after batch without pause.

The following recipes have a choice of thickeners: either xanthan gum or arrowroot. Although you could freeze your base without a thickener, arrowroot and xanthan gum give the dessert a creamy smooth texture, and they help keep it from melting as quickly. Arrowroot needs to be stirred into a small amount of liquid to form a slurry before being added to a hot liquid. The liquid base needs to be brought just to a boil for the thickening action in arrowroot to work. Xanthan gum is made from a tiny microorganism called *Xanthomonas campestris* and is a natural carbohydrate. You need only to blend the xanthan gum with the "ice cream" base. With most ice-cream makers, you need to chill the base before churning it into a luscious frozen dessert. For the best consistency, place the "ice creams" in a freezer for a couple of hours after making them.

Beware: Ice-cream making can become a serious obsession. I have been known to stand in front of the open freezer in a wonderful daze spooning down freshly churned ice cream. Luckily, however, you can eat quantities of the following "ice creams" without disastrous consequences.

Caramel Sauce (page 268) and chocolate sauces go well with these frozen desserts, and home-made creamless ice cream is an excellent complement to the various pies and cobblers in this book.

peanut butter and banana ice cream

This "ice cream"—and it truly has the consistency of ice cream—offers the surprise crunch of chopped peanuts. Peanut butter and bananas is one of my favorite combinations, I can't go too long without making a batch.

MAKES 1 QUART

2 cups original flavored soy milk
2 tablespoons arrowroot powder
½ cup creamy peanut butter
2 ripe bananas, peeled
½ teaspoon vanilla extract
½ cup pure maple syrup
Pinch of salt
½ cup roasted unsalted peanuts, finely chopped

• In a small bowl, mix ¼ cup of the soy milk with the arrowroot. Add the remaining 1¾ cups of soy milk to a small pot or saucepan. Bring the soy milk to a boil. Stir in the arrowroot slurry. Stir continuously, until the soy milk thickens and just starts to bubble.

• Remove the soy milk from the heat and add to a blender with the peanut butter, bananas, vanilla, maple syrup, and salt. Blend until smooth. Cool thoroughly in the refrigerator.

• Make into ice cream according to the directions for your ice-cream maker. Add the chopped peanuts in the last few minutes of churning. Freeze for a couple of hours before serving.

xanthan gum variation

Omit the arrowroot. To a blender add the soy milk, peanut butter, bananas, vanilla, maple syrup, salt, and 2 teaspoons of xanthan gum. Blend until creamy. Cool thoroughly in the refrigerator. Make into ice cream according to the directions for your ice-cream maker. Add the chopped peanuts during the last few minutes of churning.

chocolate sorbet

This is a rich, chocolaty frozen dessert, with a texture between that of sorbet and ice cream.

MAKES 1 QUART

1⅓ cups raw, unsalted cashews
4 cups water
2 tablespoons arrowroot powder
¼ cup cocoa powder
2 tablespoons instant espresso
¾ cup Sucanat or maple sugar
½ cup chocolate chips
1 tablespoon vanilla extract

• Blend the cashews and the water in a blender until creamy. (You may have to do this in 2 batches.) Strain the blended cashews through a layer of cheesecloth placed in a strainer. Bunch up the cheesecloth and squeeze to extract all of the liquid. You should have 4 cups of cashew milk. Discard the cashews.

• Reserve ¼ cup of the cashew milk in a small bowl. Mix it with the arrowroot to make a slurry.

• Place the rest of the cashew milk in a medium pot or saucepan. Add the cocoa powder, espresso, and sugar to the cashew milk. Bring the liquid to a boil, stirring every now and then to make sure the ingredients are dissolved. Stir in the arrowroot slurry. Stir constantly until the mixture thickens and starts to bubble. Turn off the heat and add the chocolate chips. Let the chips sit in the hot liquid for a few minutes before whisking to combine thoroughly. Stir in the vanilla.

• Cool thoroughly in the refrigerator. Make into ice cream according to the directions for your ice-cream maker.

xanthan gum variation

Omit the arrowroot. Make the cashew milk as directed above. To a medium saucepan add the cashew milk, cocoa powder, espresso, and sugar. Bring the liquid to a boil, stirring to make sure the ingredients are dissolved. Turn off the heat and add the chocolate chips. Let the chips sit in the hot liquid for a few minutes before whisking to combine thoroughly.

Blend the liquid (in a couple of batches; it's hot!) with 2 teaspoons xanthan gum and vanilla. The xantham gum will thicken it considerably. Thoroughly cool the liquid in the refrigerator. Make it into ice cream according to the directions for your ice-cream maker.

cashew-cinnamon ice cream

Cashew milk is the base for this vanilla-cinnamon frozen dessert. It's delicious with anything made from apples: apple pie, the apple crisp, and the streusel cakes.

MAKES 1 QUART

1⅓ cups raw, unsalted cashews
4 cups water
2 tablespoons arrowroot powder
2 vanilla beans
½ cup pure maple syrup
¼ cup canola oil
¼ teaspoon salt
½ teaspoon ground cinnamon
1 cinnamon stick

• Blend the cashews and the water in a blender until creamy. (You may have to do this in 2 batches.) Strain the blended cashews through a layer of cheesecloth placed in a strainer. Squeeze to extract all of the liquid. You should have 4 cups of cashew milk. Discard the cashews.

• Reserve ¼ cup of the cashew milk in a small bowl. Mix it with the arrowroot to make a slurry. Place the remaining cashew milk in a medium pot or saucepan.

• Slice and split the vanilla beans open lengthwise and scrape out the seeds with the tip of a paring knife. Add the scraped seeds plus the pod to the cashew milk.

• Add the maple syrup, oil, salt, ground cinnamon, and cinnamon stick to the liquid. Bring the liquid to a boil. Turn off the heat and let the mixture steep for 15 minutes. Strain the liquid.

• Return the mixture to the stove and bring to a boil. Stir in the arrowroot slurry. Stir constantly until the mixture thickens and starts to bubble.

• Remove from the heat and cool thoroughly in the refrigerator. Make into ice cream according to the directions for your ice-cream maker.

xanthan gum variation

Omit the arrowroot. Follow the recipe through step 4. Add all of the cashew milk to the pot with the other ingredients. Blend the liquid (in a couple of batches; it's hot!) with 2 teaspoons xanthan gum. The xanthan gum will thicken it considerably. Cool thoroughly in the refrigerator. Make into ice cream according to the directions for your ice-cream maker.

coconut sorbet

As simple as it is tasty, this recipe gains a lot of body from the coconut milk. It pairs exceedingly well with the Chocolate Coconut Layer Cake (page 252).

MAKES 1 QUART

3   cups coconut milk (2 14-ounce cans)
2   tablespoons arrowroot powder
6   tablespoons maple sugar or Sucanat
½   cup coconut flakes

• In a small bowl, mix ¼ cup of the coconut milk with the arrowroot to make a slurry. In a medium saucepan, heat the rest of the coconut milk with the sugar, stirring to dissolve the sugar thoroughly.

• When the coconut milk comes to a boil, stir in the arrowroot slurry. Stir constantly until the coconut milk thickens and just starts to bubble.

• Cool thoroughly in the refrigerator. Make into ice cream according to the directions for your ice-cream maker. Add the coconut flakes in the last few minutes of churning in the ice-cream maker.

xanthan gum variation

Omit the arrowroot. Heat all of the coconut milk with the sugar in a medium saucepan until the sugar is dissolved. Blend the liquid (in a couple of batches; it's hot!) with 2 teaspoons of xanthan gum. The xanthan gum will thicken it considerably. Cool thoroughly in the refrigerator. Make into ice cream according to the directions for your ice-cream maker. Add the coconut flakes in the last few minutes of churning.

glossary

achiote seed, Hard, brick-red seeds from the pods of a tree that grows throughout the Yucatán. Used primarily as a coloring agent to give food a bright orangey glow. Available in Mexican and Caribbean markets.

adzuki beans, Small, reddish brown beans with a white stripe along one edge, popular in Japan and China. Low fat content makes them easily digestible.

agar-agar, Vegetarian form of gelatin, made from a red seaweed that is processed into flakes, bars, or powder. The bars are also known as kanten bars.

aïoli, Garlic mayonnaise.

almond butter, Creamy, smooth spread made solely of almonds ground to a paste.

amaranth, Tiny, high-protein grain with a slightly nutty flavor, most frequently used as an addition to other grains.

anasazi beans, Mottled maroon and white bean most often used with Southwestern and Latin American flavorings.

ancho chile, Dried poblano, the most commonly used chile in Mexico. The sweetest of the dried chiles, with a mild fruit flavor. Name means "wide" in Spanish, and it measures 4 to 5 inches long and 3 inches across, with a dark mahogany color.

annatto seed, Achiote seed.

arame, Slightly sweet and delicately flavored sea vegetable that grows in the seas around Japan. Comes in thin strands, available in Asian markets and natural food stores.

arborio rice, Starchy short-grained Italian rice used mainly for risotto.

arepa, Colombian or Venezuelan flat corn pancake cooked on a griddle. Usually made from *masa harina*.

arrowroot powder, Root starch used as a thickener, much like cornstarch.

asafetida, Pungent spice used in small amounts. Highly valued as a digestive aid. Unsavory scent turns into an oniony aroma when cooked. Available in Indian stores.

barley, Small, stubby-kerneled grain with a lot of natural starch. Sold pearled or hulled.

barley malt, Mild sweetener with a strong, distinctive flavor, and a consistency and color like molasses. Made from sprouted barley. Add hops and yeast, and you've got beer.

barley miso, A dark miso with a rich, salty, full flavor. Mellow barley is a much milder variety.

basmati rice, Long-grain rice with nutty aroma and fluffy texture. Most-prized rice in India.

béchamel, White sauce made with a roux (an amalgam of flour and oil). Provides a thickening base and can often take the place of cream.

Bhutan rice, Short-grained rice with a nutty taste, light, fluffy texture, and dark rosy pink color. Grown in Bhutan for centuries and recently imported into the United States. Available in gourmet and natural food stores.

Bibb lettuce, Round-headed lettuce with tender, buttery textured leaves.

black-eyed peas, Earthy, flavorful, beige peas with a black eye. Also known as cowpeas. Most associated with the Southern rice dish Hoppin' John, which when eaten on New Year's Day is said to bring good luck for the year.

black mushroom, Dried shiitakes. Available in Asian markets and natural food stores.

blanch, Cook briefly in salted boiling water. Facilitates removal of skins (such as for almonds, tomatoes, or fava beans), eliminates harsh or bitter flavors (such as for broccoli rabe), or partially cooks before cooking by another method (such as with carrots before roasting them).

287

blood orange, More intensely flavored than juice oranges, with orange- to crimson-colored skin and blood-red juice. Mostly available from January through March.

blue hubbard squash, Large, ungainly looking winter squash covered with "warts," with very tasty flesh.

bok choy, Member of the cabbage family with fleshy white stem and green leaves. Mild flavor and quick-cooking; suitable for stir-fries.

bouillon, Flavorful aromatic liquid made by simmering water with vegetables. Bouillon cubes of dehydrated vegetables and salt can be used to add quick flavor in place of stock.

bouquet garni, A small bundle of herbs wrapped in a piece of cheesecloth; used to enhance flavor of stews and soups.

braise, Cook food in fat first, then simmer covered in a small amount of liquid until tender.

broccoli rabe, Greens with pronounced, somewhat bitter flavor, eaten widely in Italy. Leaves resemble those of a turnip, with little broccoli-like florettes interspersed among the greens. All parts are edible.

bruise, To release the flavorful oils in herbs or citrus peels by laying the knife blade over the item and giving it a firm smack, the way you would for peeling a clove of garlic.

bruschetta, Toasted bread rubbed with garlic and crowned with any variety of toppings.

burdock, Wild, long, thin, brown, hairy root with a deep earthy flavor and medicinal qualities. Needs only a scrubbing to remove dirt clinging to the skin.

buttercup squash, Squat, round, usually dark green winter squash with dense, sweet, orange flesh. Japanese Kabocha, honey delight, and black forest are all in the buttercup catergory.

butter lettuce, Round-headed lettuce with tender, buttery leaves.

carob powder, Chocolate alternative made from the dried, roasted, and pulverized pod of the honey locust tree that grows in the Mediterranean region. Naturally sweeter than cocoa.

chanterelle mushroom, Wild mushroom with golden or pale orange color and undulating cap. From 1 to 6 inches across.

chayote, Pear-shaped, pale green starchy fruit with smooth skin. Grown in Mexico, and increasingly easier to find in supermarkets and specialty stores.

chiffonade, Shredded leaves, most often leaves that have been stacked, rolled, and then sliced. Frequently used for basil and spinach.

chile de arbol, Tiny, dried, "tree-like" chiles. Closely related to cayenne with a searing, acidic heat. Bright red, about 2 to 3 inches long and ½ inch wide.

chipotle chile, Smoked red jalapeños with a hot, smoky, sweet flavor.

couscous, Traditional food from Morocco made from semolina wheat that is cooked, fried, and chopped into little grain-like pieces. Does not need to be washed before cooking.

cremini mushroom, Similar to button mushrooms in look and flavor but rounder and larger with tan or brown caps.

currant, Small seedless raisin used extensively for baking.

daikon, Long white Japanese radish, eaten cooked, raw, or pickled. Known for cleansing and digestive properties.

dandelion greens, Member of the chicory family with long, spindly leaves and a pronounced bitter flavor.

dashi, Japanese soup stock that usually contains kombu, a kelp. Used as a base for miso soup and other dishes.

deglaze, Adding liquid to a hot pan that has just had food cooked in it. Liquid facilitates scraping up any brown bits stuck to the bottom of the skillet and enables reclaiming the juices that have cooked down.

delicata squash, Small, elegant-looking oblong winter squash with characteristic green stripes. Edible skin is easy to peel.

edamame, Fresh green soybeans, usually prepared by boiling in salted water until tender.

emulsion, Two or more liquids that would otherwise remain separate are blended into a homogeneous liquid, generally by beating.

enoki mushroom, Clusters of pearl-tipped caps perched on top of stems. Often sold packed in the dirt they were grown in, so the last inch or so of the stems must be removed.

epazote, Pungent-smelling, jagged-leafed herb, often used in Mexican cooking, especially with black beans.

fiddlehead ferns, Tightly scrolled vegetables (the green shoots of the ostrich fern) with a delicate asparagus-like flavor. In season for only a limited time in spring; once they open and grow into ferns, they are no longer edible.

food mill, Strainer with a crank-operated curved blade used to purée food while at the same time removing stems and seeds.

frisée, Known as curly endive for its ruffled leaves. Assertive, slightly bitter flavor. Most often used as a salad green.

Gaeta olive, Italian black olive with a mild, sweet flavor and somewhat wrinkled skin.

galangal, Resembles thin-skinned ginger, with distinctive flavor and delicate floral bouquet. Widely used in Thai and Malaysian cooking, and sold in Asian stores, most always frozen.

gluten, Tough, viscid substance remaining when the flour of wheat or other grain is washed to remove the starch. Gives yeast doughs their characteristic elasticity.

grits, Coarse or finely broken-up pieces of dried corn, suitable for porridge or polenta. Available in natural food stores.

guajillo chile, Shiny, deep-orange-red-brown dried chile. Measures 4 to 6 inches long, tapering to a point. Medium heat level with an uncomplicated taste, a little citrus and tart.

habanero chile, Small yellow, red-orange, or green, lantern-shaped fresh or dried chile. Hottest in the world. Has tropical fruit tones that mix well with food containing tropical fruit.

haricots verts, Skinniest, tastiest, and most delicate French green beans.

Hass avocado, Best-tasting avocado. Small and dark green, with pebbly, rough skin and buttery, dense flesh.

hatcho miso, Dark miso made from soybeans.

hijiki, One of the most mineral-rich sea vegetables. Comes in black spaghetti-like strands and has a briny sea taste. Needs to be soaked for at least 20 minutes and cooked for at least 20 more.

hokaido, Kabocha squash. Dark green skin and squat pumpkin shape. Sweet flesh is suitable even for pies.

hominy, Dried field corn or dent corn, with larger and starchier kernels than sweet corn. Also called posole.

horseradish, Root vegetable with pungent white flesh. Can be grated and stirred into food prepara-

tions for a pungent bite. Also sold jarred, packed in vinegar.

immersion blender, Handheld inexpensive tool that can be placed directly into a pot. Great for puréeing soups or sauces (though not if they contain fibrous bits that need a real blender).

Inka coffee, Grain beverage used as a coffee substitute, made from roasted and ground rye, barley, beets, and chicory root.

jalapeño chile, Plump, shiny, bullet-shaped fresh pepper, about 2 inches long. The most widely eaten hot chile in the United States.

jasmine rice, Long-grain, high-quality, slightly sticky white rice used in Thai cooking. Has a distinct fragrance when cooked.

jicama, Round tuber with hard, brown skin. Exterior masks a sweet vegetable with watery and crunchy flesh that is best eaten raw.

kabocha squash, Squat, green winter squash with dense, flavorful orange flesh and dark green edible skin. Also called hokkaido pumpkin.

kaffir lime, Southeast Asian fruit whose rind and leaves are used to give distinctive lemony sourness to Thai and Indonesian cooking.

Kalamata olives, Large, purplish black olives from Greece. Great all-purpose olive, meaty and rich.

kanten, Vegetarian "Jell-O" made most often of fruit juice with agar-agar as the gelling agent. In bar form, agar-agar is often called kanten bars.

kimchee, Pickled and slightly fermented mixed cabbage and vegetable pickle. Mild when freshly made, increasingly pungent the more it ferments.

kohlrabi, Root vegetable with long, spindly stems coming out of a green or purple knob. Needs to be peeled. Flavor of a young turnip, and can be prepared as a turnip. Available from summer through winter.

koji, Cooked rice, barley, or soybeans innoculatd with *Aspergillus* culture. Used in the process of fermenting miso, tempeh, shoyu, and mirin.

kombu, Kelp that comes in flat, stiff ribbons and gives body to grains, stews, and soups. Natural flavor enhancer, since it is high in glutamic acid, a natural form of monosodium glutamate. Small piece of kombu added to a bean cooking pot improves the bean's flavor and digestibility.

kudzu, The powdered root of the kudzu plant used as a thickener. Kudzu has the added quality of being a medicinal ingredient, specifically used in the East to alkalize acidic conditions such as colds, nausea, and indigestion. Soothing for the belly.

latke, Yiddish word for pan-fried potato cakes most often associated with Hanukkah.

lemongrass, Herb that looks like coarse, heavy grass. Used for sour-sweet citrus flavor associated with Southeast Asian cooking.

lentilles du Puy, Tiny French lentils that hold their shape when cooked.

lotus root, Sausage-shaped root of the lotus flower, about 3 inches wide and 5 to 8 inches long, with flesh that fans out from the center like the spokes on a wheel. Crisp texture is best fresh, although it comes in a dried form in natural food stores. Available in markets with Asian produce.

lysine, Amino acid essential in human beings and animals.

mâche, Tiny leaves of a small hardy plant that grows wild in much of the Northern Hemisphere. Delicate flavor is useful addition to salad, particularly in winter. Also known as corn salad or lamb's lettuce.

maple sugar, Crystallized maple syrup.

masa harina, Fresh corn masa that has been dried and powdered. Texture is much finer than that of cornmeal. Maseca is the best brand currently available. Stored in a dry place, *masa harina* lasts one year.

masala, Blend of several aromatic spices used in Indian cooking. One of the most popular mosalas is garam masala, a blend of toasted cardamom, cinnamon, cloves, peppercorns, cumin, and coriander seeds.

mesquite, Hottest-burning hardwood, used for grilling or barbecuing.

milk pumpkin, Large, pallid, milky beige pumpkin with very sweet flesh suitable for pies. Also know as a cheese pumpkin. Mostly available in green markets October through December.

millet, Small yellow grain that is easy to digest (and is good for the stomach and spleen), and gluten-free and has a nutty flavor. Important staple in Asia and North Africa.

mirin, Sweet cooking wine made from sweet rice. Also called sweet sake. Its 14 percent alcohol content evaporates when heated. Used in marinades and salad dressings, or when a light touch of sweetness is needed to balance flavors. Good-quality, authentic mirin is made only from sweet rice, koji, and water.

mise en place, French for "put in place," or getting your ingredients prepped before you start cooking. Usually an efficient way to cook.

miso, Fermented soy paste, made by mixing cooked soybeans with koji, salt, and water, and fermenting the mixture from two months to three years. Used to make soup and as an addition to many different dishes. High in protein and loaded with enzymes that help digestion. Huge variety of misos ranges from mild and light to full-bodied and dark.

mizuna, Spindly leaved green most often used as a salad green, actually belonging to the Asian cabbage family.

mole, Thick Mexican sauces thickened with nuts or seeds. Mole poblano—the dark complex sauce made of dried chiles, nuts, seeds, spices, and a bit of chocolate—is the most common to North Americans.

moong dhal, Hulled and split mung bean, golden yellow in color. Form most widely used in Indian cooking. An easily digestible legume, it is often combined with appropriate spices such as asafetida to make it even more digestible.

MSG, Monosodium glutamate, a white, crystalline, water-soluble powder used to intensify the flavor of foods.

mulato chile, Dried poblano, similar to an ancho, although with a slighty smokier and anise-flavored heat.

mung bean, Dark green bean known as the green gram bean. Most often used in the split-yellow form in Indian cooking.

mustard greens, Pungent, peppery greens with light green, crinkled leaves that have a hot mustardy bite. Used extensively in Southern cooking.

napa cabbage, Mild cabbage shaped like a football with crinkly leafs and broad white ribs. Cooked or raw, all parts are edible. Also called Chinese cabbage.

nasturtium, Edible flowers sometimes included in a mesclun mix or often seen garnishing cakes.

New Mexican chile, Scarlet, elongated, tapered chile measuring 5 to 7 inches long and 1½ to 2 inches across. Uncomplicated red chile flavor. Sold in quantity in the form of crushed flakes and ground powders. Also known as chile Colorado.

Niçoise olive, Tiny, brownish black French olives with large pits in proportion to their size.

nori, Cultivated sea vegetable that is harvested, washed, chopped, and spread over bamboo mats to dry into paper-thin sheets. Most familiar as the sheets that wrap sushi.

oden, Japanese stew, made with a dashi that includes fried tofu and an array of vegetables. Often served at oden carts in Japan.

orecchiette, Ear-shaped pasta.

oyster mushroom, Pale, clustered mushrooms joined at the base. Delicate flavor, but the tough stems need discarding before cooking.

pasilla chile, Dark, raisin-brown dried chile measuring 5 to 6 inches long and 1 to 1½ inches across. Ranges from medium hot to hot. Literally means "little raisin," and also known as chile negro.

pattypan squash, Thin-skinned summer squash. Flat disk shape with a scalloped edge along the circumference. Shows up golden, light, or dark green, or even splashed green and gold.

picadillo, Refers to a variety of finely chopped fillings for tamales or stuffed chiles. Comes from the Spanish word *picar,* "to mince."

poblano chile, Large, dark green fresh chile with thick, meaty flesh. Varies in strength between medium and hot. Used cooked or roasted, never raw. It is the chile usually used for chiles rellenos.

polenta, Thick, savory cornmeal porridge. Staple of Northern Italy, eaten soft or allowed to cool and firm so it can be cut into shapes before boiling or frying.

porcini, Intensely flavored Italian mushroom, most often dried, which needs soaking to soften and remove sand.

portobello mushroom, Versatile large-capped mushroom with a dense texture and full flavor.

pressure cooker, Pot with a lid that locks into place, allowing pressure inside to build up, and the resulting increased boiling point speeds up cooking.

purée, Raw or cooked foods blended until smooth with a blender, food processor, food mill, or hand masher.

quinoa, Small grain about the size of a sesame seed, but round. Highest protein content of any grain. Light and easily digested. Wash well to remove the bitter saponin coating that grows on the outer surface.

radicchio, Member of the chicory family. Deep scarlet leaves that are compact like a cabbage, Has a mildly bitter flavor, eaten raw or cooked.

raita, Cooling Indian dish of yogurt with mint and cucumbers served alongside hotter dishes to soothe the palate.

ramp, Similar to a scallion but with broader, flat leaves and a small white bulb at the root end. Available in the spring for only a few weeks.

rapidura, Similar to Sucanat: sweetener made from dried granulated cane juice.

red kuri squash, Red-orange winter squash with very sweet flesh and edible dense orange skin.

refresh, Arrest the cooking process by running cold water over food or immersing it in ice water.

Rice Dream, Sweet, rich nondairy milk made from brown rice. Rice starch converts into maltose and glucose (natural sugars) during the culturing of the rice, so there is no extra sweetener added. Comes as liquid or as a frozen dessert.

rice noodles, Asian noodles made from rice flour, usually thin vermicelli or flat, ribbonlike noodles of varying widths known as rice sticks. Available in natural food stores and Asian markets.

rice syrup, Mild sweetener with a subtle butterscotch flavor made from rice. Good for savory food as well as desserts, or for those who barely want any sweetener.

roast, Cook uncovered in the oven at high heat. Vegetables are usually coated with a small amount of oil.

saffron, Dried, thread-like stigmas of the saffron crocus. A small amount flavors a whole dish and colors it a brilliant gold.

sake, Rice wine of 15 percent alcohol content. Widely used in cooking.

sambal, Indonesian term for chutney. Based on fresh fruit, ginger, coconut, herbs, spices, and chiles (among other ingredients) and soured with tamarind or citrus.

sauté, Food cooked quickly in a small amount of fat. Sauté pans are shallow skillets with either sloping or straight sides and a long handle.

sea salt, Highest in trace minerals of all salts, sea salt is either evaporated by the sun and wind or dried, additive-free, at low temperatures.

seitan, High-protein chewy "wheat meat" made of wheat gluten. Available in plastic tubs in the refrigerator section of natural food stores.

semolina, Flour made from durum wheat, a high-protein wheat suitable for pasta.

serrano chile, Smaller and hotter than jalapeños. The hottest commonly available fresh chile.

shiitake, Japan's most popular mushroom, sold fresh or dried; widely sautéed or used as a basis for stocks. Hard stems are inedible but excellent for stocks.

shoyu, Naturally brewed all-purpose high-quality soy sauce. Fermented solely from whole soy beans, salt, water, and wheat koji.

sofrito, Latin American term for a combination of tomatoes, bell peppers, garlic, and scallions sautéed in oil.

sorrel, Leafy herb with strong lemony flavor, resembling arugula. Eaten raw or cooked.

soybean, High-protein bean from which all soy products (including soy milk, tofu, tempeh, shoyu, and miso) are made. Also eaten fresh in the form of edamame.

soy milk, Liquid extracted from soybeans that have been soaked, ground, boiled, and pressed dry. Some types have flavorings and sweeteners added. Richness varies from brand to brand.

springform pan, Round, straight-sided cake pan whose sides can be unclamped from the base for easy removal without disturbing the top.

stock, Flavorful liquid made by simmering vegetables and aromatics in water until the flavor is extracted. Used for soups, stews, sauces, and other dishes.

Sucanat, "Sugar cane natural," a sweetener made from dried granulated cane juice. Only the water and fiber are removed, so the mineral salts and vitamins naturally present are retained. Moist, with a slight taste of molasses and a coarse granular texture.

sugar pumpkin, Small, bright orange pumpkin. Very sweet flesh suitable for desserts.

sun-gold tomato, Very sweet, tiny cherry tomatoes.

sweat, To cook food gently with a little oil in a covered pan until softened and moisture is released, but food not browned.

sweet dumpling, Sweet mini-squash similar to delicata with thin green stripes. Makes a good shallow container for individual stuffed squash.

tahini, Smooth, creamy paste made from unroasted or very lightly roasted sesame seeds.

tamale, Packets of corn dough wrapped in banana leaves or corn husks and steamed.

tamarind, Fibrous pod of a tropical plant native to India. Used as a souring agent in Indian and East Asian cooking. Comes pressed into cakes or as liquid concentrate in Indian groceries.

tapioca, Starch from the roots of the cassava plant. Comes as tapioca, cassava flour, or pearled tapioca, which undergoes a "beading" process that gives the pearls the pebbly texture desirable in puddings.

tempeh, Traditional Indonesian fermented soy food that has a meaty texture. The fermentation process makes the soy protein more digestible. Adapted to the United States market by the addition of different grains to the fermented soy. Cook before eating.

Thai "bird's eye" chile, Tiny red or green chile with a searing heat. Commonly used in Thai dishes.

tomatillo, Small, plum-size, tart-tasting green fruit similar in appearance (but in fact unrelated) to the tomato. Leaflike husks must be removed before cooking or eating.

umeboshi paste, Purée of Japanese plums pickled for a year with red shiso leaves; bright fuchsia color and a sour-salty flavor. Available in natural food stores.

umeboshi vinegar, Pink brine of the umeboshi plums. Used in place of vinegar and salt to boost flavor in soups, sauces, and dressings. Technically not a vinegar because it is pickled, not fermented. Available in natural food stores.

wakame, Tender sea vegetable most common in miso soup. Soaked, it expands more than other sea vegetables, transforming into a supple, broad, slippery leaf many times its dried size. Comes fresh or dried.

wheat gluten, Elastic protein formed when hard wheat flour is moistened and agitated. Gives bread its characteristic elasticity. When the starch is washed away and only the gluten is left, it can be simmered in broth to make seitan.

wild rice, Seed of aquatic grass with a deep, earthy flavor. Long black grains that burst open when cooked.

xantham gum, Natural carbohydrate made from a tiny microorganism called *Xanthmonas campestris*. Used as a thickener, especially for salad dressing and ice cream. Available in natural food stores.

Yannoh coffee, Grain beverage made from various roasted cereals such as barley, rye, and malted barley, along with chicory and acorns. Available in natural food stores.

yucca, Slender, elongated root that ranges from 4 inches to 2 feet. Skin is bark-like; white flesh has a mild flavor and buttery texture. Contains a fibrous core that needs to be removed before cooking. Also known as manioc.

resources and mail-order sources

Angelica's Herbs
147 First Avenue
New York, NY 10003
212-529-4335
All types of herbs, spices, chiles, sea vegetables, agar powder, hominy—a wonderful place to visit when in New York City.

Bridge Kitchenware
214 East 53nd Street
New York, NY 10022
212-838-1901, ext. 3 (in New York);
Information and customer service 212-838-6746, extension 5
Fax 212-758-5387
Catalogue orders only:
800-BRIDGE K (800-274-3435), ext. 3
or website www.bridgekitchenware.com

Chef's Catalogue
3215 Commercial Avenue
Northbrook, IL 60062
800-338-3232
Good equipment resource; All-Clad pots and pans; mail order available.

Cooking By the Book, Inc.
11 Worth Street
New York, NY 10013
212-966-9799
Web site: cookingbythebook.com
A cooking school. Inventors of the microplane zester, cheese grater, and spice grater. Mail order available for zester and graters.

Coyote Cafe General Store
132 West Water Street
Santa Fe, NM 87501
505-982-2454; 800 866-HOWL, extention 4695
Wide variety of Southwestern products, including chiles, hominy, masa harina. Mail order available.

Dean and DeLuca
560 Broadway
New York, NY 10012
800-221-7714
website: www.dean-deluca.com
Spices, dried beans, rice, masa harina, walnut oil, cookware, and more. Mail order available.

Fillo Factory
P.O. Box 155
Dumont, NJ 07628
800-653-4556
Mail order available for fresh filo.

Foods of India
Sinha Trading Company, Inc.
121 Lexington Avenue
New York, NY 10016
212-683-4419; Fax 212-251-0946
Large variety of beans, grains, spices, chickpea flour, tamarind concentrate. Mail order available.

J. B. Prince Company, Inc.
36 East 31st Street
New York, NY 10016
212-683-3553; Fax: 212-683-4488
Large selection of baking supplies; mail order available.

K. Kalustyan
123 Lexington Avenue
New York, NY 10016
212-685-3451
website www.kalustyan.com
Enormous selection of spices, beans, grains, chiles, and products from Middle Eastern and Indian cuisine; catalogue.

King Arthur Flour Baker's Catalogue
P.O. Box 876
Norwich, VT 05055-0876
800-827-6836
Vast array of flours (including tapioca), sugars, baker's supplies, and equipment. Mail order available. Baking advice available.

Kitchen
218 Eighth Avenue
New York, NY 10011
212-243-4433
Mail-order catalog: 1-888-468-4433
For southwestern ingredients in particular, this is an excellent source. Stocks
every kind of dried chile and chile powder, corn husks, hominy, masa harina
de maiz, epazote, achiote seeds, black
and white jasmine rice, large selection
of beans. Has a large selection of
other products including saffron, dried
galangal, hot sesame oil, sushi mats,
plastic squeeze bottles, and more.

Melissa's World Variety Produce, Inc.
P.O. Box 21127
Los Angeles, CA 90021
800-588-0151; website www.Melis-
sas.com
Exotic products from around the world;
will ship fresh lemongrass.

Mountain Ark Trading Company
120 S. East Street
Fayetteville, AR 2701
800-643-8909
Mail order available for macrobiotic
food and kitchenware.

New York Cake and Baking Distributor
56 West 22nd Street
New York, NY 10010
800-942-2539 or-212 675-CAKE
Large selection of baking supplies;
mail order available.

Omega Nutrition
800-661-3529; e-mail omega
@istar.ca; website
http://www.omegaflo.com
Superior oils, including coconut oil.

Penzeys, Ltd.
P.O. Box 933
Muskego,Wisconsin 53150
414-679-7207; website
www.penzeys.com
Stock of 250 spices and spice blends,
including dried chiles and vanilla
beans.

Poseidon Bakery
629 9th Avenue
New York, NY 10036
212-757-6173
The best-quality fresh filo; no mail
order available.

Udom Corporation
Thai and Indonesia Grocery
81A Bayard Street., New York, NY
10013
212-349-7662
Galangal, kuri leaves, Thai chiles.

Uptown Whole Foods
242 Broadway
New York, NY 10024
212-874-4000
Large natural-food store that carries
specialty items like agar powder. Mail
order available.

Wildoats Markets
Website: Wildoats.com
Wildoats has 110 natural food stores in
22 states and Bristish Columbia. They
carry many specialty items, including
agar powder. Contact their Web site for
a listing of their stores and for online
ordering.

Williams-Sonoma
Mail Order Department
P.O. Box 7456
San Francisco, CA 94120-7456
800-541-2233

Index

conversion chart
Equivalent Imperial and Metric Measurements

American cooks use standard containers, the 8-ounce cup and a tablespoon that takes exactly 16 level fillings to fill that cup level. Measuring by cup makes it very difficult to give weight equivalents, as a cup of densely packed butter will weigh considerably more than a cup of flour. The easiest way therefore to deal with cup measurements in recipes is to take the amount by volume rather than by weight. Thus the equation reads:

1 cup = 240 ml = 8 fl. oz.   ½ cup = 120 ml = 4 fl. oz.

It is possible to buy a set of American cup measures in major stores around the world.

In the States, butter is often measured in sticks. One stick is the equivalent of 8 tablespoons. One tablespoon of butter is therefore the equivalent to ½ ounce/15 grams.

liquid measures

Fluid Ounces	U.S.	Imperial	Milliliters
	1 teaspoon	1 teaspoon	5
¼	2 teaspoons	1 dessertspoon	10
½	1 tablespoon	1 tablespoon	14
1	2 tablespoons	2 tablespoons	28
2	¼ cup	4 tablespoons	56
4	½ cup		120
5		¼ pint or 1 gill	140
6	¾ cup		170
8	1 cup		240
9			250, ¼ liter
10	1¼ cups	½ pint	280
12	1½ cups		340
15		¾ pint	420
16	2 cups		450
18	2¼ cups		500, ½ liter
20	2½ cups	1 pint	560
24	3 cups		675
25		1¼ pints	700
27	3½ cups		750
30	3¾ cups	1½ pints	840
32	4 cups or 1 quart		900
35		1¾ pints	980
36	4½ cups		1000, 1 liter
40	5 cups	2 pints or 1 quart	1120

solid measures

U.S. and Imperial Measures		Metric Measures	
Ounces	Pounds	Grams	Kilos
1		28	
2		56	
3½		100	
4	¼	112	
5		140	
6		168	
8	½	225	
9		250	¼
12	¾	340	
16	1	450	
18		500	½
20	1¼	560	
24	1½	675	
27		750	¾
28	1¾	780	
32	2	900	
36	2¼	1000	1
40	2½	1100	
48	3	1350	
54		1500	1½

oven-temperature equivalents

Fahrenheit	Celsius	Gas Mark	Description
225	110	¼	Cool
250	130	½	
275	140	1	Very Slow
300	150	2	
325	170	3	Slow
350	180	4	Moderate
375	190	5	
400	200	6	Moderately Hot
425	220	7	Fairly Hot
450	230	8	Hot
475	240	9	Very Hot
500	250	10	Extremely Hot

Any broiling recipes can be used with the grill of the oven, but beware of high-temperature grills.

equivalents for ingredients

all-purpose flour—plain flour
baking sheet—oven tray
buttermilk—ordinary milk
cheesecloth—muslin
coarse salt—kitchen salt
cornstarch—cornflour
eggplant—aubergine

granulated sugar—caster sugar
half and half—12% fat milk
heavy cream—double cream
light cream—single cream
lima beans—broad beans
parchment paper—greaseproof paper
plastic wrap—cling film

scallion—spring onion
shortening—white fat
unbleached flour—strong, white flour
vanilla bean—vanilla pod
zest—rind
zucchini—courgettes or marrow